How to Navigate the Minefield That Is Dementia with Your Loved One

A GUIDE BORN OF EXPERIENCE

SUSAN WILSON KRECHEL MD

ISBN 978-1-0980-6850-9 (paperback)
ISBN 978-1-0980-6851-6 (digital)

Christian Faith Publishing, Inc.
832 Park Avenue
Meadville, PA 16335
www.christianfaithpublishing.com

Printed in the United States of America

FOREWORD

Mid-2018 was the darkest period in my life. I was weak, ill, and trying desperately to lift up my husband as he seemed to be tumbling into the abyss.

I needed to reinvent my life. Although I knew that my life with Oliver was not yet at an end, it was at the stage of the long *goodbye*.

I considered going back to work, either as a volunteer or in a paid position. I feared that my physical condition would not allow this. I had no stamina.

I awoke one morning thinking I should write a book. I had published many papers and one textbook, so I knew the drill.

I knew from my own research that there was no information available to the lay public, written for the lay public by a physician who had endured this dreadful process.

I had found no roadmap available delineating the steps to follow in order to get the help I needed.

I decided to make this book, a manual, in three parts.

The first part is a memoir designed to tell you who Ollie and I are and how we have lived our lives, as well as how we entered the minefield that is dementia.

In the second part, I try to explain dementia in easily understood terms. I have reviewed the scientific literature and have given you information on the latest research into cause, risks, diagnosis, treatment, and prevention.

Finally, in the third part, I have tried to give you that road map you need to get care for your loved one while protecting yourself physically, emotionally, and financially.

I hope that you find this book informative.

Susan Wilson Krechel, MD
susan_krechel@icloud.com

MEMOIR

He was my rock, my ears, and my teacher of all things not taught in college and medical school. Then he began slipping away… into dementia.

INTRODUCTION

I had just picked up my husband, Oliver, from the fourth nursing home in which he had resided in the previous five months. This one had actually stabilized and brought him back almost to his baseline condition prior to entering the first facility.

As we drove toward the restaurant we had chosen for our lunch date, he said to me, "We have had such great times." "Yes," I agreed, "and I am going to do everything in my power to keep them going." "That's all I can ask," he replied.

At the time of this conversation, my best friend, lover, and husband of thirty-eight years, Oliver Anthony Krechel, was already right on the verge of late-stage dementia.

In spite of this, while entering and leaving the restaurant, this gracious gentleman held the door for me to proceed before him.

While our journey through the minefield that is dementia began in 2006, I was powerfully impacted by the 2008 movie *The Curious Case of Benjamin Button*, starring Brad Pitt and Cate Blanchett.

The movie is based on a short story of the same title by F. Scott Fitzgerald, first published in 1922. It is the unlikely story of Benjamin Button, who was born old and spent his life aging in reverse and died as a tiny infant.

I seriously doubt if Fitzgerald took his inspiration for this story from a dementia patient, but the story is eerily like that which happens in dementia. In the natural progression of dementia, the sufferer regresses mentally and dies in an infantile state.

Considering Dr. Alois Alzheimer first described the disease (soon to bear his name) and its pathologic findings in 1906,[1] possibly Fitzgerald did have access to this information.

CHAPTER 1

The Way We Were

I will begin the description of this journey in the context of where each of us was at the time our relationship began.

My mother was a caregiver; she took care of her invalid mother when I was a child. She was the woman of the house caring for my grandfather and me both in my later childhood. At that time, we were living with my grandfather while she worked to help put my father through medical school in another state. She also cared for my father at the end of his life as he suffered with congestive heart failure. She passed that caregiver gene to me, and I cared for her after my father's death and at the end of her life. My father died in 1978, at the age of sixty-five, making my mother a widow of sixty. We both had apartments in downtown St. Louis. I was a practicing physician and assistant professor of anesthesiology at Washington University in St. Louis.

We became closer than ever, taking several trips together. She accompanied me to a few medical meetings. One in New Orleans comes to mind. Such a lovely quaint city alive with jazz. Al Hirt and Pete Fountain were the New Orleans jazz stars we were fortunate to see. Strolling down Bourbon Street, we experienced exotic sights and sounds; neither of us had even dreamed about and would never forget.

We also made the last American Express Grand tour of Europe, a personally guided tour that included all meals which could be ordered from the menu at each Grand Hotel we happened to stay.

This particular tour disappeared from the catalogs after our journey, most likely because two of the couples on the tour took it upon themselves to order everything on the menu at each stop. Aside from the wasteful four, our other companions were lovely people. Among the most memorable was a retired San Francisco opera singer who was inspired to serenade us, singing *O Solo Mio*, as we traversed the canals of Venice in our gondola. It is such a great memory.

Traveling together helped my mother move on with her life without my father and encouraged me to expand my own horizons.

My hobby was horseback riding. Horses had been in my blood since my childhood in Chicago. I had completed all the requirements for my Girl Scout badge in horsemanship but had never been on a horse. The Girl Scout leader thought that was a significant deficit, so the whole troop took riding lessons at a local stable, progressing to riding in Chicago's Lincoln Park.

After my father finished medical school, he established a practice in St. Louis Missouri, and my mother and I joined him in St. Louis. Soon after, I had my first horse and my first golden retriever. I was in junior high school at the time. My love for horses inspired my mother and father to purchase a minifarm in St. Louis County. I was no longer a city girl; I had become a country girl. We soon had several horses and even a few young calves. My father's love for racing and racehorses soon became my own passion. I knew the bloodlines and race record of every competitive thoroughbred in the country. There were two racetracks in Southern Illinois, right across the Mississippi River, from our home. During the racing season, my parents and I spent nearly every night at the racetrack. I did my school homework between races. Early the next morning, I would be up and in the saddle on one or more of the racehorses my father had acquired. I was my father's exercise jockey. This usually meant I would miss the school bus, so my father would drive his jockey to school. I was on top of the world. I probably would have attempted to become the first woman professional jockey, but I could never have made the weight.

I had to settle for becoming a medical doctor.

Not surprisingly, once my formal education was complete and I was gainfully employed, I once again started riding. The stable where I boarded my horse offered lessons in hunter-jumpers, so I dived right in. After six months or so, learning the basics, the instructor Mark Andreasen moved on to another location where he would both board horses and offer riding instruction. I decided to move my horse to his new facility. The location was in south St. Louis county; it was a lovely fifteen-acre spread called Oak Trails Ranch. From childhood, I had dreamed of owning a place like Oak Trails Ranch. Soon I learned that the owners really wanted to sell the place. My dream came true. My mother helped put the deal together while I continued my duties at Washington University. This was 1979, and I was thirty-four years old. Having been through a few not-so-healthy relationships with other physicians, my attitude toward potential suitors was pretty negative; so my mother and I pooled our resources, bought Oak Trails Ranch, and moved into the ranch house together. We hired Mark to manage it for us.

No house is a home without a dog, so we added a golden retriever, Samsun. Life was good.

So what was Oliver's story prior to our meeting?

Ollie graduated from Hancock High School in Lemay, Missouri, in the spring of 1945 at the age of seventeen. With encouragement from one of his teachers, he took a test offered by the army. His score qualified him to enter the army immediately after graduation as part of the Army Specialized Training Corp.[2] Qualification included a Stanford-Binet type IQ test score of at least 115 (an IQ above 115 is considered above average).

His above average IQ did not protect him from the ravages of dementia in later life.

After boot camp at Fort Bliss, headquartered in El Paso, Texas, he was shipped to Brookings, South Dakota to begin an accelerated college degree program (a four-year program in one and a half years). Qualified candidates could go on to medical school or pursue advanced engineering degrees. Others, completing the course, graduated as officers.

Notable Alumni

- Mel Brooks, American actor, filmmaker
- Bob Dole, US senator, Senate majority leader, and presidential candidate
- Henry Kissinger, US secretary of state and Nobel Prize winner
- Ed Koch, US congressman and New York City mayor
- Gore Vidal, author
- Kurt Vonnegut, author

OLIVER IN HIS ARMY UNIFORM, NOTE THE INSIGNIA OF
THE ARMY SPECIALIZED TRAINING PROGRAM ON HIS LEFT
SHOULDER: THE LAMP OF KNOWLEDGE SUGGESTED ACADEMIC
LEARNING AND THE SWORD REPRESENTED THE MILITARY
PROFESSION THE INSIGNIA WAS. AFFECTIONATLY REFFERED
TO BY HIS CLASSMATES AS THE PISS POT AND THE SWORD.

A few months after the end of WWII, in August 1945, the undergraduate program was discontinued. Ollie found himself on a troop ship headed for Japan as part of the occupation forces. He was discharged from the army in May of 1947 as a private first class. He went to work for the Maune Company in St. Louis, initially installing playground equipment. He began working his way into sales of residential windows manufactured by Maune. Soon, he married Geraldine, the younger sister of a high school chum Ed Morgan. They were blessed with three children: Claudia, Keith, and Gloria. The kids and Ollie were fortunate to spend nearly every weekend fishing the Current River near Van Buren Missouri. The family owned a second home there, right on the riverbank, which enabled this idyllic life.

Unfortunately, an act of Congress in 1964 brought this to an end. In this act, Congress established the Ozark National Scenic River Ways National Park designed to protect the Current and Jack's Fork Rivers in Missouri. Their property was purchased by the National Park Service, and the park was dedicated in 1971.

Family vacations to Pensacola, Florida, developed into a love of gulf fishing along the coast. Income-producing properties were purchased in this lovely area, and eventually, a second home was built in Pensacola with gulf access.

After the kids were grown and married, Jerry stayed in Florida full-time while Ollie continued working in St. Louis, spending weekends in Florida. He spent weeknights with divorced daughter Gloria and granddaughter Heather in a little house on West Felton Avenue in Lemay, Missouri. The arrangement proved hard on the marriage, leading to a separation.

In the fall of 1978, daughter Gloria and granddaughter Heather moved to Gerald, Missouri, where Gloria married Robert Flottmann. This left Ollie alone in the little house on West Felton, with his Yorkie Trooper.

To pass the time and nurture his inborn creativity, Ollie took community college classes in art and produced two nice oil paintings. A business-related trip to the Colorado Rockies inspired a landscape painting, and the other painting was an abstract. After we were married, these paintings graced our home for thirty-seven years. Near Ollie's death, I passed them on to his son Keith.

The Colorado Rockies trip not only inspired the landscape painting; it also inspired a physical fitness campaign. He became a runner, spending many hours jogging in Jefferson Barracks Park, just a short jog from home.

In the summer of 1979, Ollie began a journey of reflection by hiking a section of the Appalachian Trail in North Carolina. He spent a week hiking, tent camping, fishing for dinner, and deciding how to move forward with his life. It was at this point that our paths began to cross.

Next door to the West Felton house lived Gladys Orzel and her daughter Anna (my goddaughter). Anna and her mother provided babysitting for Heather and dog sitting for Trooper. Heather, and hence the whole neighborhood, called Ollie Grandpa.

In her early teens, Anna decided that Grandpa and her godmother would make a cute couple, so she made sure to tell Grandpa all about her doctor godmother and to tell me all about her neighbor Grandpa. Not having met him, my vision of Grandpa was that of a grizzled old man. Then one Sunday, as my mother and I picked up Anna for a day of horseback riding at Oak Trails Ranch, Trooper got out of the yard and onto the street. Ollie came out to catch him. "There's Grandpa," my mother said. "That can't be Grandpa," said I. Before me was a redheaded, red-bearded good-looking man in great shape with a nice tight butt.

Yes, I was one of those women who appreciate well-toned gluteus maxima on guys. My interest was piqued.

The Maune Company had expanded into commercial windows and exterior curtain wall and took on the new name of Profile Systems. Oliver Anthony Krechel was named vice president of the company in 1979. This was a big move for a little company. The industry leader at the time was Cupples Products Inc., also based in St. Louis. Among the most famous of the buildings clad by Cupples are the John Hancock Center and the Sears Tower in Chicago, as well as the World Trade Center Twin Towers in New York City.

In addition to studying architecture at Washington University in St. Louis, as a night school student, Ollie also studied Cupples work on a regular basis, often being present at stress tests for their mock-ups. He marveled at the mock-ups of the World Trade Center, the most advanced of the time. A few of the buildings with windows and or curtain wall systems (exterior cladding) provided by Profile Systems as a result of Ollie's sales efforts were the Edison Brothers building on North Broadway in St. Louis, Missouri, Nordstrom's building façade in San Francisco, California, and the inn of the Spanish Pavilion in St. Louis.

The Spanish Pavilion was a jewel of the 1964 World's Fair in New York. St. Louis Mayor Alfonso Cervantes arranged to have the pavilion gifted to St. Louis by the Spanish government, along with most of the interior items which made it successful at the World's Fair. Then with the help of some St. Louis businessmen, the mayor moved the pavilion to St. Louis, where they hoped to operate it as a tourist attraction.

The building was reconstructed in St. Louis at the corner of Broadway and Market Streets in downtown St. Louis and dedicated in 1969.

The project was not successful; and the foundation, which owned and operated it, was soon bankrupt.

In 1976, the developer Don Breckenridge bought the building to convert it into a hotel. A twenty-five-story tower was constructed over the open courtyard.

Since Oliver worked with Profile Systems, it was Oliver's system design for the curtain wall containing the heat and air-conditioning conduits that helped make this hotel a reality.

The Breckenridge Inn was purchased by the Marriott Corporation in 1979. They completed the hotel conversion.

This project had great personal significance to Ollie and me, and we held our wedding reception and spent our first night as husband and wife in this iconic hotel.

CHAPTER 2

The Beginning

In the fall of 1979, Goddaughter Anna began asking Grandpa to take her to Oak Trails Ranch so that he could watch her ride her new horse.

I had purchased a beautiful bay mare for Anna, and she had named her Anna's Debutante and called her Debby. In the years Anna owned Debby, they were successful in many horse shows.

ANNA AND DEBBY SHOWING OFF A FEW OF
THEIR PLACEMENT RIBBONS

I met Ollie a few times when he brought Anna to the stables. Then in early 1980, he took the plunge and asked me out. The date was a trip to Gerald, Missouri, to have lunch with his daughter

Gloria, her husband Bob, and his granddaughter Heather. I came very close to saying no, and I was really not interested in another relationship of any kind. But I did accept, thinking, "It's just lunch."

Ollie was apparently very unsure how to manage a date with a doctor. So on the way to Gerald, he stopped at Senate Grove to show me his grandmother's grave after spending most of the drive telling me stories of his childhood on his grandparents' farm.

A trip to a cemetery is an unlikely top ten destinations for a doctor on a first date. Strange as it might sound, it worked well for him. I decided that he was the most sensitive man I had ever met. A few dinner dates followed. An avid gardener, he invited me to dinner at his house where he prepared a lovely meal and introduced me to Brussel sprouts from his garden. Things were still working well for him. In early March, I was scheduled to fly to Orlando, Florida, to present a paper at the Southern Society of Anesthesiologists. Ollie insisted on driving me to the airport. We parked, and he accompanied me into the airport terminal, where he announced he was going with me and proceeded to buy a ticket on the same plane. A little overwhelmed, at this point, I decided he was not only the most sensitive man I had ever met, but he was also the most confident. I did not say no.

I was the speaker at this medical convention, so the organizing group had reserved a room for me at the convention hotel. Amazingly, it was a suite with plenty of room for two.

OLLIE AND SUSAN AT THE HOTEL IN ORLANDO FLORIDA
FOLLOWING HER SCIENTIFIC PRESENTATION

After my presentation, we were free to explore Orlando and Disney World. I had the time of my life, and I am pretty sure Ollie was pleased he had come along for the ride. The bookish academic anesthesiologist with the relatively boring life was learning two could have a lot more fun than one. Upon our return, I invited Ollie to have dinner with my mother and me. My mother fixed chili. With the first bite, we were all fire-breathing dragons; mother had mistakenly used cayenne pepper instead of chili powder. Was she consciously or unconsciously trying to discourage this relationship? Ollie solved the problem by taking the three of us out for dinner. Samsun also had a problem with this new person in our lives. He took forever to warm up to Ollie. Eventually, he did, and we all breathed a sigh of relief. Dogs are good judges of character.

It was about this time in our relationship that one of the otolaryngologists with whom I worked took me aside one day and suggested that I might benefit from hearing aids. I had been deaf in my right ear since age five apparently due to childhood infections. I had been diagnosed with measles, chicken pox, and scarlet fever occurring within days of each other. After my recovery, it was noted that I refused to use the telephone on my right ear. Testing in the Chicago public school system noted profound deafness in the right ear and suggested I always be seated in the front of the classroom. They also gave me lip-reading lessons.

A year or so before I met Ollie, I had been giving a lecture to a group of residents and became alarmed at the fact that I was having difficulty fielding questions from the audience. I consulted another otolaryngologist who brutally diagnosed hysterical deafness. Fortunately for me, my surgical colleague was a bit more perceptive and suggested hearing aids. This changed my life. I had begun to lose hearing in my left ear. It was the left ear that could be fitted with an aid. The right ear was too badly damaged to benefit from an aid.

I was amazed after receiving my new hearing aid that there were birds outside my bedroom window. It had been years since I had heard the birds. Communicating became a lot easier too.

Ollie and I continued dating—going to indoor soccer games, shopping trips, camping, fishing, and general outdoor exploring. We also enjoyed many live theatre performances. He taught me to play golf, taking me to his golf club in Joachim, Missouri. He was actually a fine golfer, and I just enjoyed walking the course more than hitting the ball, but he was patient, and we always had a fun time. We finished one Saturday night at the mall, just browsing. Knowing that Ollie had an elephant statuette collection (inspired by his tenure as Jefferson County Republican Committeeman), I found a small elephant painting to go with his collection. Years later, when I was hanging this picture on the wall of our second home, I happened to turn it over and read an inscription Ollie had written on the back of the picture. It said, "Found by Susan, at Harvey Wall Hangers 2/9/80. Part of a beautiful day that included a Steamer's soccer game, at the Checker Dome, dinner at OB Clark's, shopping at South County Mall and time together at home. I love her dearly." It was signed "Ollie." He was such a dear loving man.

In spite of being fifty-three years young, Ollie took up horseback riding, and since Oak Trails Ranch was mainly a hunter-jumper facility, he was soon taking fences with rest of us. Mark helped him acquire a fine palomino mare he called Honeybee. As a rider, I have to say he was better than me, and he was bolder and had better form.

OLLIE TAKING A FENCE WITH HONEY BEE AT A LOCAL HORSE SHOW

Anna remained a big part of our lives. Ollie took her to school most days, and she continued to plot ways to draw us closer. One cool late March evening, she took Ollie shopping for a pair of earrings for me. They were a beautiful pair of cameos and required pierced ears, which I did not yet have. Ollie remedied that over the weekend by doing the honors of piercing my ears. How many guys would be brave enough to pierce a doctor's ears? How many doctors would trust this small surgical procedure to a nonsurgeon? No complications occurred, and I still wear those same earrings thirty-eight years later.

As spring turned to summer, we were spending nearly every nonworking hour together. We opened the pool at the ranch and spent many hours around it. The picture below is the first of many showing clearly how much he adored me. When I visited him in the nursing home, the brightness of the look on his face lit up the room. Many have commented on that fact. There has never been a doubt in my mind that he loved me dearly and I him.

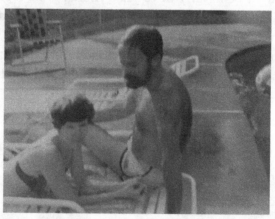

OLLIE AND SUSAN RELAXING AROUND THE POOL
AT THE OAK TRAILS RANCH HOUSE 1980

By late May of 1980, unbeknownst to me, Ollie began to question the wisdom of maintaining the Felton home since he spent all his time with me at Oak Trails Ranch. Mark introduced Ollie to a friend of his who was looking for a starter home. The friend rented the Lemay home with an option to buy. I am quite sure that in addition to Mark, both my mother and Anna were aware of this plan.

Not I, until his furniture appeared in the ranch house basement. I did not say no. This man brought me great joy.

As his divorce entered the final stages, he asked me to marry him. I said no. The divorce seemed very one sided. All of the Florida assets would go to his ex-wife, and he would pay a fairly hefty alimony, as well as maintaining a life insurance policy to protect her income should he die. Given the assets and the income I would bring to the marriage, it seemed very unbalanced. We agreed to continue living together.

CHAPTER 3

The Engagement, Wedding, and Honeymoon

We continued to have fun. For me, this was the most exciting time of my life.

As I thought more of his marriage proposal, I began to imagine myself in his ex-wife's shoes. He was treating her more than fairly, as I would want to be treated in similar circumstances. I decided that this simply spoke to the character of the man, which meant a lot more than mere assets. The age difference was of some concern as well. He was seventeen years my senior. All the men in my life were gone between the ages of sixty-four and seventy-two. Ollie was fifty-three. I decided if I could get ten good years with him, it would be worth it.

One night, I said to him, "Let's get married." He did not say no. We announced our engagement July 5, 1980. The announcement was made at a party held at Oak Trails Ranch attended by staff and residents of the Department of Anesthesiology, Barnes Hospital, Washington University, St. Louis. My mother's cautioning words were, "You will be a grandmother." My reply was, "You will be a great-grandmother." She also offered to move out, but both Ollie and I urged her to stay; Oak Trails Ranch was her home too. The three of us had ten great, fun-filled years together, and Ollie and I had more than thirty. Even during the hard years, since his diagnosis and especially the need for nursing home care, there have still been some wonderful moments together.

Following the engagement announcement, the wedding plans began in earnest. We set the date for October 3, 1980. We soon learned that we had barely enough time to put all the pieces together in order to pull off a big wedding. Three months is cutting it close. Every weekend and many week nights were devoted to wedding plans. Neither of us were regular churchgoers at the time and did not belong to any particular denomination. I had attended a Presbyterian sponsored Sunday school as a child in Chicago and felt a deep connection with God and knew I wanted to be married in church. Ollie was brought up a Methodist, attending the Senate Grove Methodist Episcopal Church in Berger, Missouri, during the summers he spent on his grandparents' farm. The adjoining cemetery is the same one he took me to on our first date, showing me his grandmother's grave. Although Ollie brought his children up in the Baptist Church and served as a deacon, he no longer considered himself a Baptist. Ollie's daughter Claudia had married a Methodist and was attending the Kirkwood United Methodist Church in Kirkwood, Missouri. She suggested we get married in her church. We visited the church and were interviewed by the pastor, who agreed to perform the ceremony.

One evening after the engagement was announced, we met in Downtown St. Louis at the Diamond Shop to pick out the engagement and wedding rings. We chose a lovely heart-shaped diamond and set it in a plain gold band. It was perfect. With my mother's help, wedding plans came together. The flowers turned out to be a bit of a problem. I wanted white roses and white orchids; the orchids were a bit tricky to get in October. A friend of my mother's was doing the flower arrangements, and she was able to come through with the orchids at the last minute. I did not know if they would be in the bouquet until I saw it on our wedding day.

We chose the Marriott Pavilion Hotel for the reception and our first night together as man and wife because of the significance the building played in Ollie's career. The Hawaiian Island of Maui was our honeymoon destination.

Since my father was no longer living, I asked my mentor Dr. C. R. Stephen to walk me down the aisle. Olli's son-in-law Bob Flottmann agreed to be his best man, and his other son-in-law Bill Rouggly agreed to be groomsman. I chose my medical school friend and roommate Dr. Dianne Hoard to be my maid of honor, and my goddaughter Anna Orzel was bridesmaid. The flower girls were granddaughters Heather Flottmann and Amy Rouggly, and the ring bearer was granddaughter Sara Rouggly. The music was provided by the church organist, Earl Naylor, and the soloist was ranch manager, Mark Andreasen. The one glitch in the wedding plans was that we forgot about ushers. On the afternoon of our wedding day, we asked my cousin Frank Liscom, who had flown in for the wedding from Reno, Nevada, and longtime friend of my parents' Ralph Olson from Waukesha, Wisconsin, to be the ushers. It was smooth sailing from there.

The reception was fun; it was a great party. The highlights included my cousin Frank, a semiprofessional drummer, sitting in on the drums with the live band we had hired. One of the guests whose last name was Wilson (my maiden name) but no relation kept the food trays full at the request of Mr. Wilson. This was not budget friendly, but the party played on. Finally, Ollie's sister Doris caught the bridal bouquet. She married her boyfriend, boss, the following spring. It was a great catch for both of them, and the marriage lasted until his death in 2018.

My aunt Frances Bonham was invited to the wedding and reception and stayed at the ranch with her sister (my mother) while Ollie and I were on our honeymoon. My mother and aunt had been estranged for many years; our wedding brought them together. My aunt played an important part in our lives over the next twenty years.

Our honeymoon was spent at the Hyatt Regency, Kaanapali Beach Resort near Lahaina, on the lovely Hawaiian Island of Maui. Lahaina is an old whaling town. We played golf, explored the lovely shops of Lahaina, and rented a car to drive the high costal road. We saw beautiful views in the unpopulated part of the island and never met another car.

We traversed the island's interior, lush countryside on horse-back. Of course, we made the climb to the observation deck of the Haleakala Volcano, the centerpiece of Haleakala National Park. The summit tops at just over ten thousand feet. The climb was cold and difficult but well worth the exertion to view this beautiful place. The volcano is dormant, not extinct. Another eruption is not out of the question.

All too soon, we had to fly home, back to work and the ranch.

CHAPTER 4

Marriage, the Early Years

We continued all the fun activities that we had engaged in before the wedding. Many weekends were devoted to Hunter Jumper competitions, and we did well.

In addition to dressage and show ring hunter-jumper offerings at the ranch, Mark added a cross country trail. Behind our property lay around fifty acres of woods. Mark cut trails and arranged barriers the horses needed to jump to continue on the trail. The course was run at a gallop. It was great fun. Of course, this was the sport that would later make Superman actor Christopher Reeves a quadriplegic.

By April of 1981, I found myself a favorite on the regional speaker's circuit, speaking to many groups of anesthesiologists and nurse anesthetists in places like Leavenworth, Kansas; Carbondale, Illinois; and Wichita, Kansas. Ollie always found a way to call on architects in the cities where I had speaking engagements and was thereby able to accompany me to these locations. This certainly made these work-related chores more fun.

My mother, too, enjoyed traveling, so we planned a trip to the British Isles for September of 1981. My aunt Frances came along to share a room with my mother; and two sisters, Frances and Dorothy, from California, whom we had met on the grand tour of Europe before Ollie came into our lives, were also going on this trip.

Frances and Dorothy had established a bond with my mother because they had also worked at the Merchandise Mart in Chicago at the same time my mother was working there, during World War II. Many government offices associated with the war effort were housed in this huge building. My mother did clerical work for the Navy Seabees.

The trip very nearly went off the rails a few days before we were to fly to London. Riding a new horse we had acquired for him, Ollie was thrown as the horse spooked. He landed in the sitting position and immediately began rolling in pain. I saw the accident and knew his back was in jeopardy. I was able to convince him to stop rolling and lie still while an ambulance was called to take him to the hospital.

An orthopedic surgeon with whom I worked at Barnes Hospital saw him in the emergency room. He did have two compression fractures. A back brace was prescribed, along with limited activities; but as long as he did not carry any suitcases, he was cleared to travel. The trip went on as planned, and he had five women carrying his bags for him. What a life!

In 1982, I was promoted to associate professor of anesthesiology at Washington University in St. Louis. This same year, I was asked to produce a textbook of anesthesiology as it pertained to the geriatric patient. I had been involved in this aspect of anesthesiology since 1975. My mentor Dr. C. R. Stephen had begun an annual three-day meeting on this topic, drawing speakers and participants from across the country. I had given several of the lectures. The textbook was entitled *Anesthesia and the Geriatric Patient* and was published by Grune & Stratton in 1984. As would be true throughout my career, Oliver was the man behind the woman.

I continued on the speaker's circuit, Ollie accompanying me. There was always an architect to call on in order to drum up business for Profile Systems. A few days in Carbondale, Illinois, followed by a few days back at my alma mater, the University of Louisville, where I gave a lecture to a group of Anesthesiologist's that included one of my medical school classmates, Dr. Don Shoemaker.

That summer, Ollie's youngest sister Virginia was hospitalized at Missouri Baptist Hospital. She spent months in the intensive care unit following surgery for Crohn's Disease. Her son Harry spent that summer with us. He was a teenager who needed to be kept busy, so we assigned him the task of painting the outdoor arena fence. This kept him busy most of the summer and convinced him that manual labor was not something he wanted to make his life's work. He figured out that he better focus on an education that would give him skills beyond manual labor. Harry went on to get a BA in information technology and an MS in managing information technology. Having had experience as an intensivist, I followed Virginia's care. The main reason for the prolonged intensive care unit stay was that they were unable to wean her from the mechanical ventilator. Although I was no longer an intensivist, I still followed the literature and became convinced that the high sugar content of the parenteral nutrition she was receiving was, in fact, the reason she could not be weaned from the ventilator. I was not on the staff at this hospital, so my suggestions were largely ignored. That is until, I sought the help of one of my former residents, Dr. Cynthia Guy. She was on the staff at Missouri Baptist and agreed to back up my suggestions. Soon after, Virginia was able to breathe without the assistance of the ventilator. She was ultimately able to go home to her son.

I presented another paper at the Southern Society of Anesthesiologists, this time in Hilton Head, South Carolina. As was often the case, we combined the meeting with a vacation, renting a car and exploring South Carolina. Among the highlights of this trip was the day we spent exploring Brookgreen Gardens near Myrtle Beach. It is a lovely sculpture garden covering many acres, amongst pathways shaded by live oak trees.

Ollie had a building project in Charleston, so we stopped by to see how that was going. We also spent an evening with Dr. Janet Walker, who was doing a family medicine residency in Charleston. Janet had been a medical student at Washington University, and I had been assigned as her faculty advisor, probably based on our common interest in horses, especially dressage. We have stayed in touch all these years. As an air force physician, she was stationed for a time in Germany, where she had the opportunity to work with Haute Ecole instructors, learning the most advanced components of classical dressage and riding Grand Prix—level horses.

In October, we joined an International Medical Meeting for Octoberfest in Munich, Germany—we being Ollie, my mother, Aunt Frances, and I. I attended the meetings while they enjoyed the beauties of Munich. I, too, was able to enjoy many of the festivities. In the street below our hotel rooms, we could see team after team of draft horses hauling loads of beer kegs to the brewery tents set up in the park. Each tent was full to overflowing with beer drinkers, singing and enjoying raucous music. Following the meetings and fun in Munich, we boarded buses to take in additional sites in Germany and Austria. Berchtesgaden is a lovely German town in southeastern Germany, near the Austrian border. Above it is Obersalzburg, which became the infamous, Adolf Hitler's southern headquarters. Nearby we toured Eagles Nest Conference center, which was built for Hitler's fiftieth birthday. Crossing the border into Austria, we visited Lustschloss Hellbrunn, in Salzburg. This is a fifteenth-century palace built by a prince-archbishop of Salzburg. We were royally entertained attending an opera at the Graz Opera House. Then on to Vienna where we tried the Sacher Torte at the Sacher Hotel. Finally, the highlight of the Vienna visit was an exhibition of the world-famous Lipizzaner stallions at the magnificent Spanish Riding School.

Another great bonus produced by our wedding was that it not only brought my aunt Frances into our lives, but it also brought her daughter Dolores; Dolores's husband, Rich; and their children, Karen, Kathleen, and Kenneth into our lives. Dolores and I had spent the summers of most of our preadolescent years together. We were as close as most sisters and only a year apart in age. While Ollie and I were married on October 3, 1980, Dolores and Rich were married on October 4, 1969. As we grew closer once again, we often celebrated anniversaries together. On the first occasion of this reunion, Rich, who was a commodities broker, was touring the grain belt with his family, looking at the crops. This brought them to Missouri. The five Latzes visited us at the ranch. The two girls were especially fascinated by the horsemanship on display. The following year, we invited Karen and Kathy to come stay with us for horse camp and swimming. They had a great time, and Kathy would continue riding near her home in the northwest suburbs of Chicago. Ollie's daughter

Claudia also hosted the two girls at her home. Claudia's two daughters, Amy and Sara, were close in age to my young cousins. The families were blending. Oak Trails Ranch was a popular venue for horse camping and swimming. Granddaughters Amy and Heather were also summertime visitors. Heather would later say that these times were among her fondest memories.

Throughout the 1980s and 1990s, Ollie and I made many trips to Chicago. He would visit architects, and I would work with the American Society of Anesthesiologists in various capacities. On most of these trips, we would take the time to visit Frances, Dolores and family, as well as my older cousin Marlene and her family.

We spent Christmas Eve 1982 (Anna's birthday) with Gladys and Anna at their home on West Felton in Lemay, near the spot I first caught sight of Ollie, chasing Trooper. Anna's sister Marguerite was there with her husband, Steve Whitten. Steve was a nondenominational minister in Southern California. I knew quickly that he had truly dedicated his life to God and would follow a righteous path and be successful. He was good at mesmerizing the room even then. It was also clear he adored Marguerite; and not just Marguerite but Anna and Gladys adored him. I knew instinctively that night that our time of influencing and guiding Anna was coming to an end. Although saddened, I felt that Steve would be a good guide in our stead. My instinct proved correct. In early 1983, Anna and Gladys were making plans to move back to San Diego, California. My instincts regarding Steve proved correct as well. He was a good guide for Anna and became very successful in his ministry. He eventually began teaching divinity at a San Diego college. He and Marguerite have four wonderful kids.

The Southern Society of Anesthesiologists called us back to Orlando and Disney World. I made another presentation while memories were recalled and new memories were made.

That same spring, we vacationed in Washington, DC. We arrived just in time to see the beautiful cherry blossoms. We were the travelling four again—Ollie and I, my mother and aunt Frances. We stayed at a lovely old Washington Hotel that was under renovation that year, making it more affordable. We took in most of the sights on walking tours.

The Eastern Seaboard was a territory where Ollie did a lot of business for Profile Systems, so we rented a car and drove to both Baltimore, Maryland, and Trenton, New Jersey. Near Trenton, we stopped for lunch at an old inn. Of course, George Washington had slept there.

OLLIE, SUSAN AND SUSAN'S MOTHER GERRY AT
LUNCH TRENTON, NEW JERSEY, 1983

One of Ollie's East Coast associates had a great trip planned for him and his wife. They were going up to British Columbia, Canada, to meet with a big game hunter in the region. This fellow ran summer trips to the high country to defray his costs as he game spotted in anticipation of the big game hunters who travelled north to hunt for the abundant wild life, caribou, moose, big-horned sheep, and bear. We were invited to join this couple on a trip of a lifetime. We were all in.

On July 1, 1983, we flew into Watson Lake, Yukon, Canada. Watson Lake is famous for its Sign Post Forest. Signposts from all over the world are proudly displayed here.

Our guide's wife picked us up in Watson Lake and drove us south along the Alaska Highway to their basecamp, located in British Columbia on Swan Lake. Here we met the couple's two daughters and were treated to a good meal and a restful night. Absent were the other couple who had invited us to join them. This adventure would be just Ollie and me, the guide and the cook.

The next morning, we hauled all our gear down to the dock, where we were picked up by a sea plane and flown to the higher elevations where we met the guide and the cook. The cook was a Colorado college student who had been hired for the summer. The guide and the cook had ridden into the mountains weeks before to deliver the riding horses and pack horses and set up the cabins for us and later the big game hunters. All was in readiness for our wilderness experience. The outhouse was only three sided, but the view was spectacular, including the bear in the valley below. The guys provided us with fishing tackle and a dinghy and sent us off to fish in Bigfoot Lake, adjacent to the cabin. Our assignment was to catch dinner for four and throw the rest back. No problem, the fish were abundant, biting and huge. We each had one on the line with nearly every cast. What a wonderful afternoon this was.

This was a part of the world that I would never have experienced without Ollie, and what a magnificent experience it was.

OLLIE WITH A LAKE TROUT, HIGH COUNTRY BIG FOOT LAKE

Back at the cabin, the cook put our gear away and cleaned and filleted the fish while we sat back and relaxed. That night dinner was wonderful, and we were regaled by stories of life in this beautiful wilderness. Nightly, we communicated by shortwave radio with the basecamp. This was our only connection to the outside world. The next morning, we saddled up the horses—or shall I say, the horses were saddled for us? All we had to do was mount up to begin the game-spotting portion of our adventure.

As we left the Big Foot campsite, Ollie pointed out some animal tracks near the trail. The track was roughly the size of a dinner plate. "Bear track," he exclaimed. "No," said the guide, "that is a wolf track." We climbed higher and higher into the Canadian Rockies. Eventually, we climbed right into a snowstorm. We had to stop to rest the horses for a while and eat our lunch consisting of leftover fish from the night before. The storm moved on, as did we.

Periodically, the guide would scour the hills with binoculars, looking for the game herds. We found several herds of mountain goat and often nearby, big-horned sheep. The guide would dismount and scurry up the mountainside to find a location for us to get close to the herd without spooking them. Climbing up was pretty straightforward. Climbing back down not so much; the guide went down fast like a mountain goat leaning back almost parallel to the terrain. Me, I went down more like one butt bump at a time. Ollie was much more graceful but held back to assist me when needed. We arrived at our next camp sight early enough to take the dingy out on the nearby mountain lake. As always, the lake trout were biting.

Dark clouds rolled in as evening approached, and the wind picked up, causing white caps in the lake, making progress to the shore difficult. To make our situation even more harrowing, the only sound we could hear were wolf howls. It was almost as if they were saying, "Looks like dinner is going to wash up on the shore before too long." We made it back to the cabin, where we could relax by the woodstove to get warm while the cook and guide tended to the chores. The accommodations were not grand, but aside from a shower, there was nothing more we could ask. This being the land of the midnight sun, we were often eating dinner at 9:00 p.m. or 10:00

p.m. and still admiring the gorgeous views right outside the cabin door. The fire would often burn down in the stove as we slept. If I got cold, dear sweet Ollie would get up and throw a couple more logs on the remaining embers. Each morning after a very big breakfast, we would mount up and continue on to the next campsite, continuously spotting game. We could see Caribou in the valleys, but there was no sneaking up on them. Each day was more glorious than the last. The horses were sure-footed and steady. Rarely would it be necessary to dismount and lead them through difficult terrain. We arrived at one of the cabins which appeared to have a recently installed floor. The guide told us that he had done an inspection tour of all the cabins earlier in the spring and found that porcupines had moved into this particular cabin and made a real mess, requiring extensive repair before arrival of guests. Gradually we made our way down the mountain, heading for base camp. In the lower elevations near the abundant rivers and streams, we encountered moose. We saw several moose cows with calves. We kept our distance but still had a magnificent view. Back at basecamp, the guide prepared the sauna for us, clean at last. We still had one more day at base camp. I suspect this was the best day of the trip for Ollie. We went fly fishing for Artic Grayling and Dolly Varden in one of the streams that fed base camp Swan Lake. We had brought only one fly rod; these hungry fish were hitting the fly two at a time. I got the fly rod once or twice but mostly watched as Ollie had the fishing experience of his life up till that point as we would go on to do many more fly-fishing trips. After ten days in that glorious place, we flew back home, with wonderful memories. As you will see, we travelled the world to many exotic places, but this Canadian Rockies trip would always remain our favorite experience.

That fall, our dear friend Mark Andreasen announced that he was giving up on the horse business and would be joining corporate America. Mark assisted us in finding a new tenant for the ranch facility. Michaela Kennedy agreed to lease the facility. She turned out to be quite the businesswoman, as well as horsewoman. Michaela's forte was hunter-jumper, riding, teaching, and training. She did, however, agree to bring in a dressage instructor specifically for Ollie and me.

The arrangement worked well for us. The ranch facility was soon full and creating a strain on the facility itself. We had been relying on cistern water supplemented by water hauled in to fill the cistern. We would need to drill a well to accommodate all those thirsty animals. The ranch was located on a limestone bluff overlooking the Meramec River. Although I worried that this location would make finding good water difficult, I was proved wrong. The well was a huge success, producing plenty of good water. The electrical system in the barns and arena needed to be revamped due to the high demand. A new hay storage area above the horse stalls was added. Ollie knew just the right people to accomplish all these renovations.

Professionally 1984 was a good year for me. The book *Anesthesia and the Geriatric Patient* was published, and I was given tenure by Washington University. In the university, system tenure is granted to those faculty members who have achieved enough standing in their fields to warrant a lifetime appointment. I continued my speaking engagements, both locally and nationally.

A new hospital was being built on the medical campus. It was officially named Children's Hospital at Washington University Medical Center and was dedicated in 1984. Several new anesthesiologists had been recruited to staff the operating rooms in the new hospital, but they still needed another faculty member with sufficient pediatric experience to fill the last position. I was asked to fill this position. I loved it; I had found my true calling.

On the home front, Ollie decided his red beard was starting to gray too much, so one Saturday morning, he shaved it off. My mother was the first to see him after the deed and exclaimed "Oh my God." With this, I came running. Poor Ollie could only say, "I can grow it back." He looked different, but he was still my guy, so I approved. I must admit, though, that night, I felt like I was sleeping with a stranger. The scratchy beard was gone.

The fearsome foursome went cruising that spring. It was the first of many cruises for Ollie and me, but my mother and Aunt Frances were already old hands at it. We sailed the Southern Caribbean on the Rotterdam of the Holland America Line. Notable ports of call included Curacao, a Dutch island in the lesser Antilles, and Caracas, Venezuela.

The summer of 1984 was interesting to say the least. My mother began having intense headaches and had herself convinced she had a brain tumor. One afternoon when I came home from work, I found her crying over one of my medical books. While I did not think she had a brain tumor, I did not know what she did have. After an extensive workup and many consultations, she was diagnosed with temporal arteritis. Left untreated, it can result in blindness. She was given high-dose steroids to treat this disease and, thanks to the debilitating effects of the steroids, spent three months in the hospital.

Ollie's mother fell and broke her hip that summer and had surgery and a short rehab in the same hospital. Not to be outdone, Ollie woke up one morning with severe abdominal pain, which I diagnosed as an acute gallbladder attack. I called one of the surgeons I worked with, and after a quick workup, Ollie was having his gallbladder removed. So that summer, every evening after work, I was making hospital rounds on my family. In 1985, Ollie's mother passed away following another fall in her home; she was eighty-three years old. We buried her at the Senate Grove Cemetery, near her mother and father. This was the cemetery where Ollie took me on our first date.

We continued to ride competitively in both hunter-jumper and dressage. I took two notable falls—one over a fence, which resulted in a concussion and an eye injury requiring stitches. The requisite hard hat did not prevent the concussion; the metal clasp on the strap actually caused the eye injury. The second injury happened when a leisurely ride on the steadiest horse in the stable resulted in a neck injury as the horse spooked at something unknown. This one would actually haunt us the rest of our lives.

Again, this year, we combined a work-related trip to the West Coast with a leisurely sightseeing drive through the southwest, taking in the Grand Canyon, Lake Mead, and Las Vegas. The photo below of Ollie leaning against a tree on the canyon edge is one of my favorites.

OLLIE, GRAND CANYON, 1985

Granddaughter Sara was the perfect age of twelve for a trip to Disney World, and since it was one of our favorite playgrounds, we spent a week there with her.

The Hancock High School class of 1945 had its fortieth reunion in June. This would be the first time; I would meet his former classmates. Ollie spoke frequently of his best high school chum Bob Engasser. Although I had never met him nor seen a picture of him and Ollie had not seen him in many years, I was able to pick him out from across the room. The two best buddies were dressed exactly alike and unlike anyone else in the room. There would be many more reunions, but this was Bob's last. He died of pancreatic cancer a short time after this reunion.

Ollie took a great trip on his own in 1985. He made a last-minute trip to Kuwait to bid some jobs which were in the works there. A last-minute visa was available to him but not to an accompanying wife. He made it up to me by coming home with some gorgeous gold jewelry from the local shops. The Kuwaitis were oil rich at the time and had shared the wealth with all the citizens, unlike most of the other Arab countries. The Kuwaitis were mostly living a leisurely life, and most of the day-to-day business was conducted by foreign nationals who were allowed to work in the country for a fixed period of time, a decade or two. Ollie's contacts in Kuwait were Egyptian Coptic Christians, and they took him under their wing for the duration of his stay. Nabil Adley was his main host, and they made a joke of Ollie's daily greeting when he was picked up from his luxurious hotel accommodations. "Nabil, another sunny day." Of course, every day in Kuwait was sunny. This phrase would be uttered many times over the years as their business relationship continued. So striking was this relationship and phrase that ten years later we would name one of our field trial competitive golden retrievers Another Sunny Day.

CHAPTER 5

A New Life, Together

The year 1986 proved to be a very eventful year. We began by planning another adventure trip. Ollie and I were going to Churchill, Manitoba Canada, to view the polar bears. The trip was planned for July. That trip would never be taken.

In the spring of that year, the new chairman of the Department of Anesthesiology mandated that I return to adult anesthesia and leave my position at the children's hospital. I felt strongly that my calling was pediatric anesthesiology. Not long after hearing this unwelcome news, I was talking to the chairman of anesthesiology at the University of Missouri, Dr. William Eggers, who promptly offered me the position of chief of Pediatric Anesthesiology at the University of Missouri. Ollie and I discussed this offer at length. Ollie offered the solution that would change our lives. The solution—find a place halfway between St. Louis, where Ollie would continue to work and Columbia, Missouri, where the University of Missouri was located. This would give each of us a one-hour, sixty-five-mile commute to work every day. Consulting the Missouri map, we concluded that the small town of Jonesburg fit this description. The idea was to build new a facility like the one we had in St. Louis. Although, Jonesburg was a town of less than five hundred persons, it did have a local real estate agent, Edgar Shelton. He showed us several properties, but only one fit the bill, a nice 120-acre farm on Hwy FF about five miles North of I-70, making it an easy commute for both of us.

Initially, we decided that we did not need the entire 120 acres, so we contracted to buy 60 acres. Later we would acquire an additional 40 acres adjacent to this property giving us 100 acres.

A mobile home was parked on the property and occupied by a couple whose family had previously owned the land; it had been lost in foreclosure. We attempted to buy the mobile home, but the price they were asking was too high, so we bought a new single wide mobile home with a bedroom at each end. My mother on one end, Ollie and I on the other along with Sam, the golden retriever and two Siamese cats. The mobile home was basically furnished, but there were a few items we needed to move from the ranch house. One of my residents, Dr. Elaine Riegle, owned a truck and offered to help us move the bulky items. Elaine has remained a true friend throughout all these years. Much of the furniture from the ranch house needed to be stored. We now basically had three households together: mine, my mother's, and Ollie's. That was a lot of stuff; some of which would need to be accessed from time to time. Bob Flottmann, who was a teamster, suggested we rent an over the road trailer and park it on the property. Bob took care procuring and moving the trailer for us, and everyone pitched in to load it the day we moved. This proved to be a great idea. The rental cost was low and accessibility was easy. The days we lived in that mobile home were among the happiest and carefree days of my life. There is much to be said for simplicity.

Much to the amusement of the entire town of Jonesburg, we built the barn with an indoor arena before we built the house. Our priorities were to get the horses settled first. We were fine in the motor home. When I look back on this time in our lives, I am reminded of the advice of my favorite twenty-first-century thinker, Jordan B Peterson. In his third rule for life, he advises, "Make friends with people who want the best for you,"[4] I can only say I really hit the jackpot when I met and married Oliver Anthony Krechel. This move was about what was best for me, not what was best for him. He made this move happen.

As a child, my father had introduced me to the sport of kings, Thoroughbred horse racing. He owned several and raced them at the tracks in Southern Illinois just across the Mississippi River from St.

Louis. I grew up loving the horses and the sport. Soon after our move to Jonesburg, there was a group of Missouri horsemen who were interested in bringing horse racing to Missouri. The money was being put up by a wealthy financier, and a large tract of land was selected just twenty miles from our new farm. That made the farm a perfect place for offtrack stabling. We laid out a plan for our property which included a half mile training track and several small barns to house the potential boarders.

We purchased a well-bred colt we named Uno, our first race-horse. We also purchased several well-bred mares and commenced our breeding program. The long-range plan was to give every new foal a chance on the track. Those that did not make the grade, we would develop as dressage horses.

Uno, registered name Tammy's Pleasure, would go on to win several races at Fairmont Park in Southern Illinois. On page 41 shows Uno winning by several lengths. Below the race photo is the trophy presentation. Ollie and I are third and fourth to the right of the horse, sporting big proud smiles for Uno. Joining us for this occasion is my mentor Dr. C. Stephen standing far right.

UNO, AKA TAMMY'S PLEASURE, WINNING A RACE AT FAIRMONT PARK AND TROPHY PRESENTATION IN THE WINNERS' CIRCLE.

Over the next few years, we would spend many hours with the horses, birthing new foals, and weekends and vacation days putting up fencing for new pastures and corals. Loving the work we did together.

Since several of our horses were black, including Uno, we named our new farm Black Horse Farm and continued to do business as Black Horse Farm (later Black Horse Orchard and Farm) well into the twenty-first century.

Soon after the move to Jonesburg, my book *Anesthesia and the Geriatric Patient* became a worldwide hit, and I found myself in demand as an international speaker and visiting professor on the topic. The first of these was a South American Regional Convention being held in Cartagena, Columbia. Ollie and I would make the trip in 1987. During the meeting, I delivered several lectures for this weeklong convention. Although, I had both high school and college Spanish, I was no longer fluent. Nonetheless, I prepared the lectures in Spanish, with a little help from one of my Argentine coworkers. The meeting actually provided translators, who would have translated my English presentations into Spanish but instead had to translate my Spanish back to English for my fellow American guest lecturers. That must have been a real trick for them.

The trip to Cartagena was not uneventful. We flew from St. Louis to Bogota, Columbia. We needed to take a commuter flight to Cartagena. The airport was crowded; and most of the male passengers were sporting handguns, machine guns, or machetes, this included those on our flight. It was a new experience. When we arrived, our luggage could not be found. Three days later, one of our hosts managed to retrieve our luggage by offering a bribe.

We still had a magnificent time; our hosts offered several trips to the small islands in the area. Two of our friends from Brazil, Carlos and Edith Parsloe, were also attending this meeting. Carlos was one of the guest lecturers. The four of us spent a lot of time together that week, as we would whenever we found ourselves in the same location. While I was busy all week with meetings, Ollie found time to explore old Cartagena. He was especially enamored with the fishing community, taking many photos of their activity. Also of interest was the community love of baseball. "These little guys were good," was Ollie's comment after spending a morning watching them play. I have often wondered if one of these little leaguers was Edgar Renteria, who played for the St. Louis Cardinals from 1999 to 2004 or any of the several major league players from Columbia playing in the late 1990s and early 2000s.

Back home, we were still living in the trailer while we were getting bids to build the house. Ollie drew the plans for the house with a little help on the plumbing specs from one of the guys at Profile Systems. I wanted a colonial-style façade and Master Suite. He wanted a window facing the field near the woods so he could shoot deer out the bedroom window during deer season. The bedrooms would be on the second floor, and the library on the lower level would be adjacent a full bath so that it would serve as my mother's room when she could no longer climb the stairs.

There were a dozen large, nicely spaced maple trees behind the trailer home. Ollie situated the new home so that the front was shaded all day by these lovely old trees and the back with a southeast exposure had plenty of sun and a view of a small pond.

They say many marriages do not survive building a house, but ours never skipped a beat. It was fun to come home from work and see the progress being made on the construction. Each new phase exceeded our expectations. Ollie had, had a lot of experience with country living; my mother and I were mostly city girls, and rural living was a new experience.

Jonesburg had no trash pickup so, we needed a burn barrel. The burn barrel would soon provide my mother and me with a new appreciation for the nature of fire.

One clear, calm summer Saturday morning, Ollie went out to the burn barrel fifty yards behind the trailer. My mother and I were standing in the back doorway watching him light the fire. A small piece of flaming debris fell out of the barrel and hit the ground at the edge of the driveway and an open field. Ollie immediately turned to me and shouted, "Call the fire department." I was aghast. It was such a small piece of burning debris, but I did as I was told and turned to the phone and called the fire department. Jonesburg had an all-volunteer fire department, so I knew it would take some time for them to get to the scene. By the time I got to the back door again, I knew why we needed the fire department: the whole field was aflame, and the fire was headed straight for one of the old barns on the property. Fortunately, the house had not yet been started, because it, too, would have been threatened. A crew was working on the roof of the new horse barn, and two men from St. Louis were there to put in an invisible fence to contain Samsun and the new beagle Chester. The two crews quickly realized that we were in trouble. All of us including my mother would fight that fire for what seemed an hour before it was out and the barn saved. The fire was out before the fire department arrived. It would be our first encounter with Freddie, the redheaded fire chief, police chief, and mail delivery person. Freddie explained that we would need to start paying annual dues to the fire district to help pay for the volunteer fire department. We gladly began making our contributions. We were lucky this time to have had extra help nearby to fight the trash fire. Ollie was a fire genius, to have detected the danger so early.

In December of 1987, Ollie turned sixty. We had a surprise party for him at the local watering hole in Jonesburg. Friends and relatives from all over came to help him celebrate.

DECEMBER 12, 1987 OLLIE'S 60TH BIRTHDAY PARTY,
JONESBURG, MISSOURI LEFT TO RIGHT CLAUDIA,
SUSAN'S MOTHER GERRY, OLLIE, SUSAN, GLORIA

Our next big adventure was the result of my being asked to be a visiting professor in New Zealand. This was a weeklong gig where I would be giving evening and weekend lectures to large groups of New Zealand anesthesiologists and spending week days with anesthesiology residents and medical students in both Wellington and Christ Church. They were particularly interested in how our board certification examinations were conducted. As a board examiner, I was able to give the insight they sought. Our New Zealand hosts were very gracious and allowed me to bring Ollie, my mother, and aunt along. They entertained all of us royally. As usual Ollie, my mother and aunt were able to see more of the countryside than I, while I was busy with my visiting professorship duties. Although Ollie did not have architectural contacts in New Zealand, he and I still walked the streets of both Wellington and Christchurch, he with an eye for the architectural features.

One Friday afternoon, we were doing just that when we stopped in front of an architectural products firm. The office workers were just sitting down to Happy Hour before taking off for the weekend. These friendly people invited us in to join them, and Ollie was able to charm them as he did anyone who met him. We ate lots of lamb in this sheep-raising country and bought some of the most beautiful handmade wool sweaters produced anywhere in the world. They still top off my winter wardrobe.

Our hosts' hospitality included a rental car to explore the South Island while traveling to the venues booked for us on some extended stay tours. So all of us were able to see the ski resorts of Queenstown and of course glorious Milford Sound, which we were able to see both by air and sea.

Since we were going to be in that part of the world, we decided to extend our trip even further and flew from New Zealand to Australia for a week on our own. We rented a caravan (motor home) and drove from Sydney to Melbourne.

What an adventure that was. Poor Ollie had to drive from campground to campground on the wrong (left) side of the road. By the time we reached our hotel in Melbourne near the airport, traversing Melbourne's many roundabouts, he could not wait to get rid of that motor home. Getting directions to the drop-off spot at the airport proved difficult. He engaged the hotel doorman in conversation to achieve this end to no avail. Although they were speaking the same language, the nuance of the dialects were so different that neither could understand the other. My mother, aunt, and I could only laugh, which did nothing to help the situation. Thankfully, a hotel manager was able to understand the problem and get Ollie on the right road to airport returns. From Melbourne, we flew nonstop to San Francisco, a very long thirteen-hour flight. A connecting flight took us to St. Louis and home.

Our careers continued. Ollie travelled frequently across the country to visit architects needing products Profile Systems could provide. I settled in quickly to the most rewarding and productive part of my career. In my new position as chief of Pediatric Anesthesiology, I would need to work closely with the chief of Pediatric General Surgery, Dr. Mary Alice Helikson. Her reputation was one of being hard to get along with. However, she accepted me without question, and our partnership would produce a number of journal articles and other work in the pediatric surgery and anesthesiology fields. For this immediate acceptance, I have much to owe Dr. Jesse Ternberg, chief of Pediatric General Surgery at Washington University St. Louis Children's Hospital. Jesse had known me from a rank intern to associate professor of anesthesiology. I had been giving anesthesia to her patients for many years, including my goddaughter Anna.

Anna had been having recurrent bouts of right lower, abdominal pain. One afternoon, while we were enjoying a day at the racetrack, she had another episode of abdominal pain. I diagnosed appendicitis and took her to see Jesse. Jesse thought it was more likely ovarian torsion, but it was indeed appendicitis. It was on Jesse's recommendation that Mary Alice accepted me without question. Jesse was a pioneering woman in both medicine and the field of pediatric surgery. I was indeed blessed to have known and worked with these two remarkable women.

Dr. Bill Eggers was a great boss; he not only recommended me for tenure, which was granted, but he also empowered his faculty and encouraged them, providing us with the latest tools. He gave each of us a personal computer, well in advance of most other medical or surgical departments having this opportunity. I had no idea what to do with it. One night when I was on call and not occupied with patients, one of my residents, Dr. Robert J. Burton, taught me the basics. What a wonderful gift that was, and I am forever grateful to you, Robert.

In 1988, the two granddaughters, Heather and Amy, were sixteen. We decided that three weeks in Europe would be a great Christmas present. The trip was actually booked for the summer of 1988; Ollie and I would go along as chaperones. We toured London, seeing Westminster Abby, Buckingham Palace, the Churchill War Rooms, and many other magnificent sites. Included were stops in Holland; Switzerland's Lake Lucerne; and of course Italy—the leaning tower of Pisa, Venice and her canals, St. Mark's Square, the glass island Murano, Milan, Florence with the great works of Michelangelo including *The David*, works of Leonardo, and Giambologna's *Kidnaping of the Sabine Women*. Florence always takes my breath away; the girls treated it with a yawn. Not enough shopping and Heather missed her boyfriend. There was also Rome, the Vatican with the beautiful Sistine Chapel ceiling by Michelangelo, and of course, the magnificent *Pieta*. My desire to introduce them to the culture and art of Europe seemed to be failing. The frustration came to boil in Paris, when I simply walked out on all three of them and went running down the Avenue Champs-Elysees. Ollie was right behind me. He calmed me down enough to return to the restaurant where the girls were waiting. We left the girls in Paris with a family who had sent daughters to Amy's family in the USA in an exchange program. They spent another week in France while Ollie and I returned home. I guess maybe a little of my efforts might have paid off, as Heather went on to get a master's degree in art history and worked in New York City with some of the many fine private collections in that city.

Back home at Black Horse Farm, the house was almost finished. That fall, we were able to move our furniture and belongings out of the over the road trailer we had rented for storage. Our friend Dr. Janet Walker showed up for a visit, just in time to help us move in. She would be the first guest in our new home. This ended our two-

and-a-half years in the mobile home. We sold the mobile home and rocked in the site and made it into a rose garden.

For our ninth anniversary, Ollie gave me a card, which I keep today. He wrote the following sentiment by hand: "They passed so swiftly, those nine wondrous and happy years, filled with love and caring, simple and priceless joys that fill my heart and soul. Yes, my love grows and grows for my dearest Susan." It was signed, "Ollie."

In the late 1980s, professional obligations took us across the country on a regular basis. Ollie was able to find business in whatever city I needed to work. We always managed to find interesting things to do in our spare time. Art museums were a special favorite. We were fortunate to be in Boston during an exhibit of the American artist Andrew Wyeth's Helga pictures. This was a stunning collection of 107 drawings and watercolors painted over a fifteen-year period using a single model. He soon sold the collection to a private collector for $10 million. A true piece of Americana that Ollie and I both enjoyed.

As 1990 rolled around, we considered ideas to celebrate our tenth wedding anniversary. We settled on an early fall trip to Glacier National Park in combination with a Trans-Canada Railway tour. This would be another trip we did not make. My mother suffered a fatal heart attack in late summer 1990. It hit both of us hard, and she had been a continuous part of our lives since the beginning. She sustained the heart attack on a Sunday, so I was present, giving initial treatment. Ollie was forced to drive to a neighbor's house to phone for an ambulance since our telephone chose that day to malfunction. I rode with her in the ambulance and stayed with her over the next five days until she died. My office at the hospital had a hide-a-bed couch. Wonderful man that he was, Ollie made the long drive from St. Louis to Columbia (120 miles) every night to stay with me. What a great comfort that was to me. Her passing left a huge hole in my heart. Gone but not forgotten, it would take years for the grief to subside.

Ollie and I continued working, running the farm operations, and I continued to ride dressage. Ollie had largely given up riding since we had moved to the farm, in 1986. Although we did not discuss it, I suspect it had much to do with the fact that he had lost his best horse in a freak accident just before we made the move. Micaela had left our horses out to free range. Ollie came home late from a trip and. not knowing this, left the gate open. Our two horses got out on the road. His was hit by a car and killed. It was our saddest memory of the ranch. Ollie supported me in every way, working with the horses and building the facility, but never rode.

We made a trip to Lake Ouachita near Hot Springs Arkansas. Ollie's son Keith and his family were vacationing there, so we drove down to see them. At that time, they were living in Louisiana but would soon become Texans. We had a great little reunion. The next year, Ollie and I decided to cruise the inside passage from Fairbanks to Vancouver. This was a cruise land tour package, which included a train trip to Denali National Park. One of the horses had injured him while he was cleaning her hooves. Of course, he failed to mention this to me until after the ship had sailed. He had thrombophlebitis by this time and was at high risk of a pulmonary embolism. Yes, I would have cancelled the trip had he told me before we set sail. Fortunately, I was able to treat it adequately, and no complications occurred.

We saw the Alaska pipeline, watched Iditarod mushers train their dogs, sailed Glacier Bay, and visited Sitka, an old Russian settlement. We visited gold rush towns like Fairbanks and Skagway, also native fishing villages like Ketchikan.

We chartered a deep-sea fishing boat out of Juneau with another couple we had met on the cruise. He was a general surgeon from Oklahoma, and he tried hard to recruit me into his group practice. My heart was still in academics, especially the work I was doing in pediatric anesthesia, so I respectfully declined.

CATCH OF THE DAY, OLLIE AND OUR SURGEON FRIEND

We saw and photographed abundant wildlife in Denali National Park.

Nice as it was, it did not compare to our experience on the game spotting, fishing excursion in British Columbia.

The cruise ended in Vancouver British Columbia, where we spent a couple of extra days to see the sights. We were fortunate to get tickets to Andrew Lloyd Webber's *Phantom of the Opera*. It was our first time to see this wonderful musical, but I will always believe it was the best.

We also spent a day in the amazing Butchart Gardens.

CHAPTER 6

Opening Another Chapter in Our Lives

The year 1992 was another big year of change in our lives. Profile Systems had moved its operations to Gerald, Missouri. Ollie no longer needed to drive into the sun both ways but now needed to contend with an equally long drive but on narrow winding roads. Since his work still required frequent flights around the country, I was still coming home to an empty house many weeknights.

One of the Maune brothers had retired, and his pension was a drain on the company. Ollie could see the handwriting on the wall and worried that the company would fold within a year or two. He did not want to continue selling jobs that might not be delivered, thereby letting down his loyal representatives and clients. He decided to retire. No pension was available. At first, he considered doing some consulting work, but as his sixty-fifth birthday approached, he decided to develop his truck-farming talents instead. He began planting sweet corn, tomatoes, beans, squash, potatoes, pumpkins, and many more saleable crops. He joined several Farmers' Markets and spent many days a week selling his produce. Even I got in on the act on weekends when he needed to be in two places at once.

My life was changing too. I had developed severe headaches which were often precipitated by riding the horses. After consulting a neurologist and neurosurgeon, it was determined that I had a neck injury which at this point did not endanger my spinal cord but could certainly do so with any further injury. Rather than risk being a quadriplegic like Christopher Reeves, I made the decision to give up riding. Some of those previous falls had caught up with me. In addition, our dreams of making the farm an offtrack stabling site were shattered when Gov. John Ashcroft opposed bringing horseracing to Missouri; the legislature could not come up with the votes to override a veto.

What God taketh away he often gives back in another form.

My good friend Dr. Elaine Riegle had raised a litter of Labrador retriever puppies and had a chocolate male available. Although golden retriever Samsun was still living, we decided to take on the challenge of a new puppy. Mac joined our lives and put it on a whole new trajectory. "Labrador retrievers are hunting dogs and need to be trained as such," explained my friend Elaine. She introduced us to Sue Hawxhurst, a local dog trainer who conducted Saturday classes for people wanting to train their own dogs. This introduced us to a whole new world of AKC (American Kennel Club) competitive dog sports—obedience, conformation, hunt tests, and field trials.

Now that Ollie was retired, we had even more flexibility to seek out new adventures. One of the operating room nurses was a great fisherman and suggested we try fly fishing for salmon in the Pere Marquette River in Michigan. He recommended the Pere Marquette River Lodge in Baldwin Michigan for lodging, outfitting, and guides. The Michigan State Division of Natural Resources had begun stocking Lake Michigan with Salmon in the late 1960s.[5] The salmon found perfect spawning conditions in the rivers feeding Lake Michigan, including the Pere Marquette. This adventure was almost as good as the Canadian Rockies. We would come here several times over the next ten years. We loved it.

SUSAN AND OLLIE, EACH WITH A BIGGER FISH

My reputation in the field of geriatric anesthesia came calling again when I was asked to chair the panel on geriatric anesthesia at the World Congress of Anesthesiologists in the Hague, Netherlands. We took our granddaughter Sara Rouggly on this trip. While I was working, she and Ollie would tour the Hague and nearby Belgium. When the meeting was over, the three of us had a day to explore Amsterdam. Having read Irving Stone's *Lust for Life* at an early age, I was captivated by the Van Gogh Museum in Amsterdam. We also visited the Rembrandt Museum there.

True to form, we once again combined pleasure with business, making our way to Liverpool, England, where we boarded the cruise ship *Crystal Harmony* to cruise the Baltic Sea. We experienced the beautiful Norwegian fjords and ports in Finland, Sweden, Denmark, and St. Petersburg, Russia. The Soviet Union had collapsed by 1991. This made our ship one of the first tour ships into this region after the collapse. They were very pleased to see us and the money we brought into the economy. We saw bread lines everywhere. Although it was summer, the windows in every building were filthy,; it looked like they had not been cleaned in many years. It was sad. As Ollie put it, "There is no work ethic in socialist countries. Washing windows is always someone else's job." We also experienced a bit of history at our next stop, Gdansk, Poland. It was here that Lech Walesa, then president of Poland, had helped form the first trade union in a Warsaw Pact nation. It was known as Solidarity. As a movement, Solidarity had helped display the weakness of Soviet-style Communism and helped to bring it down. Monuments to this movement and its leader were prevalent.

Back home again, I began my most productive years in pediatric anesthesia. Much of the work was presented at meetings of the American Society of Anesthesiologists (ASA) and the New York Society of Anesthesiologists. The ASA meetings were in major cities all across the nation. The New York Society always had their meetings on Manhattan in December. We loved December in New York, the Broadway plays, the Metropolitan Museum of Art, the Guggenheim, and so much more. There were marvelous restaurants within walking distance of the hotels, and Christmas was in the air everywhere.

I began a collaboration with one of my colleagues, Dr. Eugene Worth. He was a wizard at setting up interactive exhibits for teaching various aspects of anesthesia care. I provided most of the material, and he developed a program for hands on learning. These exhibits were immensely popular and several earned first prize at the meetings. The department's residents (postdoctoral students) and staff nurses assisted in the research and were encouraged to present the work at their own scientific meetings. It was an exciting time for all of us. I believe that my most important work was the CRIES score. This was an assessment tool to judge neonatal pain. CRIES is an acronym of five physiological and behavioral variables previously shown to be associated with neonatal pain: *C* for *crying*, *R* for *requires increased oxygen administration, I* for *increased vital signs, E* for *expression,* and *S* for *sleeplessness.* One of the neonatal nurses Judy Bildner and I validated the score in the University Hospital Neonatal Unit and published the results in 1995.[6] All this activity received media attention.

On Valentine's Day in 1995, the headline on the front page of the *St. Louis Post-Dispatch* read, "Test Sheds New Light on Infants and Pain." The story gave a nice account of the history of pain in infants and the improvement in care offered by the CRIES score. The previous year, NBC had sent a crew to film us utilizing some of our innovative infant anesthetic techniques in the operating room at the University of Missouri Hospital. The resulting footage appeared on *NBC Nightly News* on April 11, 1994, and the *Today Show* the next morning.

Back on the farm, we needed a new business plan. Offtrack stabling and developing dressage horses was no longer a viable plan.

Ollie loved the land and the self-sufficiency it could provide. He was a twentieth-century Johnny Appleseed, planting fruit trees everywhere he had lived. Black Horse Farm was no exception. We planted several hundred apple and peach trees. In addition, we converted one of the pastures into a field of blackberries and raspberries, another into blueberries. One large pasture was planted in Scotch Pines to sell as Christmas trees. Last but not least, we planted four hundred walnut trees. If well managed in forty years, they would be worth a small fortune in lumber. While they were growing up, we practiced agriforestry by planting strawberries in rows between the trees. Black Horse Farm was now Black Horse Orchard and Farm, with year-round sales. We also became licensed dog breeders, producing several litters of Labrador retrievers and golden retrievers every year. With so many trees coupled with Missouri's hot dry summers, we needed irrigation, so we acquired the forty acres adjoining the farm and cleared much of the woods to put in a deep lake for irrigation. Fruit trees need bees for pollination; this required a few beehives to insure we would have a crop each year. One of my residents, Dr. William Stark, gave us the first hive along with some pointers on beekeeping to get us started.

A VERY HAPPILY RETIRED AND BUSY OLIVER ANTHONY KRECHEL

All this outdoor activity came with a price. Ollie soon had his first tick-borne illness. This time it was ehrlichiosis. Ten years later, it would be Rocky Mountain spotted fever.

Ollie had many fond memories of his time in Japan with the occupation forces, and he wanted to see it once again. So we found a great land tour combined with an ocean voyage on the Crystal Harmony once again, sailing from Yokohama to Honolulu. Prior to sailing, we were able to add on a short excursion to Hong Kong. Since it was due to be returned to China, in a couple of years, we wanted to see this vibrant city before the transfer from Britain to China occurred. It was truly a vibrant city full of young entrepreneurs. While there, we took a hydroplane to Macau, at that time a Portuguese protectorate which also would be returned to China in the coming years. Casinos were the great attraction here. We were just passing through, having booked a guide to take us into China for the afternoon. First, we had to pass through a huge wall, showing our passports of course. Our guide explained the purpose of the wall was mainly to keep the Chinese in, not to keep anyone else out. The economic prosperity of both Macau and Hong Kong were a stark contrast to this poor rural area of China on the Communist Chinese side of the wall. This was our second experience in a communist country. Construction projects were unfinished and clearly had been for some time. This reminded us of the filthy windows we had seen in St. Petersburg, Russia. Our impression was that people had no incentive to perform beyond minimal effort. Everyone received the basics, food and some type of shelter, although overcrowding was apparent. The people were friendly and seemed happy to visit with us, perhaps a break from monotony.

In April of 1995, we celebrated my fiftieth birthday. Claudia threw me a party in her home in Sycamore, Illinois. My cousins Dolores, Rich, and Karen came down from Chicago to celebrate with us. It was a fun day.

When I began the practice of medicine, I set an arbitrary goal of retirement at age fifty as an associate professor. The truth is now that I was here at the peak of my career with all the requirements for full professorship, I wanted it and more. A power play was underway in the department at the University of Missouri. The dean was asking Dr. Bill Eggers to step down, and a new chairman was being sought. Dr. Eggers had at one time told me I was his likely successor, but that was not to be. I did throw my hat in the ring as a candidate, but so did another qualified member of the department. He was chosen to be the new chairman. Immediately he began aggressive moves against me. I should have been promoted to full professor that fall, but he neglected to put in the paperwork. He also hired someone else to be chief of pediatric anesthesia. I had a choice to make. It would not have been hard to find a position in another academic institution, but it would most likely be somewhere like Chicago, New York, or Los Angeles. Ollie had already made one move for me, and he loved the farm and what he was doing; we both loved the farm. I did not think asking him to move was an option; neither did I think commuting back to the farm on weekends was a viable option either. Another important consideration for me was the fact that Ollie was seventeen years my senior, and if we wanted to spend our golden years together, it better be now.

We sat down at the kitchen table and took a good look at our finances and discussed the possibility of my joining him in retirement. To make this work, we would need to live off his IRA and anything we could make on the farm. We would continue breeding Labrador retriever and golden retriever puppies. I would offer dog training in obedience, hunting, and hunt tests. When we sold a puppy, we would offer to board it when the new owner needed to be away. Since we had whelped the puppy, the boarding fee would be less than area wide fees. It was a kind of doggie bed-and-breakfast. We would continue with the raising of produce, fruit and Christmas trees.

I was eligible to receive a reduced pension from the University of Missouri. I would have needed to work another five years to receive full retirement. I would also be able to access additional funds at fifty-nine and a half and sixty-two. We thought we could make this work. We knew we would not be able to do much traveling but had our heart set on doing something special for the new millennium. So before I put in my notice, we booked a cruise through the Panama Canal for this occasion and paid in advance so we poor farmers could make this special trip.

We continued to dot all the i's and cross all the t's in anticipation of my early retirement. When everything was in place, I gave my notice. The new chairman was surprised and expressed regret for his prior actions. Things were not going well for him. Our plan was in place; I would retire just before Christmas of 1995. I never regretted this decision and never looked back.

CHAPTER 7

Life on the Farm

At the time of my retirement from the practice of medicine, the horses were gone, and we had whelped a couple of puppy litters. We had acquired a female black Lab named Molly and a golden retriever named Nugget; they were our foundation stock. Thanks to Mac, our chocolate Lab, we were well grounded in AKC hunt tests and obedience trials. I was ready for the dog business.

Farmer Ollie continued with his agrarian pursuits. We helped each other. I picked raspberries, strawberries, and blackberries; and he threw ducks and pigeons for the dogs I was training. He also began raising ducks and pigeons so that I always had an ample supply. Once the bird pens were erected, it was a simple matter to add a few chickens and a couple of turkeys.

It wasn't long before the local teachers began to notice Blackhorse Orchard and Farm. They asked Ollie if they could bring their grade school classes to see the place and picnic on the front lawn in front of the house. Ollie was a master at entertaining these kids. Dressed in bib overalls, he showed them everything, but the highlights were always feeding the catfish in the pond and looking at our huge sixty-five-pound turkey. They were also intrigued by watching him handle Mac to a bird that Mac had not seen fall. This involved sending Mac for a retrieve, stopping him on a whistle and using hand signals to guide him to the bird. We both studied and took the state-mandated tests in the proper application of pesticides we needed for the orchard. Certification was required before the pesticides could even be purchased.

Several times a year, Ollie would mount a sprayer on the tractor which was operated by the tractor PTO (power take-off). He would carefully measure the chemicals and add the proper amount of water to get the desired concentration of pesticides. Then he would essentially dress in a hazmat suit and helmet with a built-in breather pack before operating the sprayer in the orchard. This was hot, tough work but resulted in healthy trees and great fruit. He could do anything.

We became joiners, joining a state group of apple and peach growers. We attended annual meetings at various orchards to learn new ways of production and sales. We also helped man the groups booth at the Missouri State Fair for several years, passing out locally processed apple cider.

We joined the Golden Retriever Club of Greater St. Louis, attending and helping out with many of their functions. As our dog training grounds were developed, we hosted training days, trials, and picnics.

At the time, there was no active Labrador retriever breed club in the area; so with the help of some local Labrador retriever enthusiasts, we started our own club, the Spirit of St. Louis Labrador Retriever Club, registering it with the AKC so we could hold AKC sanctioned events. Clubs such as these are important for upholding accepted breeding standards. The dogs we bred had all the health clearances recommended by the local breed clubs, and in addition, we obtained AKC performance titles on the dogs we bred. Such titles included Junior Hunter, Senior Hunter, Master Hunter, obedience titles such as CD and CDX, and Utility Dog. These titles all appear behind the dogs registered name on pedigrees. Ultimately, our dogs would sport the coveted front-end titles of FC (field champion) and AFC (amateur field champion). We tried our hand in the breed show ring and took a few lessons in tracking. However, we never really caught the fever for these sports nor for agility, another popular dog sport.

Our desire to travel the world continued; so in April of 1996, we turned in our frequent flyer miles and a timeshare week and took off on our own for Athens, Greece, immersing ourselves in the ancient culture and mythology. In addition to the iconic sites of Athens such as the Parthenon and the Acropolis, we visited Panathenaic Stadium, which hosted the First Modern Olympic games in 1896. This was the one hundredth anniversary of the stadium. Traveling to Delphi on Mount Parnassus on Mainland Greece, we visited the Temple of Apollo and listened to tales of the Mystic Oracle. By boat, we traveled to and explored several of the smaller Greek islands. It was a lovely week.

Not long after our return home, we learned the tragic fate of TWA Flight 800. In July 1996, it exploded in midair shortly after takeoff from JFK in New York. Prior to this scheduled flight to Paris, France, this plane had landed at JFK from Athens, Greece. I was convinced at the time and still am that this was the very plane we had been aboard in April.

I spent a lot of time on the road in these early years of dog breeding and training. Many trips to hunt tests and obedience trials, mostly in the Midwest but often further east into Ohio and Pennsylvania and west into the Dakotas and Nevada. Some of the trips involved picking up dogs we had purchased or delivering dogs we had sold.

I made two trips to South Carolina with Nugget, so she could be bred to an outstanding golden retriever.

The drive through Appalachia was magnificent. Always one to push the envelope, I often drove twelve to fourteen hours straight, stopping only when I just could not go any further.

It wasn't long before Ollie decided that farming and Farmers' Markets were not nearly as much fun as working with and traveling with the dogs. He gave up the vegetable and berry businesses but kept the apple and peach orchards going, as well as the new Christmas tree acreage. Having him along for the ride made it lots more fun for me too.

In late December of 1996, I began to have some gynecologic problems and needed a hysterectomy. I picked my surgeon and anesthesiologist from my friends at the University of Missouri Hospital. Although this was my first surgery, since we had a new litter of Nugget puppies, I bravely insisted that Ollie just take me to the hospital that morning and return home to look after the puppies and Nugget. This was not a good idea, since my courage soon evaporated, and I could really have used his support as I waited for the procedure. Fortunately, my anesthesiologist, Dr. Nila Gupta, added some injectable courage; and I drifted off. I had requested the adult version of one of the anesthetic techniques I used on my pediatric patients. I was pain-free for thirty-six hours and required minimal pain medication for the entire recovery process. What worked for the babies worked for me too. I was ready to go home the same day, but the surgeon insisted that I stay overnight. The next morning, my anesthesiologist drove me home. Now that is service.

Now that Ollie and I would be traveling together, we needed help on the farm. Someone needed to be there to care for the dogs that were not traveling with us and to feed the ducks, pigeons, and turkey. Initially, our dear friends Rick and Janis Dunlap looked after things for us while we were away. Eventually, they introduced us to one of the young men in the neighborhood, Tim Gruenefeld. Tim soon worked his way up to become a full-time employee.

We began annual migrations—south in the winter and north in the summer. The first trip was south to Alabama, where pro trainer Rick Stawski had acquired land and lodging. Rick's home base was Minnesota, near Minneapolis. We spent many pleasant hours in the company of Rick and his wife, Barb, training and trialing young dogs, both winter and summer. That first trip south was eventful. We had started home in early spring in our Saturn wagon, pulling a small dog trailer carrying two young golden retriever puppies when Alabama and Tennessee got hit with an ice storm. After creeping along about ten miles per hour on the interstate for a while, we elected to get off the interstate and try to find a motel. We considered ourselves fortunate to get the last available room at a no-name motel.

While the puppies were plenty warm in their insulated aluminum dog trailer, they were none too happy that the ice prevented them from running and playing when we let them out to feed and take care of business. We called the Alabama Highway Patrol to find out when the roads would be cleared and were told, "When the weather warms up." True to their word, that is exactly when the roads where again passable.

AKC hunt tests were fun, but it was not long before we decided field trials were more challenging for both the dog and handler (Ollie and me).

We joined Mississippi Valley Retriever Club, a local club promoting the field trial sport, hoping to learn more. We met a wonderful group of people through this club. Several of the members recommended Bill Eckett, a very successful field trial trainer, to help us get into the sport. We sent him two of our young Labrador retrievers, who unfortunately did not make the grade. The bar is pretty high, and not just any dog has the talent and desire it takes to be successful. We did learn many of the tasks that these canine athletes need to perform. We began developing our property to contain the features that were needed to train competitive dogs. Ultimately, when national competitions came to our area, our grounds were utilized for training. There were several owners who credited the success of their dogs to the training they did on our grounds. Around this time, our dear friend Dr. Elaine Riegle came to us with a proposition. She asked us to sell her five acres so she could build her dream house in the country. Having been born and raised in Iowa, she could think of no better location for a house than one facing a cornfield and overlooking a lake off the rear deck. We had just the location for her. So our good friend became our neighbor. Years later, she would purchase an additional fifteen acres surrounding this first five acres, including the lake.

The new millennium rolled around, and it was time for us to take that special millennial cruise we had planned and paid for back in 1996. It was everything we could have hoped for; the New Year's Eve party on board was spectacular. We were on the top deck at midnight, watching the fireworks on the Atlantic side of the Panama Canal.

OLLIE AND SUSAN RINGING IN THE NEW YEAR 2000

In the morning, we began the canal transit. We were aboard the first cruise ship to transit the canal under the auspices of its new owner, Panama. The canal had been built by the United States, and the US had a lease agreement with Panama which gave it control of five miles on either side of the canal. This agreement was terminated by President Jimmy Carter in 1977, in a treaty signed with Panama, giving Panama sole control of the canal beginning in 2000.

As we exited the canal, on the Pacific side, we were greeted by a Panamanian band in celebration of this historic moment.

The history of the canal is fascinating. It was well documented by David McCullough in his book *The Path between the Seas*, first published in 1977. Ollie and I had both read this book and were delighted to see firsthand the solutions to the problems overcome in this engineering triumph.

Life on the farm continued with dog training, trialing, and holding events on our grounds.

Much of the serious retriever training was done on water. These magnificent animals were asked to do many intricate tasks involving water. Hardest were retrieves which required entering the water, getting back on land, and then reentering the water before finally emerging from the water to get the bird.

OLLIE WITH HIS SCYTH TO CONTROL THE
VEGITATION AROUND THE TRAINING PONDS

Consequently, we had several training ponds with the appropriate features to train our dogs to do this work.

In summer, the vegetation growing up on these ponds needed to be cleared away. This was tough manual labor, which Ollie always tackled with a smile. In late fall of 2000, following a routine mammogram, I was diagnosed with breast cancer. At the same time, Ollie began having prostate issues. Normally, I went to all of his doctor's appointments and he to mine; our relationship was this close. In this case, the day of my biopsy to confirm the diagnosis and his appointment with the urologist were on the same day at the same time, so we were each alone on this occasion. This would prove to be significant because he hid from me the fact that he needed prostate surgery in order for us to focus on my breast cancer issue. I wanted to avoid both radiation and chemotherapy, so I opted to have the breast removed. The oncologist still recommended chemotherapy because the tumor was larger than average at the time of diagnosis. I refused. Since my tumor was fueled by estrogen, I did agree to take the antiestrogen (female hormone) drugs. Nearly all drugs come with unintended consequences, and one of these drugs would contribute to my osteoporosis later in life.

It is of interest that a 2018 study published in the *New England Journal of Medicine* shows that chemotherapy does not provide a better outcome than no chemotherapy in tumors like mine. Surgery and antiestrogen therapy appear to be sufficient.[7]

The previous summer, one of the cruise lines had made us an offer we could not refuse, so we had booked a cruise to Tahiti over the Christmas and New Year's holidays. My surgeon urged me to take the trip. A couple of weeks' delay, she said, would unlikely change the outcome. My surgery was scheduled for early January 2001. Since the cruise departed Los Angeles and returned to the same port, we decided to drive to California. This would allow us to stop in San Diego and visit Gladys, Anna, and Marguerite as we did every time; we found ourselves in California.

Gladys had been through breast cancer a few years before and provided encouragement. Marguerite, Steve, and their growing family lived in a lovely home at the top of Yahweh Street in San Diego, where we spent an evening catching up. Anna and her husband, Issa Arnita, were now in Central California, where Anna had a great job with Intel, so we were unable to see them but talked a while by phone.

We drove on to Los Angeles where we boarded our ship for Tahiti. The cruise was lovely, but a cloud hung over it. I was frightened and in tears several times, but Ollie was always there to comfort me. We returned home relaxed and ready for the forthcoming surgery. The surgery went fine, and I was home recuperating, left arm in a sling. We were sitting on the sofa one evening watching TV when Ollie began shivering uncontrollably. He had a fever of 104 degrees. Because of his past history of prostate problems, I suspected he had urosepsis, which is a medical emergency. He, however, refused all my efforts to take care of him and was in fact belligerent. I called our farmhand, Tim, who came over but seemed to assess the situation as a marital dispute and was not helpful.

The nearest hospital was sixty-five miles away, and I was not able to drive with my left arm affixed to my chest. He finally agreed to accept aspirin, antibiotics, and a sponge bath to cool him. With the fever under control, we slept, and the next morning, I was able to make an urgent appointment with his urologist, and Ollie was able to drive us to the appointment. He received an additional antibiotic and was scheduled for surgery the next week. We were now both convalescing. We used this time to organize the suitcases full of photographs into albums, making memory retrieval easier. Eight weeks later, we were almost as good as new and ready to catch up with our dogs that had been in training with Joe and Scott Harp in Mississippi.

Life was good that spring. Black Horse Cancun Condo (call name Condo) reached her potential, placing second in the open and winning the amateur at the Mississippi Valley retriever trial held at the Busch Wildlife Area in Weldon Spring, Missouri. This was our first real success in the field trial game. Condo would win another open that spring, which qualified her for the national retriever championship in the fall, held that year in Cheraw, South Carolina.

OLLIE, SUSAN AND CONDO AFTER FINISHING SECOND IN THE OPEN AND JUST BEFORE FINISHING FIRST IN THE AMATEUR STAKE AT THE MISSISSIPPI VALLEY SPRING TRIAL 2001

Nugget had had three litters of golden retriever puppies for us and was retired. Through my aunt Frances, we heard that my cousin Frank in Reno, Nevada, was looking for a golden retriever. As a kid, I had been impressed with Frank's love of dogs and had seen firsthand the good care he provided. Nugget was a perfect fit. Ollie and I were never comfortable letting our dogs fly cargo, so I took off for Reno with Nugget in tow.

Ollie stayed home to take care of spring orchard care and kept an eye on the weather for me. Going west in the spring can sometimes bring unexpected weather events.

I took the southern route that spring of 2002. That meant I would go north over the Hoover Dam toward Las Vegas. I had made that trip many times in the past. Never was it like this one. The post-9/11 security was impressive and the traffic slow down exasperating but understandable. The dam is an important structure to the southwest.

Nugget safely delivered, Ollie guided me back I-70 through the Plains States.

As we became more known on the field trial scene, Ollie and I both became in demand as workers and judges to help make these trials possible. We were also asked to work at the national competitions. We made many wonderful friends. Most field trials are three-day events, Friday through Sunday. This meant many weekends at motels. Trips north in the summer and south in the winter required lodging also. We took the plunge and bought an RV. If not cost-effective, it was at least more comfortable. I loved it. Ollie loved it, too, as long as we were parked. He was none too comfortable with me driving the RV, with him driving behind me in the dog truck.

We used two-way radios to communicate back and forth along the way. As was my habit, I tended to drive until I simply could not drive one more block. We found ourselves parked in many an unusual spot. I would set up camp and prepare meals while Ollie took care of the dogs' needs. We usually had between four and six dogs with us at any one time.

Our trips south now were usually to Texas, where we found time to visit Keith, Donna, and family between trials and training.

Trips north were Minnesota, Michigan, or South Dakota, sometimes all of the above. We always had a great time and avoided most of the very cold and very hot weather and stayed active outdoors.

We were fortunate to be able to be away for these extended periods of time. Our farmhand, Tim, was at home taking care of the other dogs and making sure the farm kept running.

In spring and fall, we stayed home, training with friends on our own grounds. This was an active outdoor life we both loved. Spring and fall also brought visits from Anna and her son, George. She flew in from California to see friends and family. It was a pleasure to see them. George was always treated to the farm tour—dogs, cats, turkey, ducks, and pheasants, as well as the catfish-feeding frenzy.

OLLIE, SUSAN AND TWO-YEAR-OLD GEORGE AT THE CATFISH POND

I would make one more trip west by myself, with Ollie carefully watching the weather. This was to pick up a golden retriever puppy sired by one of the few amateur field champion golden retrievers. The puppy was a gift to me from the sire's owner, Bob Benko.

Bob had trained with us the week before Snapper earned his AFC and came to stay with us on several occasions when he was travelling on business.

I was picking up my puppy and another one for a fellow field trial enthusiast in Sedalia, Missouri.

It was late fall; the trip out to Colorado was easy in two days. The trip home was difficult, as a cold front was descending on me. Ollie was mapping my route to keep me out of snow and ice. It was so cold that when I stopped to let the puppies out to relieve themselves, they could only stand there and shiver. They cried the whole way, making it difficult to hear Ollie on the phone as he guided me. I had planned to stop for the night, but the puppies were so noisy that I was afraid I would be asked to leave any motel in which I tried to stay. This I thought would be worse than driving straight through, so drive I did. Ollie had arranged for me to stay with the fellow trialers in Sedalia when I delivered their puppy, but I was now close enough to home; I just wanted to go home, so drive I did with Ollie still guiding me. We were all exhausted and fell into bed about 2:00 a.m. Even the puppy slept well.

In October of 2005, we celebrated our twenty-fifth wedding anniversary. We departed the USA on October 15, for Beijing, China. While there, we saw the Forbidden City and Tiananmen Square, well remembered by US citizens as the sight of a brutal massacre of Chinese dissidents. Our guides knew nothing or admitted nothing of this. We also accessed a part of the Great Wall of China near Beijing. The wall, of course, extends across China for two thousand miles and was begun more than two thousand years ago. It was designed to keep out invaders from the north, notably the Mongols. It is magnificent still. Leaving Beijing, we boarded a small cruise ship for a four-day cruise upriver, a small stretch of the mighty Yangtze. To prepare for this epic journey, we read *The River at the Center of the World* by Simon Winchester. This mighty river starts in the mountains of Tibet and flows 3,900 miles to the East China Sea. Among the highlights was a look at the Three Gorges Dam Project. This is the largest water conservancy project ever undertaken. The project was designed to alleviate the catastrophic death and destruction caused in river flooding in the lower Yangtze. According to the editors of the *Encyclopaedia Britannica*, the 1931 flood killed more than 300,000 people and left 40 million homeless. The floods of 1954 and 1998 were less destructive, with 30,000 and 3,650 deaths respectively.[8]

A secondary benefit of this project is the generation of hydro-electric power. Although the project was not yet complete at the time of our visit, it was already generating power to supply the city of Shanghai. Controversial, to say the least, at the time of completion, 570,000 acres of farmland would be underwater, and 1.5 million people would be displaced. Much of the riverbank we saw and photographed would be gone by 2012. We disembarked the cruise ship at Chongqing. Here we visited the Stillwell Museum commemorating the efforts of General Joseph W. Stillwell and the Flying Tigers in defeating the Japanese on Chinese soil during WWII.

After the museum visit, we flew to Xian. Here we visited the tomb of China's first emperor and viewed the legendary terra-cotta warriors guarding his tomb. That afternoon, we visited a Chinese Herbal Market. The market was interesting, but of even more interest to me was a Janssen Pharmaceutical factory across the street. As an anesthesiologist, I was very familiar with Janssen as the makers of Fentanyl. Today, I often wonder if the expertise learned here by the Chinese is what is helping to fuel the opioid epidemic in the USA, with Fentanyl from China crossing our southern border. It also brings to mind the opium wars, which China fought against the West, mainly Britain, to stop the flow of opium into China. Is China's sponsorship of the drug trade into the USA retaliation against the West?

Our final stop was Shanghai, a beautiful city which we wandered freely. If we looked the least bit lost, the Chinese people would try very hard to help us. We felt honored by their warmth and welcome.

CHAPTER 8

The Beginning of the End

The spring of 2006 was wonderful. Because Condo was such a champion, we had purchased a half sister, Dyna. Dyna was an even better dog because she was so willing to please. She became a superstar that spring, winning three amateur stakes and thereby qualifying for the national amateur competition that summer in Klamath Falls, Oregon.

Ollie and I and Dyna made the long drive to Oregon. On the way out, we made a special point to see cousins Frank, Margie, and Robin in Reno, Nevada. We had a great visit with my cousins and Nugget too; she was happy to see us, but saying goodbye, she made it known she really liked living with Frank and Margie.

While in Oregon, we did some exploring and discovered Crater Lake National Park, one of the many jewels in our National Park System. Following the National, we returned home to more training and trialing with great fun and reasonable success.

That fall, we had a training group coming to the farm so we were preparing the dogs, collecting the ducks, and getting ready to receive our guests. Ollie came into the house in obvious distress. He said he had a bad headache and was going to take an aspirin. My doctor antenna came up and began to think possible stroke, but the aspirin was exactly the right thing to do if it was more than just a headache. Our guests arrived, and as we set up to train, I noticed Ollie's behavior was erratic. He was bumping into things with the

ATV, and his words were not flowing properly. I told him we need to go to the hospital immediately because I believed he was having a stroke. He refused and continued to refuse as I tried to convince him to go to the hospital. There was little I could do at that point but to continue training. He went to his assigned position and began loading the shotgun to shoot a duck. We waited and waited, and finally he said, "Let's go to the hospital." When he realized he was trying to put the shot shell into the gun backward, he realized he had a problem. He had been loading shotguns since he was twelve.

Leaving our bewildered friends behind, we drove the sixty-five miles to the hospital. I called ahead while driving to notify them I was bringing in a stroke patient. I dropped him at the emergency room door. They were ready for him. By the time I parked the car, he was already in the CT scanner. His blood pressure was extremely high, and they quickly got that under control. The CT scan of his head showed a new infarction along with several old infarctions. These other infarctions, signs of previous small strokes, were silent; no symptoms had occurred. The only thing that had been curious in the months leading up to this event was the fact that he had lost his sense of smell. In retrospect, this was probably a result of one of these small strokes.

The neurology resident rattled off a series of tests they wanted to do in order to look for treatable causes of this problem. I made the suggestion that they all be done today. He complied, and all tests were completed that day, ending well after normal hours. I was grateful. The next day, he was better but still had speech problems. No treatable causes were found, so he was discharged on a variety of medications to prevent further episodes. In the following weeks, he received speech therapy and occupational therapy to recertify him for driving. Our dog training and trialing continued.

In December of 2007, Ollie turned eighty. We celebrated this milestone a little early with a late summer, early fall Mediterranean cruise. We flew to Istanbul, Turkey, where we boarded our *Oceania* cruise ship. First stop was Ephesus/Kusadasi, Turkey. Ephesus is an ancient Greek City (tenth century BC) located in modern Turkey. Many Roman features could be seen dating from the first century BC. Rhodes, Greece, was followed by Limassol and Nicosia, Cyprus.

Located in the central Mediterranean between Sicily and North Africa is the island chain of Malta. We visited its capital, lovely Valletta. For us, the highlight of this cruise was North Africa, our first trip to this continent. First stop here was beautiful Alexandria, Egypt; you could almost feel Cleopatra's presence. A very long bus ride took us to Cairo, Egypt, to view the Great Pyramids of Giza, as well as the iconic Sphinx. From here, we sailed to Tunis, Tunisia. The ancient Phoenician capital of Carthage is located nearby. The Arabs took possession of the territory in the seventh century. The French made Tunisia a French protectorate in 1881. It gained its independence in 1956. Its Constitution, brought by its first president, made it a very liberal and tolerant society which included the emancipation of women.

Islam is the primary religion, although Christians and Jews were prevalent when we visited in 2007, and the French influence was widely visible. Once again, part of the tour took us to a rug-making facility; the first such encounter was Kusadasi, Turkey. Unlike the woolen rugs of Turkey, the Tunisian rugs were silk and hand woven on site. When they showed the rug, depicting the history of the Berber people (the original settlers of North Africa in 1,200 BC). The Berbers brought horses to Africa. My love of art and history and horses prevailed and demanded that I have it as a wall hanging. It graces my wall to this day.

In late 2010, the Arab Spring began in Tunisia. I fear that much of what we, as Westerners, found so enchanting about this country is gone.

Finally, we did some Spanish island hopping—first, the Canary Islands and then the Balearic Islands where we visited Mallorca.

Back home again for December 12, 2007, Claudia invited us to Kansas City, along with Gloria and Bob, where we had a family birthday party. By fall of 2008, we were ready to go again. Ollie was especially enamored with the Great Rivers of the World and so impressed with our Yangtze River cruise that we decided to cruise another of the Great Rivers, the Amazon. Since this was a Miami-to-Miami cruise, we drove to Miami, staying one night with granddaughter Amy and family in Jacksonville, Florida. They treated us to a lovely day in St. Augustine. After leaving the car in long-term parking, we had one more night in Miami before boarding our *Oceania* cruise ship.

We sailed directly across the Atlantic to northeast Brazil and sailed upriver into the Amazon after picking up our pilot boat. This river changes greatly with the seasons, and a pilot boat can help avoid all the seasonal hazards.

We traveled past the cities of Belem and Santarem soon after entering the river. Industry, commerce, and recreation along the river were in evidence as far as Santarem. After that, we saw mainly jungle with small villages along the way until we reached Manaus. Manaus is the capital of the Brazilian state of Amazonas. We spent two days exploring this city of two million and the surrounding territory, taking small boats up several of the small tributaries joining the Amazon. Here, we were able to observe much of the daily lives of these people. On our way back to the Atlantic Ocean, going downriver, we were treated to glimpses of the Amazon pink dolphins. We also stopped long enough to visit one of the larger jungle villages we had passed on the way upriver.

Once back in the Atlantic, we made several more stops. First was Devil's Island off the shore of French Guiana. This harsh French prison colony operated for nearly one hundred years and was made famous by *Papillion*, the film starring Steve McQueen and Dustin Hoffman. Most of the original buildings are still there.

On the island of Tobago, part of Trinidad Tobago, we visited the rainforest of the oldest preserve in the western hemisphere. This area has been protected since 1763.

We toured the islands of Dominica and St. Lucia and finally the Mangrove swamps of the Dominican Republic. It is hard to believe that this beautiful lush, tourist haven country, occupies a portion of the same island (Hispaniola), as the impoverished, deforested Haiti.

After returning home, we continued our usual activities at the farm. Ollie began having recurring fevers and increasing confusion. This always led to hospitalization. Each time, a full workup was done which included a head CT scan. I had access to all of his test results. The first time I read the head CT results, I felt like I was hit by a train. Even at this early stage of dementia, he had severe brain atrophy. His brain was shrinking. In every case, the cause of his fever and confusion was a urinary tract infection. With each infection, he lost more of his ability to function in a normal capacity. I knew that this was going to be a long difficult journey.

As Ollie's dementia worsened, it became obvious to me that we would need to cut back on some of our business ventures. First to go was dog breeding. This, of course, cut down on the doggie bed-and-breakfast and dog-boarding operation, but we still had some clients. His quality of life was still very good. He was able to read and enjoyed reading. He read the *Wall Street Journal* every day, and I kept him supplied with nonfiction works on topics he enjoyed. He loved Sudoku and went through many puzzle books. He still enjoyed watching TV, especially PBS programs and sports—baseball, football, and golf. He was still able to do some of the farmwork, feeding and cleaning up after the dogs and keeping the training grounds mowed and clear of brush. Until that changed.

By 2009, the Ford tractor we had purchased in 1985 was problematic; it was down for repair more than it was in operation. We needed a new tractor, so we went to the local farm machinery dealer, and Ollie and the dealer picked out one that would be suitable. The new twenty-first-century tractor was a lot different from the old Ford. Ollie was not able to grasp the new technology, so the new Kubota became Susan's tractor. Along with it came the job of keeping the training grounds in shape as well as mowing the yard.

The apple-and-peach-tree business was next to go. Ollie had wisely quit spraying them. We still had some apples to sell and a few loyal customers, but the handwriting was on the wall. I read an advertisement for a company in Kansas City that wanted apple trees to produce Applewood BBQ chips. They offered to pay for the trees and would send a chipper truck to cut the trees and chip on site. The business and the trees were gone by fall 2010. We were watching the fabric of all that we had built unravel.

We began listing the property with some local realtors who specialized in highly developed property such as Blackhorse Farm. There were several qualified buyers, but the deals always fell through usually due to cutthroat realty dealers talking buyers into similar properties elsewhere. The Great Recession was still in full swing, and the real estate market was especially competitive. At this time, we were not sure where we would go. Southeast Texas, East Tennessee, and North Mississippi were all places we considered.

I began listing and selling valuable equipment we no longer needed. I also knew we would need to sell some of the dogs. We were getting to the point that we could only keep a few. This was hard, but the young ones still had a future. The retired competitors would stay with us until they died. March, Happy, and Fax were three competitive dogs that we would keep for training and trialing as long as we still owned the property.

Our training buddies became scarce, in part because they had found new grounds and new companions perhaps aided by the fact that I was stressed enough at this point to be less than pleasant on occasion. It is possible for two people to train field trial dogs; Ollie and I had done it many times in the past, but it required the person throwing the birds to sequence many tasks. It soon became obvious that Ollie was not able to do this anymore. I had always been the trainer, he the bird thrower.

We needed to make another change. We put Happy and Fax in training with a local professional trainer, Greg Lister. This put us in a new training and trialing group. We had some success with both dogs.

Happy was Ollie's dog, and he won a qualifying stake with him.

HAPPY AND OLLIE WIN QUALIFYING STAKE AT
MISSSISSIPPI VALLEY FIELD TRIAL

After the spring trial season of 2011, we packed our bags and headed for Yellowstone National Park. I had made the hotel reservations the prior winter. We stayed one night in a log cabin just outside Jackson Hole and explored the Grand Teton National Park as well. This was still very early park season. Many of Yellowstone's lakes were still iced in, and the fishing season had not yet begun. The wildlife was abundant. Many Buffalo and Elk had calves by their sides. This is truly a breathtakingly beautiful place.

We continued to train and trial that fall. One of the last trials of the season was in Paducah Kentucky. On Saturday, I was still in the amateur competition with Fax and due to show on Sunday morning. Rather than eat at one of the restaurants in town, we decided to pick up something at the Walmart deli. That night, we both got food poisoning. It was so serious that I considered calling 911, but we managed to make it through till morning. We were in no shape to compete, so we called our professional trainer and asked him to pick up the dogs and find another of his clients to finish the trial with Fax. We were also in no shape to drive home, but we did, stopping frequently to hydrate. On Monday, I called both the Walmart in Paducah, as well as the Kentucky Health Department. Neither were interested in this incident. This is a pretty sad commentary for Paducah.

One of the field trial clubs that Ollie and I had helped to start held a fun field trial one weekend in late fall. Ollie and Happy got third place; it was a fun-filled day for all of us. Both Fax and Happy remained in training with Greg Lister. In the early spring of 2011, I reminded Ollie that it was time to enter the field trials for spring, and we needed to decide which trials we wanted to compete in. He said he did not want to do any.

It was time to leave the field trial game behind us. We brought Fax and Happy home, and I began advertising them for sale. Both were young and accomplished, so they sold quickly.

Dogs were always an important part of our lives, and so we would keep March and a young golden retriever female as pets.

That December, we once again opened the Christmas tree lot. Sales had been declining for several years. Partly due to other growers in the area, partly due to the trending artificial trees, and partly due to the trees not getting all the attention they needed to be desirable Christmas trees. Although our employee Tim took care of most of the sales, on occasion, a customer would come in while he was away. One such time, I sent Ollie out to help the potential customer. He was reluctant to go. In retrospect, I think he did not feel that he was able to manage the chain saw and tree baler that were needed for a sale. He did go out and show the man what we had available. There was no sale. The man rudely told him he did not have anything worth buying. What kind of person treats an old man like that at Christmastime or any other time for that matter? We were both upset. When Tim came back that afternoon, I told him to cut down all the pine trees. We were now out of the Christmas tree business, and Black Horse Farm was no longer a business.

Ollie was clearly slipping further into dementia's cognitive dysfunction. This fact was brought into focus even more clearly when I asked him to burn some papers that I was clearing out from our nearly thirty years on the farm. As I discovered only later, he decided the best place to do this was in the hay storage barn. Our good friend and neighbor Rick Dunlap begged to differ. He used the barn to store his hay. This frightened me. Ollie had gone from a fire genius to a fire fool. The saddest part of this journey through dementia with the love of my life was the fact that he clearly knew what was happening to him. He managed to convey to me when it was time to make a change, each time there was a decline in his ability to function. He knew when it was time to stop driving, when to stop working the orchard, when to stop training and trialing, and finally when to give up the Christmas trees. After selling the additional fifteen acres to Elaine, we still owned ninety-two acres with the house and three large outbuildings. Clearly, all tasks would now fall on me. It was no longer economically feasible to employ Tim, since the businesses were no longer in operation. We needed to move closer to St. Louis, where hospitals and needed services were available. We needed to find a place that I could take care of on my own and still be able to care for Ollie. Leaving the farmstead unoccupied was not an option.

While pondering our new realty, I discovered a new cruise opportunity that would take us to two places still on our bucket list, the Valley of the Kings in Egypt and Israel. In April of 2012, we began a thirty-five-day cruise, beginning in Hong Kong and ending in Athens, Greece. This would prove to be our last trip together, but it was awesome. We left St. Louis midmorning and flew to Los Angeles. There we boarded our flight to Hong Kong departing LAX at 1:30 a.m. Los Angeles time; that flight was another ten hours. It was a long day.

Before boarding our ship, we were treated to a tour of Hong Kong. It did not appear to have changed very much since our last visit. Chinese rule had not changed it substantially on a superficial basis. Unlike the last time, we did not have much contact with the local people.

Once on board and unpacked for our long journey, we had time for dinner and to watch from the deck, as we left Hong Kong behind. Our first stop was Da Nang, Vietnam. This is the area where troops stationed in Vietnam during the Vietnam War went for R&R. Here we visited beautiful China Beach. Next we sailed around the Vietnam peninsula to Saigon, now Ho Chi Minh City. That morning, we had awakened early as usual and gone up on the top deck to exercise. While walking, one of the runners forced me to the inside, where I tripped on one of the railing supports. I sustained a concussion and was in and out of consciousness for about thirty minutes, finally awakening to one of the ships staff inquiring if I needed a doctor. "Oh no," replied Ollie, "she is a doctor." I probably would have said yes. I had also sustained trauma to my left hip. The pain was significant, but I soldiered through it. I did not want to be hospitalized in Vietnam.

Saigon (Ho Chi Minh City) is now a beautiful modern city. We were welcomed warmly at the dock. We took our tour to the interior regions, which included lots of transfers to busses and boats. By midafternoon, I was begging for Ibuprofen. This injury made me realize that Ollie, who had always felt the need to be my protector, was just not able to do so anymore. He could not leave the cabin alone for fear of getting lost. Room service was not as available as it should have been. Fortunately, we had a couple of sea days, and I was in much better shape when we arrived at our next destination, Bangkok, Thailand. Following a day tour of Bangkok, we boarded our ship for an overnight sail to Singapore, the jewel of Southeast Asia. Singapore is an island city state. The Merlion Fountain is the symbol of Singapore, a lion head on a fish body. Standing in Merlion square, Ollie was enthralled by the amazing, unique architecture of this very cosmopolitan city. It reminded us of Manhattan, just cleaner. Our guides reminded us that littering is a crime, and it is punished; fines can be stiff.

The next stop was Phuket. Thailand, where we boarded buses, for Phang Nga Bay, much of which is protected as a national park. We spent a lovely day exploring many of the beautiful limestone caves, accessible by water.

Rounding the Southern tip of India, we dropped anchor in Cochin, India. Here, we boarded a small boat to cruise the nearby, Indian backcountry. We glimpsed the idyllic everyday life of the small villages, which consisted of fishing, swimming, collecting water, washing clothes and dishes all in the same river.

Once again, we boarded the ship for an overnight sail, this time to Bombay, now called Mumbai. Here Colonial India is on display. Sadly, it appears that the infrastructure of the city has changed very little since India was given its independence from Britain in 1947. Here, Ollie and I celebrated my sixty-seventh birthday. At dinner that night back on board, the dining crew presented us with a birthday cake and a multinational rendition of "Happy Birthday." At our favorite cocktail lounge that night, Constantine the Ukrainian pianist sang a better rendition of "Happy Birthday." It was the end of a perfect day.

From the Indian Ocean, we sailed into the Gulf of Aden on our way to our next stop Salalah, Oman. Here we became Somali Pirate bait. Both the ship's crew and the passengers began pirate drills, which continued for several days until we reached the Red Sea. Passengers practiced retiring to the ship's interior, away from all windows. The crew dragged out the water cannons, which would remain on deck until we were safely sailing the Red Sea. The US military was now monitoring our position and maintained contact with the Bridge crew until we were out of danger. They were prepared to assist us if needed. We felt safe.

Docking in Oman gave us our first taste of the Middle East. Camels were everywhere, bedded down in trailers, traversing the city streets, and running wild on the lovely beaches. The highlight here was Al Mughsail Beach. Leaving the Gulf of Aden, we entered the Red Sea, destination Aqaba, Jordan. This port city's nearest neighbor is Eilat, Israel. We could see this bustling city just across the harbor. From Aqaba, we drove overland to the world heritage site of Petra. Petra is located in the Valley of Moses, where legend has it that Moses struck the rock, bringing forth water. This ancient site was occupied as early as 9,000 BC, well established by the fourth century BC and a prominent city of commerce in the first century AD. The remains visible at this time are from first century AD.[9]

As we neared the ancient city of Petra, we passed through the new city of Petra, built to house the Bedouins who were inhabiting the site at the time it was designated a world heritage site, in 1985. It also houses the many workers needed to support this magnificent tourist attraction. The entrance to Petra is a three-fourth-mile gorge, called a Siq. Transportation was available by horse-drawn cart, horseback, and an occasional camel ride, all for an exorbitant fee. Stubborn to a fault, I elected to walk. I had packed two bottles of water each for Ollie and myself. Unfortunately, I discovered well into the Siq that Ollie had left his water on the bus.

True to form, I made sure he remained well hydrated—me, not so much.

The walk through the Siq, itself is a walkthrough history, but the end of the Siq, as it opens up to Petra, is breathtaking. Located here is the memorable treasury building well-known from the *Indiana Jones* film. We spent another hour exploring this beautiful site. Although transportation was available for the trip back to the busses, I once again chose to walk. This was a huge mistake. About three-fourth of the way back, I was feeling very hot and weakened. Now completely out of water, we sat on one of the available benches. A Jordanian couple approached us. The woman dressed in a long heavy black robe with hijab was curious about us. Her husband allowed her to converse a little with us. Her English was rudimentary, but we managed to gain a little insight into each other. I was exhausted and wearing lightweight clothing. I could not imagine being dressed in the heavy black robe and hijab she wore.

By the time we reached the entrance to the archeological site, I was suffering heat exhaustion. All the benches were occupied, so leaning against a wall in the shade, I told Ollie I was going down. "No, no, I won't let you," he said as he held me up. Always my protector, sometimes in spite of myself, Ollie was always there to protect me and took his job very seriously. A European couple from another cruise ship were watching us and gave us not only the bench but also a bottle of Gatorade. This and the additional water we were able to get at a nearby hotel rehydrated us, so we were good as new for the trip back to the ship. On the trip back to Aqaba, we passed several Bedouin encampments. Our guide told us these encampments house as many as thirty people and they move several times a year seeking more grazing for their animals. They often cross borders from one country to another, knowing allegiance to none.

Once again, we sail to Egypt. This time the destination is Luxor and the Valley of the Kings. After docking at Safaga, we boarded a bus for Luxor. Here we saw the temple of Luxor including the remaining obelisk (its twin was moved to Paris, France). West of Luxor is the Valley of the Kings, where we explored several of the tombs. Nearby, we visited the Temple of Queen Hatshepsut and the Colossi of Memnon. The next morning, we would transit another great man-made canal. This time the Suez Canal. Although very different than the Panama Canal, it was no less magnificent.

Ollie's passion had always been the great rivers and canals of the world. We experienced many of them in our lives together.

The crown jewel of this trip was Israel. We docked at Haifa and spent the next three days touring this incredible place. The first excursion was to the stone fortress Masada.[10] It lies in southeastern Israel, near the Dead Sea. Herod, king of Judaea, under the Romans, made Masada a royal citadel. Militant Jews captured Masada from the Romans by surprise in 66 AD, and the garrison of one thousand including women and children became the last stand for Jewish rule in Palestine after the fall of Jerusalem and the destruction of the second temple in 70 AD. These brave men and women held out against Roman assault for nearly three years. In the end, they chose death by suicide over enslavement.

We took a brief trip to a Dead Sea resort and enjoyed wading in this super salty body of water. As we rode in the bus travelling from one site to the next, our guide pointed out landmarks, where various Bible stories took place. Israel is indeed a living bible. Ollie was fascinated and amazed by the Israeli ingenuity enabling the desert to bloom. Drip irrigation provided water without wasting this precious resource. Pesticides were not used in this fragile environment. Instead, crops were grown in huge mesh tents kept under positive pressure so pests could not enter. This was the highlight of his trip.

The next morning, we made our way to the Mount of Olives and the Garden of Gethsemane. In this lovely cool garden, we walked among eight-hundred-year-old olive trees. The view of the old city from the mount is nothing short of spectacular. Passing through the Valley of the Shadow of Death, we entered the old city of Jerusalem through the Jaffa Gate. We freely wandered the Christian and Jewish quarters of the divided city. We walked the Via Dolorosa ending in the Church of the Holy Sepulcher. This is a truly moving experience for any Christian.

The Temple Mount is the site of the first and second temples of the Jews. Both temples, long since destroyed, the only part of them which remains for the Jews is the Western Wall or Wailing Wall. On the other side of the wall is the Muslim quarter of Jerusalem, controlled by the Palestinian authority. The Dome of the Rock towers above it all. The Rock is considered sacred to Muslims, Christians, and Jews.

After exiting the old city via the Dung Gate, we were bussed to the Church of the Nativity in Bethlehem. This Holy Christian site is located in the central West Bank, so it is also under the control of the Palestinian authority. We were welcomed by our Palestinian guide who carefully and respectfully showed us this lovely church which holds so much meaning, for Christians.

Our last day in Israel was spent visiting the city of Nazareth—the Mount of Beatitudes; the Golan Heights, (where Israel shares a border with Syria); and finally Yardenit, a site along the Jordan River just south of the river's outlet from the Sea of Galilee. Many believe that Yardenit is the site where Jesus was baptized. It is the site of many baptisms now.

Back on the ship, it was time to rest up, pack up, and prepare for the journey home, on a flight from Athens, Greece. The journey home was anything but uneventful. As usual on cruises, many of the passengers developed head colds. The virus spreads quickly to other passengers, and this cruise was no exception. On departure day, Ollie was beginning to show signs that he was the viruses next victim. There were apparently few if any restrictions to the number of carry-on items passengers could carry aboard the flight. Consequently, by the time we boarded, there was no space in any of the overhead bins, anywhere near us. I finally found a bin twenty rows in front of us, where I stored our two carry-on bags containing our medication cache. I was barely able to reach high enough to get the bags stowed.

After takeoff, Ollie began to be very agitated and confused, behavior he exhibited mainly when he had a fever. I was worried that either he had a bacterial infection associated with his head cold, or it was another urinary tract infection. Well into the flight, Ollie announced that he wanted to get off the plane and began trying to get up to do just that. I managed to calm him somewhat, explaining that we over the Atlantic Ocean at about twenty thousand feet cruising level. He clearly had a fever now. He still wanted to get off the plane. I asked the stewardess for Tylenol, but she could offer only aspirin. He could not take aspirin, because he already took blood thinners to prevent another stroke. I told her that I had the Tylenol in my carry-on twenty rows up and would she help me get it. Her answer was, "No, I cannot help you." After explaining to Ollie that I was going to get him some medicine and making him promise to stay in his seat until I got back, I set off to get the Tylenol. Directly beneath the bin containing my bag sat a very large man who looked like a pro football linebacker. As I struggled to open the bin and bring down the heavy bag, he did nothing other than scowl at me.

Finally, I got the bag loose and started to bring it down. It was too heavy for me, and I very nearly dropped it on the linebacker's head. Now he was clearly angry. I quickly retrieved the Tylenol and zipped the bag up and prepared to return it to the bin. The linebacker got up, grabbed the bag, and threw it up into the bin without a word. "Thank you," I said.

Twenty rows back, Ollie was still in his seat. I gave him the Tylenol, and soon he was calm again, and the fever appeared to be under control. I wish I could say that this was the worst thing to happen on the return trip, but it was not. We landed in Philadelphia to clear customs and catch a connecting flight to St. Louis. All went smoothly until we needed to go through a TSA checkpoint before boarding the flight to St. Louis. Ollie went through first without incident. They stopped me because I was wearing a lymphedema sleeve. This is an elastic sleeve I wear on my arm when I fly to prevent severe swelling due to the breast cancer surgery. They detained me in the scanner for a good ten minutes, refusing to listen to explanations or my concerns for Ollie wandering off or losing our belongings including tickets and passports. When Ollie tried to approach me, most likely because he sensed my obvious distress, they pushed him away. I was in fact extremely agitated, and I am usually quite calm under duress but not this time.

Finally, a TSA supervisor arrived with some kind of chemical that he applied to my arm, presumably to test for explosives. Declared nonthreatening, we were allowed to proceed. We arrived home late that night, after a very difficult journey. I gave Ollie more Tylenol and started him on an antibiotic for the infection. Following treatment, all was well for a few weeks until once again, he began having symptoms of agitation, confusion, and fever. He was admitted to the hospital in Columbia, Missouri. The Infectious Disease Department was ecstatic to have him as a patient. Here was a man with a fever who had recently travelled to Southeast Asia, India, and the Middle East. Every test possible was run to rule out all the exotic possibilities for the fever. In the end, it appeared to be a urinary tract infection.

Ollie's son Keith had come up from Texas due to the apparent seriousness of his dad's condition. It was at this time that I explained to all three of his children about the more serious diagnosis, hiding in plain sight, that is dementia. An instance in which all three children were together with me and Ollie was not present did not occur very often. This hospitalization was the opportunity I needed. They had not guessed. Claudia told me that I had hidden it well. I guess I did. If he forgot a word, I always came up with it for him in a seamless fashion.

After ten days in the hospital, on IV antibiotics, Ollie was allowed to come home. It was our great fortune that Keith was there and staying at our house because the morning after arriving home, he suddenly lost the ability to stand. Keith was able to pick him up and put him in a chair. He was only semiconscious and clearly needed to go back to the hospital. Since we were more than an hour from the hospital, it was faster for me to drive him than to wait for an ambulance. Keith carried him to the car, and I took off, with Keith following in another vehicle. When we were only ten minutes away from the hospital, he said to me, "I am not going to make it." "Yes, you are," I replied. "We are almost there."

When we arrived in the emergency room, he was in septic shock. He would not have made it much longer. This was less than twenty-four hours after being discharged from this same hospital. His condition was stabilized, and another round of IV antibiotics was begun. The urologists were consulted, and plans were made for Ollie to have some minor surgical procedures designed to cut down on the number of urinary tract infections he was suffering.

This time when he was discharged, he stayed infection free for nearly a year.

CHAPTER 9

Back to Where We Began

While we had tried several different listing agents, we still had not sold the farm. Claudia and Bill were devotees of Dave Ramsey, a radio and Internet personality, who has helped millions with his common sense approach to money management. Dave, with his large network, is able to recommend ethical businesses, including real estate agents. Claudia was able to get the name of an agent in St. Louis and St. Charles County. Previously, we had used agents from the more rural counties specializing in large tracts of land. Terry Gannon, the agent recommended by Dave Ramsey, specialized in suburban homes. We had nothing to lose listing with Terry.

Using the experience we had gained in selling off small parcels of the land to Elaine Riegle, I had devised a plan to subdivide the land into two smaller parcels. This would allow three listings: one for the whole farm, one for the front one-half of the farm which included the home and all of the outbuildings, and one for the back half of the farm which included road access and three of the lakes. Terry had an extensive advertising network, as well as photographers who could make the listings look especially attractive. Terry agreed to list the properties, and we signed a contract for the listing.

There were some but not a lot of interest in the listings in the remaining months of 2012. We continued selling things we no longer needed and disposing of papers and items we no longer needed. Early in 2013, a young couple drove up the driveway. I went out to speak with them and determined that they had seen the listing and wanted to take a quick look at it before asking their real estate agent to request a showing. I explained about the three listings and asked about their occupations. The young woman told me that the young man was a dog trainer. "Oh," I said, "I have trained many a dog in the large kennel building." I invited them to look at the kennel building and explained how to drive out the back gate to see the back part of the property. This looked like a match made in heaven. I called Terry to tell her about the contact.

Nothing happened for six weeks, and I began to think that the couple were not really interested. Then Terry called and told us they had made an appointment to see the whole property including the house. The viewing went well, and we were assured that they were indeed interested and that a contract was imminent. It was crunch time. We needed to make up our mind about where we were going. We had looked in the Festus area since Claudia and Bill were there and had expressed interest in our being nearby. We had found a nice subdivision home in nearby Pevely, Missouri, but it still gave me the feeling of isolation.

While this was on our minds, my sister-in-law Carol Krechel invited me to a Women's Fellowship luncheon at her church. On the day of the luncheon, we were driving to Carol's house where I would leave Ollie with his brother Roger. As we were driving by St. Anthony's Hospital, near Carol and Roger's house, I thought, "This is where we should be." Our old ranch, Oak Trails, was just down the road five miles. As I sat in the church sanctuary, near the new pastor, I experienced a calling to return to this beautiful church.

Ollie and I were both excited about the prospect of returning to this familiar neighborhood. That evening, we looked at real estate listing in the area and found a home in Lemay, where Ollie had lived when we met. Lemay was an old and very economical place to live. The listing we saw described a newly remodeled home, near his old place. I called Rob Shanks, the agent who had an advertisement on the same page as this listing. I made this call on a Friday morning asking to see the home on Saturday. Surprisingly, although he did not have the listing on this home, he agreed to meet us there on Saturday.

We arrived first and walked around the place. It was not ideal for the two dogs we still owned, and the electrical grid reminded us of India.

When Rob arrived, we went inside to look at the home. It was newly remodeled but not very well, and as we looked around the basement, Rob pointed out the fact that it also had termites. Clearly, we were not going back to Lemay. We arranged to spend the following Thursday with Rob looking at other listings in the South County area in the moderate price range we had selected. Rob's assistant sent us new listing daily, and as we sat in his office waiting to begin touring, a new listing came up.

It was on the south side of Suson Park and overlooked Suson Lake. Roger and Carol lived on the north side of Suson Park, and this home was only half a mile from Oak Trail Ranch. We immediately added it to the list of homes we would view that day. It would be the second property we looked at that day. We learned that the owner had built the house in 2002 while she was working in St. Louis and had been unable to sell it in 2008 when she was offered a better position on the East Coast.

One family had rented it until recently, when she decided to test the market again. The walls were newly painted, and new carpet had been laid. There were a number of problems that remained including sunburned wood flooring and vanities that had been damaged. The kitchen appliances were either missing or damaged. The view of the lake was spectacular. Since we were leaving a lake-view home at the farm, this was an important consideration. We were the first people to view this home after the listing. An open house was scheduled for the following Sunday.

We spent the rest of the day looking at a dozen or more homes, and nothing really appealed to us as much as the lake-view home. At the end of the day, there was one remaining home to be viewed, but it could not be viewed until the next Saturday. We arranged to meet Rob again on Saturday. Before we returned to Jonesburg, we drove by the home overlooking Suson Park. The neighborhood was active now with kids home from school and parents home from work, and dogs out in the front yard, so happy to see their families back home. It looked like a neighborhood we would enjoy.

Another potential buyer was looking at the home as we drove by. We went home wondering if it would be sold before we had completed our search. The home we viewed on Saturday was beautiful. Everything was state-of-the-art and tastefully done. It had a tiny backyard not really suitable for the dogs and no appealing view. Worst of all, it was occupied by smokers. The moment I entered the home, my chest tightened up, and my asthma became a problem. Rob told us we would need to repaint the entire home to eliminate the odor and residual nicotine.

The lake-view home overlooking Suson Park was still available, but the open house was scheduled for the following day. Ollie and I decided that we really did like this home and that we could afford to make the changes we felt necessary. We did have a contract on the front half of the farm, so with Rob's help, we made the decision to offer a contract for the lake-view home contingent on the sale of this contracted farm property.

Since we were asking for a contingency contract, we offered the asking price. In order to avoid a bidding war, Rob suggested that we ask for acceptance of the offered contract by 10:00 a.m. Sunday. This was before the scheduled open house. The contract was accepted. Ollie and I were delighted. We began the long arduous process of downsizing. The new home was half the square footage of the Jonesburg home. Many furniture items needed to be sold or given away. Traditional charities would not drive as far out of town as Jonesburg. We no longer needed two vehicles, since Ollie was no longer driving. There was no room for the pool table. Grandson Josh helped us sell these items. Camping equipment, golf clubs, old medical books, and more needed to go. One of the tractors went to our friends the Dunlaps, and the new tractor and the ATV went to Tim.

The inspection process for the Jonesburg home and buildings went well, and only a few easily remedied problems were noted. The well and septic inspection did not go so well. The well was fine, but the septic system was no longer up to code. We agreed to put in a septic lagoon.

Dale Brower was a local well-and-plumbing contractor in the area with whom we had dealt since we moved to Jonesburg. He would do the lagoon work, and he hired Tim as his full-time helper, a job that Tim holds today. All that behind us, we had a closing date target with occupancy immediately after closing. We were set to close on both properties, that is the one we were selling and the one we were buying on the same day. With that date in mind, we hired the movers. The closing date was set back. We were forced to store the furniture until after closing. The art work would stay until we moved it ourselves. So far, this sale was costing us money, and now we had storage charges to pay, and we were looking at staying in a motel and eating out every day until closing. This was not looking good.

Fortunately, our friend and neighbor Elaine offered to let us use the visitor's suite she had in her basement. In exchange, I would do all the cooking. This was a wonderful gift. We were able to carefully pack all the artwork and store it in the basement of Elaine's home. To keep Ollie busy, Elaine brought out her puzzles; unfortunately, he was unable to figure them out.

She went to the store and picked a puzzle designed for six-year-olds. This he was able to manage. Sadly, this was the first time we had a brain age set for Ollie. This brain age would continue to decline. We were comfortable, and Elaine really liked my cooking, but our stay kept getting extended as the closing date kept being moved back.

After six weeks of living with Elaine, we got the final closing date. At 7:00 p.m. the evening before closing, Terry called and told us the deal was off. The young couple's loan officer had done a final credit check and discovered a missed auto payment. Ollie and I were devastated. Elaine got up and made us a batch of chocolate chip cookies. I will never forget that kindness.

That night, I asked God to give me the strength to put all the pieces back together. Getting the moving company to move the furniture back to Jonesburg would be easy but expensive. The house would be half empty. We would need a new tractor and ATV. Again expensive.

The next morning, we set about putting things back together. The first order of business was to go to Walmart for toilet paper, paper towels, soap, laundry detergent, and other items we would need as we prepared to move back into the Jonesburg home. We had just left the store with our purchases when my cell phone rang. It was Rob, telling me the deal was back on and we should be at the title company office at 3:00 p.m. I was astounded, and Ollie simply collapsed his head on the shopping cart in disbelief.

I called Terry to confirm this new twist, and she told me that she had called the loan officer and told him what a lowlife he was for leaving us stranded this way when he had no obligation to pull that last credit report. Overnight, the loan officer had a figured out a way to allow the deal to move forward. The young couple was already closing on the farm purchase as we were speaking, and Ollie and I would have the money at 3:00 p.m. to close on our new home in South St. Louis County.

We packed our toilet paper and other supplies into the car; they would be going to our new home.

We would spend a few more days with Elaine as we set the date for the movers to take our furniture to our new home and arrange for help moving the art work and other small items we had stored in Elaine's basement. Elaine told us she was sorry to see us go, but she understood why we needed to move on.

Once everything was, at last, in our new home, we began the daunting chore of unpacking all the boxes that we had carefully packed more than two months previously. The exact location needed to be chosen for each piece of our art collection. Each piece needed to be carefully mounted. I did the hammering and screw setting while Ollie spotted me on the step ladder. Books, dishes, linens, and all the other small items that make a house a home needed to be unpacked and located. This took many days. We had to purchase all new appliances and have them installed. Now we could actually eat at home. We put in a fence to give us a fenced backyard for the dogs, who were still being boarded with Greg Lister. It was a long two months for them as well. Now we could bring the dogs home and, once again, be a real family. They settled in quickly, but Ollie had a much more difficult time. For months, he would wake me at night to ask, "Where is the bathroom?"

Moves are extremely difficult for the dementia patient. Unfortunately, Ollie would require several more. We hired nephew

Mike Hezel to be the general contractor on all the remodeling projects which needed to be done. Mike had been flipping houses for several years and was experienced in remodeling. Most of the work, he was able to do himself.

We chose to replace the sunburned wood flooring in the kitchen and breakfast room with ceramic tile. We updated the kitchen with quartz countertops and a complimenting backsplash. We replaced the vinyl flooring with ceramic tile and replaced the broken vanities and mirrors in each of the bathrooms. The custom cabinetry was beautiful. There were no window treatments in the house, and we definitely needed to remedy that situation. Ollie loved light, and like the Jonesburg home, this new home was full of sunshine on sunny days.

He specifically requested window treatments that would allow him to see out without the neighbors, seeing us. We managed to find lovely blinds, which accomplished just that. We replaced the red wooden front door with a white wood and stained-glass door. New coach lights on the garage added to the curb appeal. Several loose pavers were left outside the walk out basement door. Since they were attractive, we decided to put in a patio using this type of paver. When completed, it exceeded our expectations. We now had a lovely covered patio from which to enjoy our lake view.

Our new home had a lovely gas log fireplace but no vent or flue. Oddly, this passed inspection with the caveat that we open the windows if we used it. This situation needed to be rectified. We had the gas capped off and converted the fireplace to a nice electric log with a forced air heater.

Projects remaining for 2014 and 2015 included repairing and bringing the deck up to code. The deck anchor beams were set in bare dirt rather than in concrete, as code required. We were surprised that this, too, passed inspection but knew we would need to deal with it at some time in the future. This was a three-bedroom home, but we had designated one room an exercise room and one a library, leaving no guest room. People still wanted to visit, and we soon learned that air mattresses were not the answer.

The answer was to install a Murphy bed cabinet combination in the exercise room. This room had a walk-in closet which we converted to a cedar closet. Finally, by the end of 2015, our new home had all the special features of the home we had built in Jonesburg.

Ollie and I worked together on the selection process for all these projects. It was fun for both of us. At this time, he was still willing and able to make decisions.

As his dementia progressed, one of the things I would miss most was making decisions as a couple. Two heads are better than one, and his suggestions were often extraordinary, even into the moderate dementia stage.

We joined the church, St. John's EUCC, the church I had felt called to join. Pr. Steve Westbrook visited us at home while we were in the midst of the remodel and found us a good fit to join this church family. Although we had not discussed the fact that Ollie was suffering from dementia, Pastor Steve knew the signs well and pulled me aside one day to be sure that I was aware of my husband's condition.

Ollie and I always remained equal partners in whatever project we worked on, and there were many who never guessed that he suffered from dementia. Ollie's brother Donald had been diagnosed with Alzheimer's disease in midlife and had died of this disease nearly twenty years earlier.

Roger brought this up one night at dinner, and it became clear that he and Carol were not aware that his remaining brother was also suffering from dementia. Since I never spoke of this diagnosis in front of Ollie, I had to send them an e-mail to let them know. Even though we never discussed it, Ollie was well aware of what was happening to him. He woke up every morning and put one foot in front of the other and did the very best he could do. This was his approach to life, even in late-stage dementia.

Ollie began falling on the way to the bathroom at night and developed the habit of sleeping sideways in our king-size bed. We decided that he would be better off sleeping alone with the lights remaining on while he slept. This was hard for us as a loving couple but was at the time the only safe option for him. We often discussed trips to national parks we had not seen. Most often, he was enthusiastic about these trips until it was time to actually set a date. Then he would tell me that he did not want to go. The reason for this behavior became clear in 2015, when my third cousin Christopher Latz was graduating from medical school in Texas. We were planning to drive to Texas to attend the graduation and visit son Keith while in the Lone Star State.

Ollie had a full-blown panic attack, including a very fast heart beat and chest discomfort. While waiting in the doctor's office, he admitted that he was afraid to go, because he did not think he could take care of me if something went wrong. He told me that he felt he could take care of me if something happened near our home because he knew the area so well. Needless to say, we did not attend the graduation. Ollie's physical health remained problematic in the years after the move, and it was comforting to have St. Anthony's hospital two and a half miles down the road, instead of sixty-five miles to the nearest hospital when we lived in Jonesburg.

He was hospitalized several times for urinary tract infections. As we had previously experienced, each time he was hospitalized, he lost a little more cerebral function. We also began seeing "behaviors." In Ollie's case, it was combativeness. He became a danger to himself and others. As the infection cleared, the gracious, kind gentleman I knew my husband to be reemerged. We were both now dealing with loss on an ongoing basis. Keeping busy was important to us both.

Through the church, we became involved with Feed My People, a food bank in Lemay. I became a member of the governing board. This involved quarterly meetings and helping with their fundraisers, which were food drives, fashion shows, trivia nights, chef challenges, 5K runs, and more.

They kept us busy; and when Ollie, who was with me at all the meetings and events, asked for a badge, they made him a member of the board. This was especially important to me because they were aware of his dementia but chose to be accepting. He, too, was grateful, for the opportunity.

Work was always important to Ollie. Even as his abilities declined, he constantly wanted to work at something, anything. This was true, even in late-stage dementia. We both joined a new working committee at the church called Standing on Holy Ground. This group was tasked with overseeing all new projects in the church and on the church grounds. When the original team leader became ill, I was asked to lead the team. We accomplished a lot on our watch, including rejecting an offer to buy or lease a part of the grounds for a Pediatric Urgent Care Center, bringing in a team of building inspectors and architects to evaluate our hundred-year-old building and putting in a Community Dog Park.

In 2016, I began having my own health issues. Although I had experienced asthma attacks in the past, they were mild and associated with significant triggers such as cigarette smoke and strong perfume. Now they were frequent and severe, and triggers were less apparent. I now required preventative treatment, as well as a rescue inhaler. Unfortunately, our golden retriever was an obvious trigger. The Lab was also but much less so.

I was able to find a really good home for the golden retriever, but the Lab, March, was a Condo son and twelve years old. He would remain with us until his death. Sadly, this was all too soon. Ollie and I were both heartbroken with March's passing and decided to try life without a dog. That resolve lasted all of a month. I began looking for a poodle. Although few people realize it, poodles like Labs are duck dogs and can compete in AKC hunt tests. They also do not shed and were far less likely to trigger my asthma. A local breeder has an eighteen-month-old female available; she had not worked out in her first home. Before looking at her, the breeder warned me that this dog did not relate to everyone.

"No problem," I thought. "All dogs love me." Not so with this one. She wanted nothing to do with me or Ollie. I was heartbroken. The breeder brought out another dog and asked me to consider him. He clearly loved me, Ollie, and probably all humans. His name was Nelson, and he had been the foundation sire of many of her litters but was now sterile. She did not have him advertised for sale, but she thought he would be a good fit for us.

We were, at first, reluctant because of his age of, eight and a half. We had just lost March, and no matter how many dogs you have in your lifetime, their passing is always hard.

After careful consideration, we decided to take him home. What a joy he has been.

NELSON, THE DUCK DOG

I also required surgery to relieve pelvic prolapse, and the asthma would make the procedure somewhat more complicated. At the time of the procedure and during the recovery, I would not be able to take care of Ollie. The family urged me to put him into an assisted-living facility or respite, memory care. We explored this option. Ollie was very willing to make a move, if we moved as a couple. I did not think this would work, because I would find myself still being his primary care giver in this situation.

Respite, memory care was not available.

We found an assisted-living facility nearby, which he agreed to only after assurances by me that it was a temporary measure. After completing the extensive paperwork and soliciting our Jonesburg friends to help move the furniture he would need in his apartment,

Ollie got cold feet and made it clear he did not want to make this move under any conditions.

Out of any other options now, I called Visiting Angels and asked if they could provide twenty-four-hour care for Ollie while I could recuperate from surgery. We had employed this home health care service once before when Ollie was persistently waking me up during the night, every night. At that time, they provided someone to sit with him all night so that I could sleep. After these nighttime episodes passed, we were able to manage without their help. Visiting Angels were able to provide twenty-four-hour care but could not administer medication. I would need to prepare envelopes with his medication, and they could hand him the envelope at the proper time. Clearly, I would need to oversee his care.

Fortunately, my recovery was less arduous than I had expected. However, it was complicated by Visiting Angels. In spite of my stipulation that the caregiver could not be a smoker due to my asthma, they sent smokers.

Severe coughing spells after surgery are not fun. After calling and having one of them replaced, they sent another. I asked her to leave, called the company, and told them not to send anyone else. Ollie and I were on our own. At this point, my main limitation was lifting. Ollie was strong and more than willing to lift anything.

Ollie's brother Roger discovered Rock Steady Boxing, an exercise program specifically for people with Parkinson's disease. A new affiliate was coming to our area. Since both brothers were suffering from Parkinson's disease and I was always looking for ways to keep Ollie active, we signed Ollie up for this program as well. The exercises in this program are designed to impact, core strength, and rhythm in order to improve range of motion, flexibility, posture, and gait. They are patterned after drills used in boxing. Ollie loved it, and it loved him back. His strength and agility improved as did his overall outlook on life.

On December 12, 2017, Ollie would turn ninety years old. I asked him if he would like to have a ninetieth birthday party, and he thought that was a great idea. We spent quite a lot of time in 2017 planning that party. We reserved the event center and picked the menu. The event center provided a DJ to play the golden oldies.

Ollie told them he wanted pizza, and they agreed to provide it for him, but his guests would have to eat from the buffet. By the time the date rolled around, he had forgotten about the pizza and was happy to enjoy the buffet. We made it a family affair. Granddaughter Heather, in New York, designed the invitations and had them printed. Daughters Claudia and Gloria agreed to do some extra decorations. I went through all the old photos and put together a *This Is Your Life* book. I printed all the photos and put together enough books so that there would be one book at every table for the guests to enjoy.

While all this preparation was going on, my cousin Frank in Reno, Nevada, called to tell us about the great time he had on the Honor Flight. The Honor Flight is conducted by nonprofit organizations across the country to honor military veterans by transporting them to Washington, DC, to view the monuments dedicated to the war in which they served. When I asked Ollie if he would be interested in this honor, he indicated that he would like to go on the flight. I filled out the online application for him, and within a week, he was booked on a September flight out of St. Louis.

Each veteran is accompanied by a volunteer who is their personal guide and caregiver. Registered nurses and EMTs also travelled with them. Documentation of medical history and medications were all covered. I was comfortable that he would be safe and well cared for on this trip.

The week before the flight, the group going on the flight were invited to a get together to meet and greet. Seated right next to Ollie was Vic Kohler, one of his high school classmates.

This flight consisted of all WWII veterans, which is becoming less frequent as the *greatest generation* dies off.

Honor after honor was bestowed upon these guys on that very special day. The ceremony at the airport when they returned home brought tears to my eyes, and the thought of it still does.

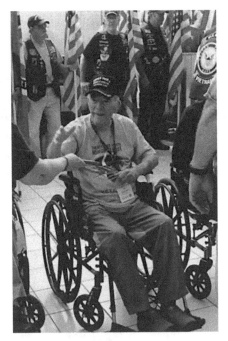

OLLIE AT THE WELCOME HOME CEREMONY ON
ARRIVAL FROM THE HONOR FLIGHT

Between the honor flight and the birthday bash, Ollie began getting more and more confused. One afternoon, after a shopping trip, I held his hand as we walked back to the car. When we got into the car, he said, "I don't think my wife would like this... She has a car, a lot like this one." This was the first time he did not recognize me.

I said, "I am your wife." He seemed skeptical.

At first, the exchange was amusing, and then it was devastating. By the time we arrived home, he seemed to accept my claim that I was his wife. It was an anxious time for me. We were expecting one hundred people, friends and relatives from coast to coast and from North to South. First to arrive was my cousin Frank, from Reno, Nevada. We picked him up at the train station in St. Louis. The next morning, the three of us went to the airport to pick up cousins Dolores and Rich from Chicago. Ollie thought the terminal was a movie theatre.

The following morning, Ollie's birthday, the five of us went to the Civil War Museum at Jefferson Barracks. As the day progressed, Ollie became more and more mentally clear. The stimulation of the extra people around seemed to be good for him. My cousin Frank agreed with this observation.

That evening, the party went off without a hitch. It was so good to see so many of our friends and relatives, many who travelled far, to be with us to celebrate Ollie's ninetieth. This included Anna from San Diego, California, granddaughter Heather, great-granddaughter Lily from New York—even one of our African family, Lydia Nickels, our great-granddaughter, who was now attending Washington University in St. Louis. Her mom, granddaughter Sara; her dad, Phil; and sister Audrey were still doing their missionary work in Tanzania.

Ollie was in his glory. He clearly enjoyed all the extra attention. It had been a very good year!

CHAPTER 10

A Very Bad Year

As the new year of 2018 arrived, I felt empowered by my new insight: Ollie benefitted by more social interaction. I decided to try Adult Day Care to meet this need. Family Partners seemed like a good fit. In fact the first time, we visited we met one of the boxers from Rock Steady Boxing. Ollie would already have one friend there and would gain many others. The plan was that. I would drive him to Family Partners, three days a week arriving at 9:00 a.m., and I would pick him up at 4:00 p.m. Two days a week, I would take him to Rock Steady Boxing.

He was thriving; I was not. This was a lot of extra driving for me, and while not his chauffer, I was still juggling work with Feed My People and Standing on Holy Ground. I was neglecting myself. I had not yet discovered Jordan B. Peterson. Rule 2 in *12 Rules for Life*[11] states, "Treat yourself like someone you are responsible for helping."

By March of 2018, I was short of breath with minimal exertion. Climbing the stairs after taking the dog out would require a time-out on the sofa. Walking the dog one block left me breathless. I would do grocery shopping while Ollie was at day care and often felt like I would pass out just pushing the cart. I felt the cloak of death near me. I reached out to Claudia and Gloria—I needed help.

Claudia really wanted Ollie to reside in an assisted-living facility Crystal Oaks, near her home. She envisioned popping in and out while he was there, both checking on him and taking him for rides and out for ice cream. I would be able to take care of myself.

After seeing Crystal Oaks, I told Ollie how concerned I was about passing out or worse while we were together, leaving him defenseless. "No, no," he said, "I will lay my body over you to protect you." I finally asked him to choose, going on as we were, with the risk that I would be gone and he would be defenseless or going to Crystal Oaks, where he would be near Claudia and safe, while I tried to heal. He chose Crystal Oaks. I have to say, sick as I was, I was disappointed with his choice.

We resigned from Feed My People and Standing on Holy Ground.

At the end of March 2018, Ollie entered assisted living at Crystal Oaks.

I went to my doctor to try to discern why I was so short of breath. My oxygen saturation was low, but a chest X-ray was normal as was an ECG and cardiac enzymes. This made a couple of bad things like lung cancer and coronary artery disease less likely, but the doctor did not make a definitive diagnosis. I was given an antibiotic, which helped but did not resolve the problem. I tried to rest and heal.

My doctor suggested pulmonary function testing and a CT scan of my chest. I found both these tests arduous. I still had the sense that with every step, I would pass out. Somehow, I made it back home after each test. The pulmonary function tests simply reflected asthma. The CT scan showed bronchiectasis. My bronchioles were dilated and full of fluid. This explained the large amount of sputum I was producing. Perhaps more worrisome was that the radiologist suggested that his findings were consistent with nontuberculous mycobacterium. Unlike tuberculosis, this disease is not contagious. It is most frequently found in slender white females who are postmenopausal. I fit this profile. It is hard to diagnose because it is hard to culture. It often requires a bronchoscopy. I was referred to a pulmonologist, and the first sputum culture grew out pseudomonas. I was placed on an antibiotic the first week in May. I was beginning to feel better when my world and Ollie's came crashing down.

On the Saturday before Mother's Day, I received a call from Crystal Oaks. They were sending Ollie to the emergency room at St. Anthony's Hospital. He had become hostile and combative; he was hitting other patients and staff alike. This usually indicated a urinary tract infection; I and everyone else had missed it. When I arrived in the emergency room, I found him sedated and bruised from above his elbows to his fingertips. I was devastated.

I was told by the nursing staff that he had arrived in handcuffs and put there by the police who had responded with the paramedics. He obviously had thought people were trying to hurt him, and the police made sure that was the case. He was strong, but he was a ninety-year-old man. Surely, there was a better way to handle the situation. He had all the usual tests, including a CT of his head. The only abnormality was a urinary tract infection. He was admitted to the hospital. He remained combative for several days, so they continued to sedate him. I asked them to place a central IV, which would allow him to leave the hospital and still receive IV antibiotics. They were unable to do this, in part due to his resistance.

Several days went by, but he continued to be combative. A neurologist was called to see him. The neurologist suggested taking him off his medication for Parkinson's and adding an antipsychotic drug four times a day. This did stop the combative behavior but made him very sleepy, and he was not eating.

I kept requesting that the physical therapist, get him up to walk. A physical therapist visited everyday but did not feel it was safe to walk him. He was not a large man; 145 pounds was his normal weight. The muscle mass that he lost at this time would take six months to recover.

When they began to discuss discharge, it was clear that he needed to go to a rehabilitation unit. It was also clear that he would never be able to return to Crystal Oaks. Crystal Oaks was a level 2 assisted-living facility, which meant he needed to be able to walk without assistance in case of fire.

We were now approaching the Memorial Day, holiday weekend. Facilities were short staffed and not taking new patients. The social worker advised that he be sent to Alexian Brothers, Sherbrooke

Village. I had been to this facility as a visitor and knew that it was clean and attractive. They were woefully ill-equipped to handle him.

The new environment was distressing to him, and he became confused and uncooperative when he was not sitting with his head on the table due to the heavy dose of antipsychotic medicine.

The first night he was there, I was called to come in to help settle him down. I did this, and he was fine when I left. Later, I was called and asked to stay all night. I knew my own health would suffer if I tried to do this, so I refused. The next night, they called very late to tell me he needed to go to a hospital. "Take him to Missouri Baptist Hospital," I said. The next morning, I called the hospital emergency room and was told that they had done yet another CT of his head and found his urine to be clear of infection. Since he was in exactly the same condition as he was when he arrived at Sherbrooke, they sent him back to that facility. The personnel at the facility were not happy.

After the Missouri Baptist Hospital emergency room visit, our doctor called, and she suggested a social worker who should be able to help us. The social worker called to tell me that she was unable to help, because once a patient is in a facility, only the social worker at that facility can orchestrate transfers. The nursing administrator at Sherbrooke became involved at this time. She thought he should be in a psychiatric hospital. In lieu of that, another rehabilitation facility better able to handle him. We talked at length about dementia and Parkinson's disease. She seemed knowledgeable and professional. She suggested a facility in north St. Louis county called the Estates of Spanish Lake and assured me that they had the best rehabilitation program in the area.

They would not take him over the Memorial Day weekend, but they agreed to take him the Tuesday after the holiday. I went to check the place out on Saturday of the holiday weekend. They were very well staffed, and the person who showed me around said all the right things. The facility was old but clean and well maintained. I agreed to let him go there.

In the seven days Ollie was at Sherbrooke, I was called four times because he had fallen. Each time I visited him there, he would say, "Where are they?" I took this to mean, where were the staff? There were never more than two nurses and one aid and a handyman to care for fifteen patients. The Estates sent a van to pick him up on Tuesday. The van broke down on the way to the facility. They sent another van quickly, so his arrival was not delayed too long. When he arrived, the first thing that he said to me was, "They are everywhere." There were staff everywhere.

His weight now was 120 pounds. He had lost 25 pounds, most of it muscle mass. He still had not received any physical therapy. I left that day thinking he was in the right place to receive that therapy.

Oh, how wrong I was.

Claudia made her first visit to the Estates on Friday. She found him still in bed at 10:00 a.m. She let him sleep. Hearing this, I decided I had better go in on Saturday. I arrived on Saturday morning to find him sitting in a wooden wheelchair, head on chest, dressed in someone else's clothing, unshaved, and without shoes. When I could arouse him, he would only say, "This place is different. I want to go home." There were no nurses in sight and only one aide on the unit of sixteen patients. I was more than a little upset. I drove home and called the facility administrator. He assured me that he would take care of the problem and call me back. He never called back.

I spent the rest of the weekend crying and calling every nursing home and rehabilitation center I could reach on a weekend. By Monday, I had some answers. Avalon Memory Care had a new facility very near our home. I was told that they had a semiprivate room available for $7,500 per month.

Assisted-living facilities were charging $4,500 per month, but Ollie was well beyond that and needed skilled nursing.

I scheduled a tour of Avalon and spoke to the nurse on duty. Staffing was thin, and there were not a lot of activities. It was beautiful and clean. It was a bird in the hand; no other places seemed to be available.

Ollie needed to be out of the Estates. I told the nurse I wanted to move my husband to Avalon. I was honest about his condition, and the nurse said they would need to review his medical records before he was accepted.

Tuesday morning, I received a call from the Estates, saying Ollie had fallen backward out of his wheelchair and he was being sent to Christian Hospital. This was the second fall he had, had at the Estates but by far the most serious.

I found him in the emergency room at Christian Hospital, waiting for the results of the third CT scan of his head in three weeks, as well as a CT scan of his neck. He was still dressed in someone else's clothing, but they had shaved him. It looked like they had used an axe to accomplish this. They had been given his electric razor but quite obviously had not used it. Considering, what he had been through, his spirits were good. Mine, not so much.

While I waited for the results of the tests, which based on my own physical exam were likely to show no injury, it dawned on me that he was now in another institution with social workers who could help us. I asked to see a social worker and was well rewarded by a lovely young lady who listened to my sad story, including the possibility of a bed at Avalon. She agreed to help. Soon, she came back to inform me that there was no available bed at Avalon, because someone else had already put a deposit on the bed. No one I had talked to the previous day was aware of this fact. The social worker suggested Parc Provence, instead. She was well aware that I did not want him to return to the Estates, so she agreed to ask the doctors to admit him for a two-day short stay until I was able to get him signed up at Parc Provence. That night, I received a call from Parc regarding their policies and procedures. A semiprivate room would cost nearly $10,000 per month. They required a one-month deposit, as well as the first month payment in advance. It would cost nearly $20,000 to get my poor husband out of the hell he had been sucked into.

The next day, I visited Parc. It was a lovely place and seemed to have a large staff, as well as many activities. It was our only option. That afternoon, I visited Ollie at Christian Hospital and told him the plan. I told him I had to give them all our money, but I thought he would be in a safe place. He was scheduled to be transported to Parc the next morning.

It is worth noting that a few months after Ollie left the Estates facility, there was a murder there. One patient murdered another.

I was grateful we were able to get him out of this "highly rated facility."

Gloria and Claudia joined me in waiting for Ollie to arrive at Parc. Christian Hospital had done a marvelous job. He was clean, shaved and in a hospital gown. I was overjoyed to see him this way, as were Claudia and Gloria. At long last, rehabilitation would begin. Parc was a very large facility with many patients in different stages of dementia. They were very careful to keep patients among their peers with similar function.

Those in late-stage dementia were housed in the Rose Garden unit in the basement.

His first assessment put him at a mental age of 2.8 years. He was now in late-stage dementia. It was my hope that with rehabilitation he would prosper and be able to move up to one of the higher-functioning units.

The focus in the Rose Garden was to keep the patients calm and serene. Real activity was minimal and replaced by many musical sessions.

Much of the variability you see among nursing homes and the seeming awareness of the patients is most likely due to the philosophy of the house doctors. Those who believe in heavy medication for example antipsychotics and antidepressants will have patients very sleepy and not active. This was the philosophy of the physicians at Parc.

The first few times that I visited him at Parc, he was barely awake, sitting with his head on his chest while the music was playing. This was not a quality life. I called his doctors and expressed my concerns and asked that they begin backing off on the medication they were giving him. I also asked that they put him back on his medication for Parkinson's disease because he had developed rigidity. The Sinemet would relieve this rigidity. Gradually, he came out of the stupor. This, however, made him more active. The staff was not too happy, because when he got up, they would need to get him to sit back down. I was asked to pay extra for chair and bed alarms. Their greatest fear was that he would fall.

My philosophy is you venture to live, you venture to fall. I knew that mobility was very important to Ollie. I did agree to pay extra for the alarms. I continued to call the doctors periodically to ask that the medication dosage be reduced. When they complied, he kept getting better and more alert, and along with physical therapy, he began walking some.

One of the aides related that earlier in the week, he had said to her, "Half my brain is gone, and now they have me in diapers," and then he stomped off. This was a very sad sign, that he was well aware of what was happening to him. Throughout this ordeal, his caregivers consistently told me he was sweet and gracious. I looked on and wondered, where does he get this grace?

As time passed and the drug dosage was reduced, Ollie became more and more alert and ambulatory. He was now the highest-functioning patient in the Rose Garden. He tried hard to communicate with other patients but without success. He did communicate with staff, other patient families, and visitors from our church, Bob and Joyce Taylor and Pastor Steve.

Claudia and Gloria visited regularly and brought their kids when they were in town. Heather visited, and when he saw her, he said "New York." New York is where Heather lives.

It was still my goal to get Ollie moved to a Parc unit where he was with others who were able to function as well as he did. Since the main activity in the Rose Garden was still listening to music, when I visited, I brought games to play—Domino's, Clue, and others. He was able to play with cueing.

Anna came to visit in July. When we arrived in the Rose Garden, Ollie was asleep in one of the chairs. We woke him gently. When he saw me, his face lit up. Anna commented, "That look expresses such great love." This is the look I would get each time he saw me for many more months. That look brought me joy.

Ollie recognized Anna that day, and we spent time playing Domino's. This was great fun for all three of us.

I began taking Ollie out twice a week for lunch. He would take his walker, but rather than use it, he carried it. When we were out, it mostly stayed in the car. Holding my hand was enough to steady him and give him confidence. After lunch, we began stopping by our house. He was able to visit Nelson, our poodle, and watch some sports on TV. I also began putting him on the treadmill to help strengthen his legs. He loved using the treadmill.

One Sunday, after a day together which included church and a meal at home and the treadmill exercise, returning him to Parc was not so easy. When we arrived at Parc, he refused to enter the facility and became verbally abusive to me. This was something, I never saw unless he was ill from a urinary tract infection.

The doorman called for nursing assistance, and when they arrived, he calmly went with them.

I was extremely upset and found myself not wanting to see him again right away.

However, the next day he had an appointment with our primary care physician, whom I had asked to take over his care while he was at Parc Provence. Obviously, he needed this appointment, so off I went to take him to see his doctor.

When I arrived, he greeted me fondly. I said to him, "You were not so nice to me yesterday. Do you remember that?"

He replied, "Of course, I remember that, and I am ashamed of myself."

Dementia patients often understand and remember things you might not expect. Always speak to them as though they had no disability, and you will be pleasantly surprised.

While we were driving to the doctor's office, he brought up the previous day's incident again, saying, "How could I have behaved so badly? Those kids treat me well there."

I told him, "I forgive you." We never spoke of it again.

His doctor did start him on another course of antibiotics for a urinary tract infection. His attitude soon became the characteristic one of gratitude rather than resistance.

Ollie was now very mobile, and this was alarming to the staff at Parc. They asked me if they could put him in a Merry-walker chair, this was a seat suspended on a set of PVC pipes on wheels. I agreed because it allowed him to roam the halls at will, no more setting off the alarms when he got up and being told to sit back down. The disadvantage of this device was that it distanced him from the staff; they no longer had conversations with him. He was free but isolated. He called the device his cage. In spite of this label, he did not seem to resent the Merry-chair, because it gave him freedom to wander, and he loved that freedom. It became clear that the staff at Parc had no intention of moving him up a level. As long as he was at Parc, he would remain in the Rose Garden.

I began looking for alternatives. I investigated Mattis Pointe, an Americare facility, only three miles from our home. It was slightly less expensive than Parc but still $7,000 to $8,000 per month. They had several beds available in the memory care unit. I was straightforward with his history and the fact that I wanted to place him where he would have a better quality of life. Although they preferred to get all his records before seeing the potential resident, they agreed that I could bring him for an evaluation.

In late July, we visited Mattis Pointe, and although I had carefully explained why we were looking at this place, he was confused. He was convinced that we were there to look at a puppy. Perhaps because so much of our lives had been devoted to dogs and puppies, whenever confused, he reverted to dogs and puppies. At this time, the other residents were functioning at a higher level than Ollie was functioning. On the way back to Parc, he asked me when we would pick up the puppy. He was so convinced that we had purchased a puppy, and it was weeks before he quit asking me where the puppy was when we were home.

Things did not go well the next week.

I had agreed to host two teenage boys from Germany who would stay several days with our church group as part of an exchange program. I was picking them up at our church one evening when I received two phone calls. The first was from Parc, saying Ollie had eaten one of his hearing aids, and the staff had been able to retrieve most of it, including the battery. Since they had retrieved the battery, anything he might have swallowed would likely not hurt him. It was, however, distressing because he now had only one remaining hearing aid. I believe firmly that it is important to preserve hearing and vision in dementia patients so that they can maintain firm contact with their surroundings. They are also very costly devices. The second call was from Mattis Pointe. They were not interested in having Ollie reside in their facility. Private facilities, that is those that take only self-paying patients and no Medicaid patients, are free to pick and choose their residents. Difficult patients will not be accepted. Difficult patients can also be asked to leave at any point.

I also looked at senior living facilities that had both independent living for me and memory care for him. This would allow us to be close together. Most of these places tell you that you can stay there from independent living through assisted living and into memory care. Base fees are high, and add-on fees are numerous. Once your money is gone, you must move to a facility that accepts Medicaid. This was not appealing.

Clearly, I needed help once again. I needed to find a way to both care for Ollie and not make myself destitute by spending large sums of money on his care. I also needed help in finding a facility that would accept Ollie and would allow him both freedom to move around and socialization opportunities. Help with the former came in the form of elder care attorneys Reuter and Merkle. Dan Reuter worked me through my options for preserving wealth while caring for my husband. All options had pros and cons. He helped me with some estate planning, but best of all, he recommended the Missouri Veterans Homes.

I began placing Ollie on waiting lists for admission to several memory care facilities just to keep our options open. Gloria and I visited the Missouri Veterans Home in St. James, Missouri. She, too, had heard good things about this place. We were greeted at the door by several of the resident veterans who spoke highly of the facility and called it a spa. Everyone looked alert and content. The admissions officer conducted the tour and filled us in on the details of everyday life at this facility. She also told us that the usual wait for admission once the veteran was officially on the waiting list was one year. The monthly cost was $2,050.

Gloria and I both left St. James thinking this was a really good option for Ollie and me. The main drawback here was that St. James is a ninety-minute drive from our home. I checked out the Missouri

Veterans Home in Cape Girardeau, Missouri, and found it to be very similar, but the veterans were much more sedated and less active than those I had seen in St. James. I filled out the extensive paperwork to place Ollie on the waiting list for St. James. He was officially placed on the list in mid-September.

Help with finding a facility that would both accept him and help me achieve for him the quality of life I thought possible came from Rob Howe. Rob was recommended by our primary care physician. I met with Rob in mid-September. He gave me two good options: one was the Family Partners group home. Ollie had gone to the Family Partners Day Care center early in the year and loved it. In the group home situation, eight residents lived in a lovely group home and were transported to the day care center five days a week. The staff at both facilities were the same. The meals were chef prepared and extraordinary. The monthly base price was $7,500, but lots of services would be extra. This was an expensive option but one that could possibly give him the quality of life I wanted for him.

The second option was Garden View care center. Skilled nursing here was $7,000 per month. Lots of activities were available, and the residents appeared well cared for and content.

We arranged for tours of both of these facilities for Ollie. He remembered the day care center and was ready to go to the group home. However, they did not have a bed available. I placed him on the waiting list. He was at the top of the list, but beds did not turn over frequently. They were building a second group home that would be ready in a year and a half.

Garden View had a room available immediately. Ollie seemed to think the place was acceptable. After watching Ollie interact with the various staff members at both facilities, Rob asked me if he was always so polite. The answer of course was yes, Ollie was always a gentleman.

My goal was to get Ollie out of his cage at Parc and into a situation where he could be completely mobile and be able to interact with other residents. Since Family Partners was not available at the time, I chose to move him to Garden View. His primary care physician agreed to care for him while he was at this new facility.

We moved to Garden View in late September. Claudia and Bill helped with the move. Ollie looked around and said, "I guess this is where I live now." He participated in a group activity that evening and the next day told me what a great Bible study group they had here. He walked in with his walker but put it in a corner and never used it again. Risk taking is a human need, so says my favorite twenty-first-century thinker in Rule 11.[12] Other patients reached out to him, and he responded. I had hoped that the staff would either help him with some of the activities such as bingo or seat him near a proficient player who could help him. This was not the case, so most activities were of little benefit. He was free to walk, and walk he did. He wore an alarm bracelet to signal staff if he wandered out a door. He grew stronger and more confident. While he might be confused about a lot of things, he always seemed to know about my significant health issues and what other activities I was engaged in. Visitors were told about the book I was writing. He was still the man behind the woman.

I continued to take Ollie to church on Sunday and out to lunch one other day of the week. He often expressed the desire to be home. The nursing staff was concerned about the small dose of antipsychotic drug remaining. I had successfully lobbied to remove most of the psychoactive drugs that had been prescribed. He was visited by a nurse practitioner working under a psychiatrist. The drug in question had a black box warning for use in elderly dementia patients. It was associated with higher death rates and infection because it was associated with a decreased white blood cell count.

The nurse practitioner and I spoke about the pros and cons of leaving him on this drug. His lab work, including his white blood cell count, was normal. He still had recurring urinary tract infections, which he had experienced for years. He still suffered from hallucinations, not uncommon in Parkinson's disease patients, and the drug in question was specific for the hallucinations. The decision was made to keep him on the small dose of this drug.

He continued to have severe urinary tract infections while at Garden View. One of these was resistant to all oral antibiotics, requiring the use of an intravenous line to administer the antibiotic.

Ollie was devastated to learn this fact. He did not want to have this line placed. I explained to him that the choice was his but if he did not have the line placed he would die of the infection. He chose to have the line placed.

In October, as the weather turned cooler, I began having severe asthma attacks; several were life threatening. My doctor prescribed a long-acting inhaler, which stopped the life-threatening attacks, but milder attacks still occurred. At the time of my annual bone density exam, in early November, it was determined that I should consult a bone specialist. Before recommending one of the many available drugs to treat osteoporosis, she ran some additional tests. I had two fractured vertebrae in my back and a marker for multiple myeloma, lymphoma, and Waldenstrom's in my blood. All of these are blood cancers, requiring chemotherapy. I now needed to see an oncologist.

It would be a few weeks before I could see the oncologist. I needed to break the news to Ollie. He showed clear signs of worry, a deep frown on his face and looking downward. "How can I help?" he asked. I explained to him that I would not be able to visit him if I had to have chemotherapy. "Can we talk on the phone?" he asked. It had been a very long time since he had used a phone, but this was a very good idea. What is truly remarkable is the fact that even in late-stage dementia, he could process information and do some minor problem-solving.

It is so important to communicate with your loved one suffering from dementia. They can often process and respond.

It was at this time that Garden View decided to raise their monthly rate to $7,500.

The fourth quarter of 2018 was very bad for the stock market. Some of our income and all of our savings were dependent to some extent on the stock market. I was facing increased costs and decreased income. This was just another stressor for me and coupled with the possibility of chemotherapy and not being able to see him in the nursing facility, I began to consider the possibility of bringing him home. I mentioned this to my beautician one day, and he told me about Molly, one of his other clients, who did home health care. Women's beauticians are like men's bartenders. They know most of your problems and often have sage advice. I spoke with Molly, and together we devised a workable plan. She would come to our house at 7:00 a.m. six days a week and bathe and dress Ollie. Monday through Friday, she would take him to Family Partners day care by 9:00 a.m. and pick him up again at 5:00 p.m. She would take him out on Saturday for some activity, like walking or bowling. I would need to take care of him every evening and get him to bed.

In the event that I needed chemotherapy, Molly would take care of me also.

Ollie was very happy to be going home. He did, however, ask me to prepare tips for his caregivers at Garden View; he wanted to show his appreciation. According to his wishes, I prepared twenty-five envelopes with five dollars in each envelope and left them at the nursing station for distribution. He was again showing us that gracious, appreciative Ollie. I brought him home for Thanksgiving, and we entertained our Jonesburg friends, the Dunlaps, and Elaine Riegle. Ollie's sister Doris also joined us. The Dunlaps and Elaine would join us for Christmas as well.

I was so happy to have Ollie home for the holidays and his birthday, December 12.

Ollie soon began to have more urinary tract infections. In fact, he seldom went more than two weeks between episodes. His behavior always deteriorated when he had one of these infections.

He often did not recognize the house, not the outside and not the inside. He would ask me if I bought this house. I always needed to show him where the bedroom and bathroom were located. He would wander aimlessly in the evening, moving things from place to place. I learned early on not to get between him and the object he was attempting to move. He would grip my arm with way too much force. Once I had to tell him I would call the police if he did not release my arm. I am sure Alexa would have been only too happy to dial 911. I had to make an exception to this rule when he attempted to move the dog bed with the dog in it. Loudly demanding that he stop seemed to work. For the most part, he would not take any suggestions from me. Sometimes it was difficult to get him to take his medicine.

On New Year's Day 2019, he bit me while I was trying to get him to take a pill for his Parkinson's disease. He bit my left thumb at the nail base, and it bled freely. Human bites require antibiotic treatment, especially in my case, since I had undergone a mastectomy and node dissection on the left for breast cancer treatment. Severe permanent swelling in the arm can result from infection in these circumstances.

I called Molly and asked her to come to the house to look after Ollie while I went to the emergency room. Fortunately, I recovered without incident.

Ten days later, I received a call from Family Partners day care, telling me that Ollie had blood in his stool. That night, I examined him, and he most certainly did have blood in his stool, quite a lot of it. I took him off his blood thinner and called his doctor the next morning. Keith and Donna were concerned and drove up from Texas. By the time we saw his doctor, the bleeding had stopped, but he had lost enough blood that he was anemic. The blood thinner was discontinued permanently. It now represented more of a risk than a benefit. Keith installed a chain lock mechanism on each of the outside doors to prevent his dad from walking outside and getting lost and hypothermic.

Ollie had only just figured out how to open these doors and had done so a time or two. I watched closely, but this extra layer of protection was welcome. Ollie's behavior at day care was similar to that, which I saw in the evenings. He walked all day and moved the chairs around a lot. He was not benefiting from the activity program they provided. More episodes of physical violence occurred. One Saturday, Molly took Ollie to Lemay to drive around the old neighborhood. At some point, he grabbed the seat belt protecting Molly and choked her with it. She was close to the beauty shop and was able to drive there and get help from David, our beautician. They called me, and I was able to coax him to my car and took him home.

There were several incidents where Molly would bring him home from day care and pull into the driveway, and Ollie would refuse to get out of the car, because he did not recognize the house. The first time this happened, he did recognize me and agreed to come into the house. The second time it happened, he did not recognize me, and it took forty-five minutes to get him out of the car. Finally, in frustration, I said to him, "You are making me feel bad." He got right out. I guess making a woman feel bad was not acceptable behavior.

In January of 2019, there were several Artic blasts, which caused subzero temperatures. I was grateful that this episode did not occur during one of those Artic blasts. That would have been dangerous for all of us. I asked Molly, several times if she was still willing to continue helping me take care of him. She always said yes, but I wondered when enough would be enough. There was no way that I would be able to take care of him by myself.

Eating was becoming a problem—which utensil to use was always a mystery to him. Deciding what foods could and should be eaten with his fingers was also perplexing. Suggestions from me were ignored. Sometimes, he seemed to give up on the meal in frustration.

Toileting was often more of problem than I was able to imagine. One morning, while I was home alone with him, he asked to go to the bathroom. I took him there and tried to pull his pants down, as always. He kept pulling them back up. Finally, I convinced him the pants needed to come down. The phone rang. I left the bathroom to answer the phone. On the other end of the phone was the admissions officer from the Veterans Home in St. James. She wanted to know if I was still interested in placing Ollie in this facility. My answer was *yes*. While my answer to her was yes, I was not really sure. This was early February, and I was not expecting the call so soon.

While some moments could be very frustrating, others were loving, sweet, and tender. I was living for the latter moments and wanted them to continue.

I would wrestle with this dilemma for the next two weeks.

During this time, Ollie had several melt downs, often in public, where he would be hitting and kicking Molly and her cousin and calling for someone to rescue him. Each time I thought, "God is giving me previews of coming attractions." This was his answer to my prayers, asking for guidance.

I finally came to terms with the decision to place him in the Veterans Home. To prepare Ollie for the coming move, I told him the army wanted him. They had a job for him. He accepted this without question and with no resistance. Claudia, Bill, and Gloria all helped with the move. It went smoothly. When we visited after the move, Ollie always seemed peaceful and content. There were no episodes of bad behavior reported. One of their activities was peeling potatoes. They joked about their KP duty. His appetite was good; and on the occasions, I sat with him at lunch, he had less difficulty eating. I was still blessed with some of those loving, sweet, and tender moments when I visited. In late March, Anna came to visit. She took this photo of us at the Veterans Home, St. James.

OLLIE AND SUSAN AT THE VETERANS HOME, ST. JAMES, MISSOURI FORWARD TO THE END

I call it Forward to the End.

CHAPTER 11

Our Final Chapter

Ollie did well at the Veteran's Home until late April of 2019. In fact in early April, we had scheduled one of our monthly family luncheons in St. James so that Ollie could join us. It was a great outing for him, and he was able to interact with at least twelve of the Krechel clan. A couple of weeks later, I began to notice weight loss. Whenever I was with him at mealtime, he seemed to have a good appetite. Dessert was always the first item on the tray to disappear. Although he no longer called me by name, he always showed recognition. At this time, he began to have falls. They were always minor, without evidence of injury.

Near the end of May, the Veteran's Home staff involved in Ollie's care met with me for the quarterly review of his care. I was able to voice my concerns regarding the weight loss and increasing frequency of falls. I was told that they were concerned about daily episodes of anxiety occurring in the afternoon and seemingly interfering with his ability to eat dinner. The staff suggested adding Depakote® to his medications. This is an old drug, used mainly for seizures and bipolar psychiatric disorders. I had always resisted the use of drugs affecting the brain; however, I did not want to see him distressed by anxiety. I agreed to a trial of this medication.

By mid-June, both of his daughters and I noted that he was more difficult to engage. He was inhabiting his own little world and was not interacting with us on any level. I also noted that he was no longer eating lunch and seemed to be losing even more weight. In addition, he was becoming weaker, and we often found him in a wheelchair.

I called the charge nurse for his unit and expressed my concerns and asked if the anxiety was improved. I was told that the anxiety was improved, and we talked about getting physical therapy involved to possibly build up his strength. We also talked about switching him to a soft diet to make eating easier for him. A few days later, I received a call informing me that Ollie had fallen out of bed and was complaining of hip and shoulder pain. The nurse assured me that on physical examination, she could not find any evidence of serious injury. I was alarmed by the reports of pain. Ollie never complained of pain.

Daughter Gloria visited him that same evening and found him without complaints and looking good. The next day, I drove down to St. James to visit. I found him asleep and did not try to wake him, since I knew they would get him up for lunch soon. When the support staff arrived to get him to lunch, he did not acknowledge me at all. Two attendants were required to get him out of bed because he complained of pain in his right arm. While waiting for his lunch to arrive, I tried to engage him in conversation and got yes and no answers only. When I asked if he needed anything, he said food. However, when an orderly asked him if he wanted to have a bath before lunch, he said yes with enthusiasm. He still did not acknowledge my presence.

The idea of hospice care had been on my mind for several weeks. I had attended a medical meeting pertaining to dementia as part of my research for this book. There, I had met a hospice nurse, Margaret Terranova. She had agreed to meet me in early July to talk about hospice, not just for Ollie and our family but also for this book. It looked like Ollie would need hospice care sooner than that meeting date. Further research led me back to the very company for which Margaret was working, Heartland® Hospice Care.

Before leaving the Veteran's Home that day, I spoke to the social worker. She agreed that hospice was a good idea, and she spoke highly of Heartland® Hospice Care. I shed many tears during this discussion. Minutes later, from the parking lot, I called Heartland

Hospice Care to schedule an evaluation. I asked that his pain be addressed because it had continued to get worse. Within twenty-four hours, I was signing papers in Margaret Terranova's office, and Ollie was now on hospice care. They quickly got his pain under control with morphine and a fentanyl patch. At last, he was comfortable without pain, anxiety, or discomfort of any kind.

The next day, the hospice nurse called to tell me that Ollie was going to succumb to his illness quickly. In her estimation, within one week. One day later, she called to tell me the process was going even more quickly. Several of us visited that Friday, and he did not look good and was unresponsive. I planned a forty-eight-hour vigil. I had initially assumed that any rest I got in this period would be at a nearby motel. However, the social worker at the Veteran's Home set me up in the family room with a pull-out bed and private bath. They also provided fruit, tea, water, coffee, as well as some snacks. While the vigil was physically and emotionally stressful, this courtesy made it less so. I will be forever grateful to the staff at the St. James Veteran's Home for the care given to Ollie and me, as well as other family members. It was the ultimate in kindness and caring.

Oliver Anthony Krechel's life journey ended at 12:59 a.m., Monday, July 1, 2019. I was at his side.

PART 2

Understanding Dementia

To the average person, the term *dementia* is often poorly understood.

In the pages that follow, I will try to give you the most up-to-date knowledge of this dreadful condition in an easy-to-understand form.

Basically, dementia is a decline in mental ability, severe enough to interfere with daily life and activities. Typically, the decline in mental ability involves varying degrees of loss in the ability to think, reason, and remember. Contributing to the misunderstanding is the fact that while Alzheimer's disease is a dementia, not all dementia is Alzheimer's disease. Those who contribute to mass media seldom make this distinction. It is my belief that many physicians, without intending to do so, perpetuate this problem as they try to explain a dementia diagnosis to patients and families in the simplest possible terms.

At this time, dementia is ultimately fatal unless the patient succumbs to another fatal incident or disease first.

Figure 1

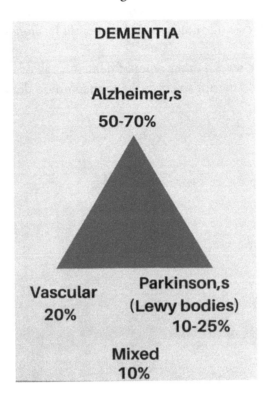

DEMENTIA

Alzheimer,s
50-70%

Vascular
20%

Parkinson,s
(Lewy bodies)
10-25%

Mixed
10%

There are three common types of dementia. Alzheimer's is the most common, accounting for 50 to 70 percent of cases. Second most common, accounting for 20 percent of the cases is vascular dementia. Third accounting for 10 to 25 percent of dementia cases is Parkinson's dementia and dementia with Lewy bodies. These are lumped together because they share three common features, that is, dementia, Lewy bodies, and a movement disorder. Finally, some 10 percent of patients with dementia have a mixed type—that is, they have features of Alzheimer's and one or both of the other two types of dementia.

I believe that this classification is an oversimplification of reality. Since dementia occurs mainly in those over sixty-five years of age, it is not surprising that there is evidence of vascular disease in the brains of dementia patients. This suggests that vascular dementia coexists with the other two types of dementia on a regular basis.

I will discuss all three types of dementia in more detail later in this section.

There are several other types of dementia, all of which are rare. I will make no attempt to cover these uncommon dementias in any detail, if at all.

CHAPTER 12

The Scope of the Problem

D r. Alois Alzheimer described the dementia which bears his name, along with its pathologic findings, in 1906.

In 1912, Dr. Friedrich Heinrich Lewy, working in the lab of Dr. Alzheimer, discovered abnormal spherical masses displacing normal cell structures within the brains of patients with Parkinson's disease. These spherical masses are now called Lewy bodies, after their discoverer. Now more than one hundred years after the earliest description of these diseases, we still do not know definitively what causes them.

When the cause of a disease is unknown, the prevention and cure of that disease become extremely difficult.

A 2010 publication of the Alzheimer's association estimated 5.3 million people in the United States are suffering from Alzheimer's dementia.[13] Due to the aging baby boom population, this number is expected to rise to 11–16 million people by 2050.

Societal costs are staggering, ranging from an estimated high of $172 billion[14] to a low of $109 billion[15] for 2010 alone, and this does not include the cost of unpaid caregivers, which is estimated to be a high of $316 billion to a low of $159 to $215 billion. The cost differences between these two reports is likely due to the methodology of the report and the subgroups of dementia studied. It is estimated that the cost of care by 2040 will be 80 percent higher. In an attempt to develop a national strategic plan to understand and combat Alzheimer's disease, Congress enacted and President Obama signed into law the National Alzheimer's Project Act in January 2011. It is important to note that this act defines *Alzheimer's* as Alzheimer's disease and related dementias.[16]

The National Plan to Address Alzheimer's Disease was born under the auspices of the Department of Health and Human Services. The latest available revision is 2017. Goal number one of this strategic plan is to prevent and effectively treat Alzheimer's disease and related dementias by 2025. The strategic plan appears comprehensive. I see evidence in the literature of the basic science research funded as a result of this plan. The published results appear to be advancing the goals of diagnosis, prevention, and cure. The goals of the strategic plan related to care, caregivers, and care facilities, although laudable, do not appear to have made it out of Washington, DC, at least not to Missouri and a few other states I have looked at. Having said that, there is an exception. The Veterans Administration is involved in implementing the strategic plan; and my experience with the Missouri Veteran's Home, where my husband resided, is positive. Elements of the strategic plan relative to care and care facilities appear to be working there.

On the light side, an initiative is underway to solicit small technology businesses to develop socially interactive and assistive robots to help serve as caregivers for patients with dementia, helping both them and their caregivers. Addressing the goal of public education, Memory Sunday, is an annual outreach to African American congregations to educate from the pulpit. This is especially valuable since African Americans are twice as likely to develop dementia, as opposed to Caucasians.[17] Not addressed in the strategic plan is the fact that Hispanics are 1.5 times more likely to develop dementia than Caucasians. The growing number of Hispanics migrating to the United States makes meeting the goals of the strategic plan even more pressing. Thanks to the strategic plan, efforts are underway to help states provide ombudsman (public advocate) services for dementia patients evicted from long-term care facilities. This is especially a problem with private pay facilities. They, unfortunately, operate outside the Medicaid rules and may not be affected by the strategic plan in any way. I was actually forced to sign a document stating that I understood that my husband could be dropped off on my doorstep if I failed to pay the bill every month; that bill was $10,000. Another problem that is not addressed is rejection of patients requesting admission. My experience has been that some of the private facilities reject difficult severely disabled patients. Some of the private facilities, including those offering a continuum of care from independent living through assisted living and into a skilled nursing care programs, will simply charge more for all services beyond a basic level. They will tell you if you run out of money you must leave. Some private facilities which charge large up-front fees amounting to $250,000 to $500,000 and up to enter at the independent-living level will guarantee that your stay will be subsidized if you are no longer able to pay. That is provided your inability to pay is no fault of your own.

Among the most important initiatives that I see in the strategic plan is a national goal to reduce the use of antipsychotic medication in nursing home residents. The 2017 update states that a 30 percent reduction has been achieved as of 2016, and new goals are being established.

You will recall from the memoir that the use of antipsychotic medication in my husband's case was a major problem in my view and a problem that I worked hard to solve.

My dear friend Dr. Cynthia Guy, now residing in Florida, shared her experience with antipsychotic drugs in dementia patients. Her husband, Stuart, a dementia patient, was given antipsychotics for behavior problems. As his disease progressed, he lost the ability to speak and no longer knew his loving wife. When she could no longer take care of him, the staff at the skilled nursing facility to which he was admitted weaned him off this medication. Suddenly, he was able to speak and recognize his dear wife. This was a joyful experience for both of them. Thanks to this initiative of the strategic plan, I have great hope for the quality of life of today's and tomorrow's dementia patients.

We must not forget that dementia is a global problem.[18] Worldwide, nearly 54 million people are expected to be living with dementia in 2020. By 2035, this number will rise to nearly 88 million. In 2050, the global estimate is that over 130 million people will be suffering from dementia. The projections for rate of growth is much higher in low- and middle-income countries while it is expected to grow at a slower rate in high-income countries such as the United States. This is likely due to better per capita health care in higher-income countries.

Worldwide costs exceeded $1 trillion in 2018, and the cost is expected to rise to $2 trillion by 2030. This figure exceeds the value of most of the world's economies. From data compiled for the World Alzheimer Report 2015, we see that dementia is appearing more frequently in the older age groups and most frequently in the oldest age group.

By way of explanation, if we were to follow 1,000 people eighty to eighty-nine years of age for one year in the high-income countries, we would find 80 new cases of dementia. Whereas if we followed 1,000 people ninety years and older for one year, we would discover 130 new cases of dementia in the high-income countries.

The later dementia occurs, the closer the person is to the normal end of life, assuring the best possible overall quality of life. We can only hope that this trend will continue.

Much work, has been done in the last one hundred years, most of it in the last twenty years. We have many clues and are opening up many promising avenues of investigation which may soon offer effective treatment, as well as possible prevention. In my view, this is unlikely to happen by 2025. I would like to be wrong.

I will attempt to increase your understanding of these investigations as we look at diagnosis, treatment, and prevention of the most common types of dementia.

Figure 2

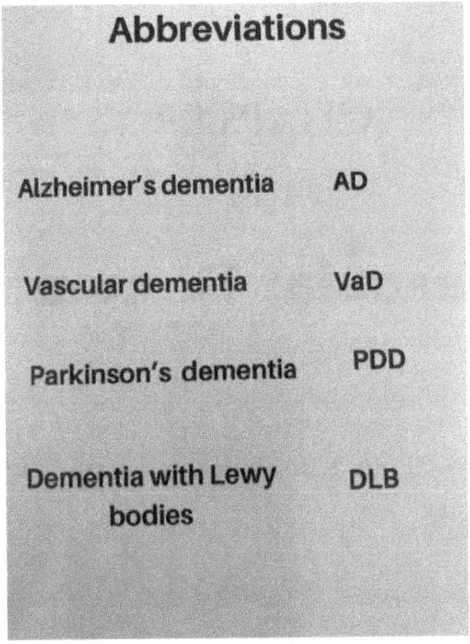

Abbreviations

Alzheimer's dementia	AD
Vascular dementia	VaD
Parkinson's dementia	PDD
Dementia with Lewy bodies	DLB

Figure 2 is an explanation of the abbreviations that will be used when discussing the common dementias.

CHAPTER 13

Vascular Dementia

Vascular dementia, by definition, is a dementia which begins following a stroke.

Figure 3[19]

Signs of stroke

S — Speech or language difficulty

T — Tingling or numbness

R — Remember any memory loss

O — Off balance coordination difficulty

K — Killer Headache

E — Eyes new vision problem

The signs of stroke are important for everyone to know. If any of the signs described in figure 3 occurs, it is a medical emergency and 911 should be notified. The diagnosis of the stroke or strokes is made by neuroimaging, that is a CT scan or an MRI. The radiologist makes the diagnosis. The stroke may or may not be symptomatic. Usually, strokes that are large occur with symptoms. Somewhat smaller strokes may occur with symptoms, which may or may not persist. There may be many, very small strokes, which can be diagnosed by CT or MRI that occur with no symptoms at all.

You will recall from the memoir that when Ollie had his stroke, the CT scan showed evidence of several small strokes that had occurred in the remote past.

Chronic cerebral infarcts (small strokes) are common in older people. They can be seen with the naked eye at autopsy in 30 percent to 50 percent of older people. The bigger and more numerous these cerebral infarcts (strokes) are, the more often the individual had been previously diagnosed with clinical dementia. If autopsy specimens are viewed under the microscope, 75 percent of older people have evidence of strokes.[20]

Nearly all dementias including vascular dementias begin with the loss of the ability to smell. So it is this part of the brain that allows us to identify odors which begins to die first. When blood flow to the brain is compromised, the supply of oxygen and glucose to the tissues of the brain is interrupted, leading to cell death. At autopsy, brains of patients who have been diagnosed with (VaD) show evidence of cell death due to vascular damage but also show the plaques and tangles (amyloid beta and tau proteins), the hallmark of Alzheimer's disease (AD).[21] Adding to the confusion, patients diagnosed with AD almost always have some vascular disease (usually involving small blood vessels).

There is a very complex interplay between VaD and AD. This overlap may increase the risk of dementia.[22] Fortunately, the brain has a huge reserve capacity and the ability to regenerate some cells in some cases. Nowhere is this better illustrated than by Jill Bolte Taylor.[23] Her recovery from a massive stroke is truly inspirational.

Let me be clear, no one with a diagnosis of dementia is at this time going to recover.

I raise the issue of reserve capacity and regeneration only to help explain how the addition of vascular injury may overcome the reserve capacity of the brain and unleash AD. It also helps explain why AD affects mainly older people and why some people never show symptoms of AD even though autopsy findings suggest that the disease is present. Those who do not show symptoms in the presence of disease findings have simply not yet used up their reserve capacity.

Risk

It appears that at this point in time, we are all at risk of developing AD unless we die of something else before symptoms begin.

Figure 4

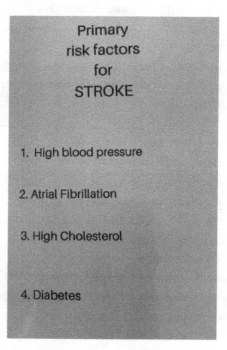

Primary
risk factors
for
STROKE

1. High blood pressure

2. Atrial Fibrillation

3. High Cholesterol

4. Diabetes

On the bright side, if we reduce our risk of stroke by taking steps to reduce high blood pressure, treat atrial fibrillation, lower our cholesterol, and treat diabetes by keeping our blood sugars under control, we also reduce our risk or at least delay the onset of VaD and AD.

There are some additional factors that are known to increase stroke risk, for example there is mounting evidence that the consumption of diet drinks (soda or fruit drinks, sweetened with artificial sweeteners) is associated with an increased risk of stroke.[24]

The ability to link specific genes (the basic physical and functional unit of heredity, the building blocks of our DNA) to specific disease states is still in its infancy. At this time, it is known that the specific gene (APOE4) can be associated with an increased risk of vascular disease but not necessarily linked to VaD. On the other hand, the (APOE 4) gene is unequivocally associated with AD. If a stroke does occur, recovery of lost function is certainly of major concern but not within the scope of our discussion of VaD.

Prevention

Two things which are relevant, however, are prevention of another stroke and prevention of VaD.

To prevent another stroke, typically patients are sent home with prescriptions for a drug to lower blood pressure, a drug to lower cholesterol (usually a statin such as Lipitor®), and an antiplatelet drug to prevent blood clots from forming, such as Plavix®. If atrial fibrillation is present, other treatments will be required.

Statin drugs are effective in preventing another stroke.[25] They are, however, associated with dementia. We will cover this in more detail later. This is a dilemma. Any further damage to the brain is likely to increase the risk of dementia, and statin drugs appear to prevent the further damage, but it is difficult to ignore the association of statins with dementia. In Oliver's case, he was given Lipitor® at the time of his stroke and continued to take it into the stage of moderate dementia at which time it was discontinued in the hope that discontinuing it might at least slow the progression. This can probably be viewed as a "Hail Mary" effort.

Of great interest is a recent (May 2019) study which suggests that two old drugs given a new purpose may actually be useful in preventing VaD following stroke.[26]

One is Pletal®, a drug to prevent clotting; and the other is isosorbide mononitrate, a very old blood vessel dilator, similar to nitroglycerin, which is used for chest pain related to heart disease. Larger, long-term studies are needed to confirm that this is indeed a breakthrough in the prevention of this one type of dementia.

The normal response of the body to any injury is inflammation. If you cut your finger, after the bleeding stops, you will notice the area around the cut is red, swollen, and warm to the touch. This is the inflammatory response seen with the naked eye. This inflammatory response continues until the offending agents (bacteria or dead cells) are removed by the bodies normal cleanup crew (specialized cells). Then healing and in some cases regeneration can occur. The cleanup crew is often overzealous and additional tissue damage occurs. As long as regeneration is possible, as is the case of skin, no real problem occurs.

The inflammatory response occurs in the brain as well and can result in more damage to delicate brain tissue, which may not be able to regenerate. Work is being done in mice with follow-up work in humans, using genetically modified proteins, to replace normal injury response proteins, produced by the cleanup crew cells, therefore attenuating the inflammatory response, thereby protecting brain cells.[27] These genetically modified proteins are in a class of drugs known as BACE-1 inhibitors, currently showing great promise in treating not just stroke victims but also victims of traumatic brain injury and other similar disorders. This work suggests that early treatment using these agents may *prevent* the damage that leads to dementia.

While this drug may be useful in dementia prevention, this is a long way from being proven and an even longer way from being available for patient care. Recently, a large group of neurology experts from around the globe have issued a call to action designed to reduce the incidence of dementia by preventing stroke. Stroke doubles the risk of dementia.[28]

This means in order to help prevent dementia, you need to part-ner with your doctor to control high blood pressure. You also need to address the other risk factors, including poor diet and lack of exer-cise, that may elevate your risk of stroke. Visiting your doctor for wellness checkups are critical and should begin early in adult life. An additional aid in prevention of dementia, following stroke is the MIND diet.[29]

MIND stands for Mediterranean-DASH Intervention for Neurodegenerative Delay. This is a hybrid diet consisting of elements of the DASH (Dietary Approaches to Stop Hypertension) diet, basi-cally a low-salt diet, and the Mediterranean diet which focuses on fruits, vegetables, whole grains, and lean protein.

Following the MIND diet requires at least three servings of whole grain daily, at least six servings of green leafy vegetables, and two servings of berries per week; and it encourages the regular con-sumption of other vegetables, fish, poultry, beans, and nuts. Olive oil is the recommended oil, and alcohol is recommended daily. Eliminated foods include red meat, fast foods, cheese, desserts, and butter.

The MIND diet not only helps prevent VaD but also has been shown to slow cognitive decline associated with aging.[30] This sug-gests that it may be useful in the prevention of other dementias.

There is no evidence that supplements work, that is vitamins and other drugstore shelf items. These are unregulated and may con-tain other substances that can be harmful. They May also be contra-indicated with some prescription drugs.

For those of you who want to check your own favorite sup-plement, www.consumerlabs.com publishes research on various products commonly promoted and found on drugstore shelves. This research is made available to consumers for a subscription fee.

Treatment

Once VaD is symptomatic, there is no good treatment. Instead, the treatment for dementia is the same for all the common dementias we will discuss.

Cholinesterase inhibitors increase the levels of acetylcholine in the brain. This is a chemical which helps carry messages among the brain nerve cells. When tolerated, this class of drugs may help for a short time. Drugs of this type are usually prescribed for mild to moderate dementia.

Moderate to severe dementia can be treated with a drug which regulates the activity of glutamate, a chemical which is involved in information processing, storage, and retrieval activities of the brain.

Figure 5

FDA approved drugs to treat Dementia

Cholinesterase inhibitors

Aricept

Exelon

Razadyne

Glutamate regulators

Namenda

CHAPTER 14

Traumatic Brain Injury

Just as a vascular injury to the brain (stroke) can lead to dementia, so can a traumatic injury to the brain (TBI).

These injuries are common. Published data for the year 2009 estimated 2.4 million emergency room visits, hospitalizations, or deaths were associated with head trauma.[31]

Even mild TBI without loss of consciousness doubles the risk of subsequent dementia. The risk more than doubles when loss of consciousness can be documented. Moderate to severe TBI nearly quadrupled the risk of subsequent dementia.[32]

The classification of severity of TBI follows the Department of Defense Coding Guidance for traumatic brain injury.[33]

Data from US Department of Defense

Figures 6

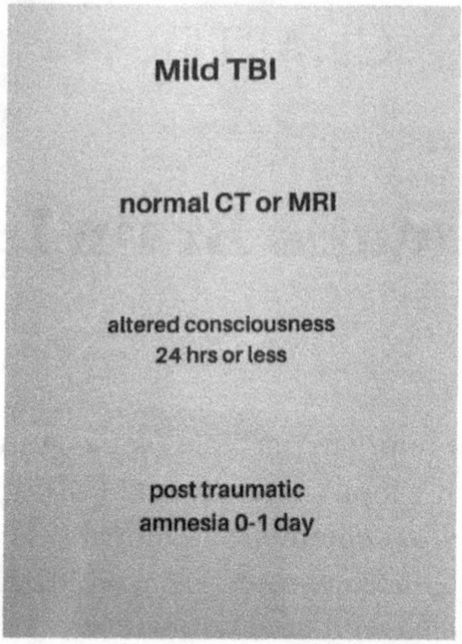

Mild TBI

normal CT or MRI

altered consciousness
24 hrs or less

post traumatic
amnesia 0-1 day

Figure 7

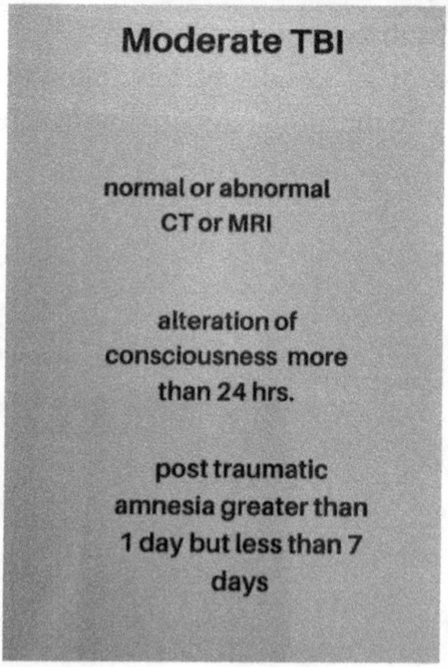

Moderate TBI

normal or abnormal
CT or MRI

alteration of
consciousness more
than 24 hrs.

post traumatic
amnesia greater than
1 day but less than 7
days

Figure 8

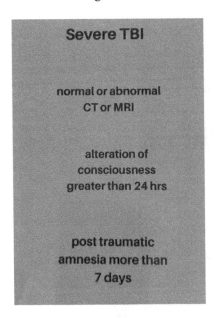

Long-standing brain inflammation again seems to be a factor. Researchers found evidence of an inflammatory response and ongoing tissue degeneration and atrophy (brain shrinkage) in autopsy specimens of patients who had sustained a single moderate to severe TBI up to eighteen years previously.[34]

Imagine what happens when multiple TBIs are sustained, for example in football, soccer, and rugby players, as well as in boxers. The concussions these athletes sustain are TBIs. In fact, following death at autopsy, the brains of these patients show chronic traumatic encephalopathy (CTE) another form of dementia. The autopsy findings seen in dementia patients with CTE when found alone are different from other common forms of dementia.

Instead of the familiar amyloid/tau abnormal protein deposits of Alzheimer's disease or the abnormal Lewy body protein deposits of Parkinson's dementia and Lewy body dementia, *abnormal tau proteins are found in isolation.*

Autopsy findings in dementia patients most often show elements of more than one type of dementia. To find any of the dementia types in isolation is unusual. Studies of patients with recurrent head trauma, mostly sports related, suggest that the average duration of exposure to the repetitive head trauma was 15.4 years.

Once the exposure to the repetitive head trauma ceased (for example, retirement from the sport), the average length of time until the patient began to show symptoms of CTE was 14.5 years. The average age at death of these patients was 59.3 years.[35]

Death occurs at a significantly younger age in these athletes. The symptoms are devastating to themselves, family, and friends.

Figure 9[36]

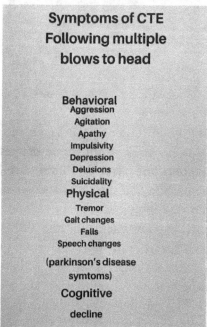

You should note from figure 9 that the behavioral symptoms of dementia associated with CTE are among the worst seen in dementia cases. The physical symptoms are very similar to Parkinson's disease. The Parkinson's like symptoms are especially common in boxers.

After painting this bleak picture of repetitive head injury seen mostly in sports, it is important to point out that not every person exposed to repetitive head trauma develops CTE. Other, as yet unknown factors, are required before repetitive head trauma leads to CTE. It is suspected that genetics is a factor.

The APOE-4 gene often associated with Alzheimer's disease has been studied but results remain inconclusive.

As we will see when we look at Alzheimer's disease, AD actually begins decades before symptoms are seen. It may be that the presence of asymptomatic AD lowers the threshold for CTE, *thus overcoming the brains reserve capacity*. Other genes and other factors may also be involved.

We have noted that even a mild TBI in young adults can significantly increase the risk of dementia in later life.

A recent study looked at older adults (sixty-five and older) and found that those who had sustained head trauma and were diagnosed with concussion were twice as likely to develop dementia within the next five years as similar patients who had sustained ankle trauma.[37]

This suggests that older adults who sustain minor head trauma may be at risk of developing symptoms of dementia sooner than if they had not sustained such head trauma. This is another example of a secondary factor seemingly *overcoming the brain's reserve capacity*.

However, this study's most important finding is that this increased risk of dementia was lowered by 13 percent if the patient received a statin drug such as Lipitor®. It is believed that the statins may prevent the inflammation associated with the injury. This suggests that prescribing a statin drug to an elderly patient who has sustained minor head trauma might be a way to lessen their risk of dementia. This is not true of younger patients in whom these drugs have not been studied, particularly in those under twenty-five years of age in whom the brain is not fully developed.

We are left with an understanding that we must do everything we can to protect our brains. Sports rules may need to be modified to prohibit using one's head to control the ball. Helmets can be helpful but do not completely eliminate the chance of TBI. Although the brain is cushioned, within the skull, if the force with which it is moved within the skull is great enough, it can result in the brain bouncing off the boney skull and sustaining injury even when a helmet is worn. Fall prevention is important. Think about your environment; identify and eliminate the hazards. Consider your footwear. Flip-flops may be cool but cause many falls. Watch your step and avoid excessive speeds. Consider your drug and alcohol use; dulled senses can lead to falls. I am sure you can think of many other ways to avoid falls and other causes of TBI. The important thing is to be *mindful.*

CHAPTER 15

Parkinson's Disease and Its Associated Dementias

This leads us to a discussion of the more common and better studied dementias.

Before delving into Parkinson's disease dementia (PDD) and dementia with Lewy bodies (DLB), it is important to give you an idea of how researchers can distinguish between these diseases. All of these diseases can be diagnosed with 100 percent accuracy at autopsy. Waiting for death is not an option to the researcher who wants to find causes and cures.

Figure 10

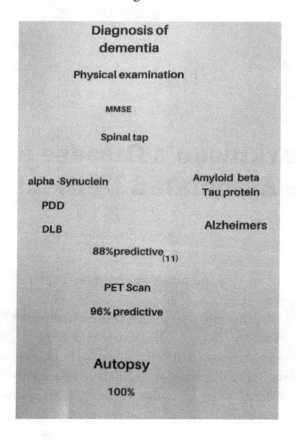

The sequence is a physical examination, the administration of a Mini-Mental Status Exam (there are several varieties), followed by a spinal tap to detect abnormal proteins associated with these dementias. With this alone, the diagnosis is about 88 percent sure. Adding a PET scan (a third generation of neuroimaging, more predictive than a CT or MRI) increases the likelihood of the correct diagnosis to 96 percent. Generally, the advanced steps of spinal tap and PET scans for diagnosis of dementia are not available to physicians except in a research setting because insurance will not pay for these expensive interventions. Their reason, a good one, is that these tests do not lead to information that can be used to cure the dementia. Today there is no cure.

Before an in-depth discussion of the dementias associated with Parkinson's disease, it is important to understand Parkinson's disease itself. Most people think of it as a movement disorder, but it is much more. As with Alzheimer's disease, the brain abnormalities can be seen in the brain decades before symptoms arise.

The protein alpha-synuclein begins accumulating in the brain cells, disrupting their function and ultimately killing them. This process is believed to begin in the part of the brain that controls the sense of smell because the first symptom is often loss of the sense of smell. Losing the sense of smell is not specific to Parkinson's disease but is seen in many other brain disorders including Alzheimer's disease.

Once this process of alpha-synuclein accumulation begins, it spreads throughout the brain much like an infection. This infection-like spread is supported by evidence that cells derived from a fetus (unborn baby) implanted in the brains of Parkinson's disease patients in hopes of curing the disease soon develop the same abnormal protein structures seen in the diseased brain.[38]

More recently, building on work done on HIV/AIDS, researchers in Sweden have discovered the precise mechanism by which the disease spreads.[39]

I mention this fact for two reasons: first, it shows that previous research on seemingly unrelated diseases can lead to breakthroughs in diseases like Parkinson's. Secondly, every bit of information acquired may prove useful in finding new drug therapy and or cures. Once the disease process has spread to the brain structures which control movement, the classical signs of Parkinson's disease are obvious.

Figure 11

Typical signs of Parkinson's movement disorder

1. RESTING TREMOR
USUALLY HAND

2. WALKING BECOMES SLOW AND
STRIDES BECOME SHORT
MAY SEE RIGIDITY LIKE COG WHEEL
MOTION AND OR FREEZING GAIT

3. STOOPED POSTURE

4. BALANCE PROBLEMS LEADING
TO FALLS

Not every resting hand tremor or shakiness is Parkinson's disease, but often it is the first sign toward making the diagnosis. A slow walking gait with mincing short strides are common. There are a number of causes of stooped or bent over posture; Parkinson's disease is one of them. Another very common cause is vertebral fractures associated with osteoporosis. Balance problems leading to falls are seen relatively late in the disease process.

During the course of his illness, Ollie also displayed all the typical signs of Parkinson's disease with the exception of the freezing gait. His brother Roger, another Parkinson's disease patient, did suffer from the freezing gait. Initiating that first step is difficult and looks hesitant. Once started, movement is relatively easy, but any break in the stride as in a doorway will bring about freezing again.

This is a symptom that responds well to physical therapy but requires 100 percent concentration by the patient.

It is not easy. Normally walking does not require concentration.

Figure 12

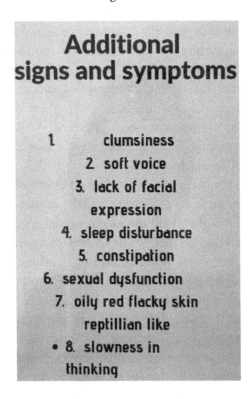

**Additional
signs and symptoms**

1.   clumsiness
2. soft voice
3. lack of facial
   expression
4. sleep disturbance
5. constipation
6. sexual dysfunction
7. oily red flacky skin
   reptillian like
• 8. slowness in
   thinking

The nonmovement-related signs and symptoms of Parkinson's disease are no less debilitating than the movement symptoms. The clumsiness can be very subtle. In Ollie's case, I attribute his giving up the game of golf to this symptom as well as his reluctance to continue competing in field trials. Fortunately for me, Ollie did not develop the soft voice until the last four months of his life. At this point, I was no longer able to hear him. This drew us further apart.

My goddaughter Anna's husband, Issa, is also a Parkinson's patient. Parkinson's disease in people under the age of fifty is uncommon. Issa was diagnosed at forty six and has been suffering with the disease for fourteen years. His speech is so soft that I am unable to hear him, and Anna is barely able to hear and understand him. Speech therapy is extremely helpful for this symptom, but it requires effort on the part of the patient, and many, including Issa, suffer from depression and lack of motivation.

Asking him to repeat what he said *twice as loud* can be helpful. Like walking, speaking does not normally require concentration, and the demands of 100 percent concentration can be daunting. Untreated patients have immobile facial features; they are unable to express themselves with a smile or a frown. Sleep disturbances and sexual dysfunction, especially erectile dysfunction, are common, as is slowness of thinking. Constipation was an especially debilitating symptom for Ollie and for me. It appeared at the same time as the tremor. We actually had some of our few disagreements over his constipation. He found it so distressing that he would wake me up in the middle of the night to tell me he could not poop. While professionally I spent years springing out of bed to attend to someone's emergency distress, I was just not able to consider constipation in that same class of emergency distress. Miralax® worked well for him, but as his dementia progressed, he often forgot when he had his last bowel movement and would demand more and more Miralax®. This also meant his stools were very loose, and mishaps in the bathroom which occurred with some frequency were unpleasant to clean up. Ollie was so fixated on his bowel movements that he often refused to go places because he failed to understand that the Miralax® would still be available.

It is important to note that mild cognitive impairment which progresses to dementia is seen in 30 percent of patients at the time the diagnosis of Parkinson's disease is made.[40]

Figure 13

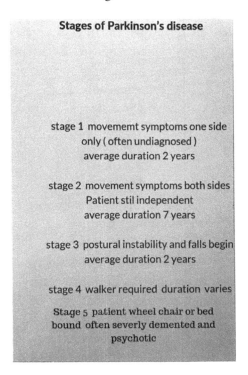

Stages of Parkinson's disease

stage 1 movememt symptoms one side
only (often undiagnosed)
average duration 2 years

stage 2 movement symptoms both sides
Patient stil independent
average duration 7 years

stage 3 postural instability and falls begin
average duration 2 years

stage 4 walker required duration varies

Stage 5 patient wheel chair or bed
bound often severly demented and
psychotic

Referring to figure 13, it is easy to discern that Parkinson's disease is a brutal unrelenting disease.

As we will discuss later, treatment in the early stages is effective but all too soon becomes as problematic as the disease itself. While I knew very early that Ollie suffered from vascular dementia and later developed signs of Alzheimer's dementia, it was the development of Parkinson's disease and the associated dementia that really started the downward spiral. I believe that this is the most brutal of the dementia related diseases.

Diagnosis

The diagnosis of Parkinson's disease is usually made at the time the movement disorder symptoms begin to appear, and it is made based solely on these typical symptoms. Confirmation that the diagnosis is correct occurs when the patient's symptoms respond favorably to the usual treatment of Parkinson's disease Sinemet®.

Sophisticated and expensive imaging tests are available and may be warranted only when the patient does not respond favorably to initial treatment.

Specifically, a (SPECT) scan is another third-generation radiologic diagnostic procedure which may confirm or exclude the diagnosis of Parkinson's disease.

Treatment

Treatment of Parkinson's disease is problematic. Traditional treatment often leads to symptoms as bad or worse than the Parkinson's disease symptoms.

This leads to the question, is it wiser to delay treatment in patients with newly diagnosed Parkinson's disease?

A 2007 study suggests that a patient's quality of life deteriorates quickly if treatment is withheld after diagnosis.[41]

The gold standard for early treatment of Parkinson's disease motor dysfunction is Sinemet®, the brand name for levodopa/carbidopa. The drug is supplied in pill form and is taken by mouth. If the diagnosis is correct symptom relief is usually excellent for months to years. Sooner or later, the patient is likely to experience OFF symptoms. These are episodes between drug doses when the drug is no longer active but another dose is not due. Parkinson's disease motor symptoms return unexpectedly. This can be very disconcerting to the patient and those around him or her. The reason for these OFF symptoms can be disease progression in the brain or disease progression within the gut. The nerve cells controlling the gut are also affected by Parkinson's disease.[42]

We noted earlier that constipation can be one of the first symptoms and may precede movement dysfunction. This is due to the slowing of bowel transit.

Also occurring as the disease progresses is slow emptying of the stomach, difficulty swallowing, and the inability to swallow the spit normally produced in the mouth. This results in staining of the bed clothes and pillows. These changes in the gut may interfere with the normal absorption of Sinemet® taken by mouth, contributing to the OFF symptoms.

Pfeiffer[43] points out that it remains unknown if Parkinson's disease begins in the gut or in the brain. In addition, as we begin to learn more about the normal bacteria found in our gut, researchers are beginning to explore what role this may play in both the disease process and the OFF symptoms.

Another factor, negatively affecting the action of Sinemet® is protein in the patient's diet. Avoiding protein in the diet is one strategy to alleviate the OFF symptoms. Additional strategies to alleviate the OFF symptoms include using a longer-acting form of carbidopa/levodopa. This drug is very expensive and therefore often not covered by insurance. There is also a form of carbidopa/levodopa that can be dissolved in a liquid. This may not only help with the OFF symptoms but is certainly justified for use in patients who have swallowing difficulties.

An additional class of drugs called dopamine agonists for example Mirapex® are available and may be a useful addition to Sinemet® in younger patients. In patients over the age of seventy, this class of drugs are prone to cause severe side effects, including sedation, hallucinations, and impulse control disorder. Impulse control disorder may take the form of hypersexuality, gambling, excessive spending, as well as other harmful behaviors.

Finally, the most commonly used strategy to control the OFF symptoms is to increase the dose of Sinemet®. This is often effective but associated with an additional complication known as dyskinesia. Dyskinesia is involuntary movement. This is often seen in the face, as in lip smacking or tongue poking. However, it may involve any part of the body or the entire body. It may look like fidgeting, wriggling, or even writhing. This can be very disconcerting to the casual observer or family member (especially the writhing), but Parkinson's disease patients usually prefer dyskinesia over OFF symptoms. The only drug available to control the dyskinesia without worsening the movement disorder is amantadine.[44]

The morning OFF symptoms can be extremely disconcerting to both patients and family members. Imagine being frozen in time and space while trying to get up and get going in the morning. This is what happens to many Parkinson's disease patients. Two new carbidopa/levodopa administration techniques may help.

DuoDopa® is administered directly into the intestine using an external pump device. OFF symptoms are well controlled, and most patients are able to stop other medications.[45] In the US, this product is available as the Duopa pump. Newer research suggests adding an inhaled form of levodopa can be effective in shortening OFF times, especially in the morning when administered after oral Sinemet®.[46]

Clinical Trials

Clinical studies are an important consideration. If we are ever to find a cure for these devastating diseases, we need two things money and volunteer patients and or subjects. The money is probably easier to come by than the volunteers, and there is never enough money.

Newly diagnosed patients and their family members should determine if there are any ongoing research trials in their area. Both Parkinson's disease and Alzheimer's disease are progressive diseases without a cure. For patients, there is little or nothing to lose in volunteering for one of these studies. What is there to gain? You might be the first to be cured, or you may add information which eventually leads to a cure for your children and grandchildren. Family members who have not been diagnosed may also provide valuable information which might lead to a cure.

I volunteer whenever there is a study for which I am eligible. I urge everyone to consider doing the same. Further information about finding studies will follow. It is only *together* that we can find the cure.

Additional Therapies

As mentioned earlier, speech therapy can be extremely useful to motivated patients. Communication is part of the essence of life. The Lee Silverman Voice Training program is highly recommended.[47]

Exercise is another extremely important way to improve the quality of life for patients with Parkinson's disease. Rock Steady Boxing is a nationwide organization with affiliates in most major cities. The group in Crestwood, Missouri, was instrumental in improving Ollie's quality of life. He even stated that the strength and confidence the program gave him were the reasons he was able to take the Honor Flight in 2017. I cannot emphasize enough how empowering this program can be to Parkinson's disease patients.

Physical therapy including intense training on concentration can help significantly with freezing gait problems. Concentration is the key word and is difficult.

Research conducted at Raboud University in the Netherlands suggests that laser shoes may assist patients with this concentration.[48]

Special shoes project a laser beam in front of the foot which is next to move forward in walking, assisting patients to overcome freezing gait. They are presently available on the market.

Surgical Solutions

Deep brain stimulation (DBS) is now the surgical procedure of choice for Parkinson's disease patients who are no longer well controlled on medication. In contrast to older procedures which remove affected parts of the brain, DBS does not involve destruction of brain tissue and is both adjustable and reversible. Removing affected parts of the brain are generally reserved for patients with dementia in an attempt to improve their quality of life.

While DBS may improve the movement symptoms by 25 to 50 percent with no OFF times, allowing for 30 to 50 percent reduction in medications, it does not work for all patients. Anna's husband, Issa, underwent the procedure and had a positive result that was very short-lived. Immediately after the procedure, Anna was overjoyed that he was able to open a door for her when they walked into a restaurant. Sadly, it did not last.

DBS does not improve freezing gait and until recently was not able to improve speech. By modifying stimulation parameters, a Canadian group was able to show some improvements in speech.[49]

Cutting-Edge Therapies

Researchers are now conducting clinical trials on Tasigna®, an old drug designed to treat leukemia. They have found that a low dose of the drug appears to rev up the immune cells within the brain to reduce the abnormal alpha-synuclein found in Parkinson's disease and thereby allow the normal alpha-synuclein to do its job, releasing dopamine when needed. The dopamine allows messages to transmit between neurons, facilitating normal movement.[50,51]

As we learn more and more about how the brain works, we discover potential new ways to interrupt the cascade of events that lead to both Parkinson's disease and Alzheimer's disease. One day, one of these new discoveries will lead to a cure or at least a slowing of the relentless disease process.

As we have discussed earlier, alpha-synuclein is the protein which becomes damaged in Parkinson's disease, and as we will discuss later, the abnormal protein in Alzheimer's disease is b-amyloid and tau. The accumulation of these abnormal proteins causes the brain cells to die. Researchers have found an enzyme AEP (asparagine endopeptidase), which seems to be the enzyme causing the damage to the proteins alpha-synuclein and tau, when AEP loses its boundaries within the brain cell.

Animal studies are showing that a drug which inhibits AEP may be useful in both Parkinson's disease and Alzheimer's disease.[52]

Researchers are also studying NAC (N-acetyl-cysteine) given both intravenously and orally. Preliminary results suggest an improvement in dopamine function, as well as a significant improvement in patient symptoms.[53]

The most exciting development of all is the testing of an implantable drug delivery system reported in a 2019 paper by Whone et al. These researchers were able to infuse a drug, in this case GDNF (glial derived neurotrophic factor), directly into a part of the brain seriously damaged in Parkinson's disease. They were able to safely use this delivery system for eighteen months. While the effectiveness of GDNF was inconclusive in this study, the delivery system makes it possible to continue to test GDNF and other drugs by infusing them directly into the brain.[54]

Causes and Risk Factors

It is not surprising that genetic factors play a part in the development of Parkinson's disease. Several families in which multiple members develop Parkinson's disease before the age of fifty have been well studied. Abnormalities within the genetic code of these individuals have been identified. These families account for a very small number of the cases of Parkinson's disease.

There are a growing number of genetic abnormalities being identified that appear to increase an individual's susceptibility to environmental factors also associated with Parkinson's disease.[55]

This makes for a very complex field of study, as genetic mutations occur on a regular basis and our environment is constantly changing.

Figure 14

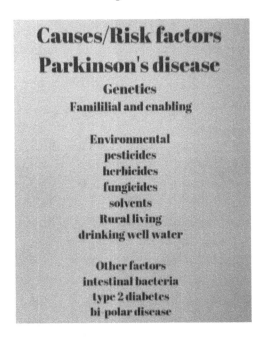

Causes/Risk factors Parkinson's disease

Genetics
Famililial and enabling

Environmental
pesticides
herbicides
fungicides
solvents
Rural living
drinking well water

Other factors
intestinal bacteria
type 2 diabetes
bi-polar disease

Environmental risk factors commonly accepted to be associated with Parkinson's disease include the use of pesticides, herbicides, fungicides, and solvents. Living in a rural environment and the consumption of well water also appear to increase the risk.[56] This can certainly be explained by the contamination of groundwater by pesticides and herbicides used in farming.

Ollie and I spent nearly thirty years on our farm. We drank well water and used both pesticides and herbicides. To purchase and use these products in bulk, we were required to take and pass a Missouri State licensing test. We did so and followed the proper procedures to the letter.

Ollie did all the commercial spraying and wore a disposable liquid repellant suit and hazmat breathing gear. I never saw him cut corners with this material, but I was not with him all the time. It is likely that the higher incidence of Parkinson's disease in farming communities represents genetic susceptibility to the environmental contaminants found there. Over the last four to five years, researchers have noticed a connection between the incidence of Parkinson's disease and intestinal disease processes. The coexistence of intestinal and brain disease is so striking that many researchers have begun to question if Parkinson's disease begins in the intestine or in the brain. The most obvious connection between the intestines and the brain is the vagus nerve.

Fifty years ago, the treatment of peptic ulcer disease often included cutting this nerve. In 2015, a group of Danish researchers found that the incidence of Parkinson's disease is significantly less in patients who had their vagus nerve cut. They theorize that an intact vagus nerve is required for the development of Parkinson's disease.[57] There appears to be a strong association between inflammatory bowel disease and Parkinson's disease. Patients with inflammatory bowel disease were 28 percent more likely to develop Parkinson's disease.[58]

Some very interesting work is being done, looking at the relationship of the intestinal bacteria Lactococcus and the viruses that infect them. Lactococcus bacteria are dopamine producers within the intestinal nervous system and regulate intestinal leakiness. This study finds that in Parkinson's disease patients, there was a depletion of

Lactococcus bacteria and an increase in the viruses known to infect it. These particular viruses are widely used in the food industry and can be found in dairy products like cheese, milk, and yogurt.[59] Are viruses the cause of Parkinson's disease? It is too soon to tell, but the thought is intriguing.

We are just beginning to understand the relationship between our own health and well-being and that of the health of the bacteria within our intestines. This has led to an entire industry toting probiotics. Without a doubt, science will one day have all the answers enabling us to know exactly which bacteria are good for us in what quantity. Until then we need to be cautious treating ourselves.

Finally, patients with both diabetes and bipolar disease, especially the depressive phase, have an increased risk of developing Parkinson's disease.[60,61]

Parkinson's Disease Dementia and Dementia with Lewy Bodies

The gold standard for diagnosing the dementias is autopsy.

Researchers using the brain banks of Europe (autopsy specimens) have determined that pure Parkinson's disease is unlikely to cause dementia. Unfortunately, VaD and AD are often found to coexist. The presence of Parkinson's disease appears to lower the threshold at which dementia symptoms are manifest.[62]

Between 50 percent and 80 percent of Parkinson's disease patients develop dementia, usually late in the course of the disease, on average ten years after the diagnosis of Parkinson's disease is established.[63]

Figure 15

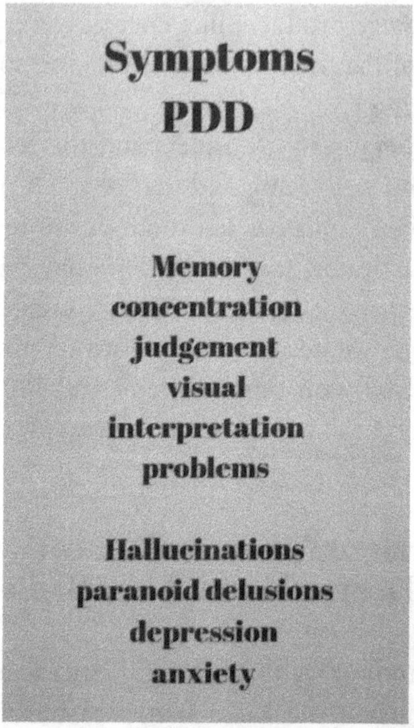

**Symptoms
PDD**

**Memory
concentration
judgement
visual
interpretation
problems**

**Hallucinations
paranoid delusions
depression
anxiety**

I observed all of these symptoms in Ollie. While paranoid delusions were the most upsetting and difficult to manage, the symptoms that most impacted his and hence my quality of life were the problems with concentration and visual interpretation. Not being able to concentrate made it difficult to read and to follow news and commentary. Ollie had been a lifelong reader; the *Wall Street Journal* and nonfiction titles were his favorite. He was also a news junkie and was always up to date on local and world events. Problems with visual interpretation robbed him of his passion for watching sports on television as well as the news outlets and his favorite PBS shows like NOVA®. Much of our leisure time together involved these activities. Losing it was hard for both of us.

Mercifully, these problems arose in the last two years of his life. Hallucinations are common in Parkinson's disease patients and may precede any other symptoms of dementia. If anything, Ollie's hallucinations were entertaining to him. They were nonthreatening and always seemed to fill him with a sense of wonder. They, too, appeared in the last two years of his life. When it appears before any other dementia symptoms, I am sure it is not in the least entertaining to the sufferer.

Anxiety was very much a part of Ollie's illness. It was manifest mostly by clinginess. As long as he could see me or knew that I was close, he was calm. I was the nonmedicinal cure for anxiety. Later, when he was institutionalized, he transferred the clinginess to the facility staff; however, changing shifts and changing faces made him less able to cope. In the end, he was given a drug to quell his anxiety. It was effective for the anxiety, but the associated side effects on balance and stability most likely caused the increasing falls which ultimately claimed his life.

Depression was evident from time to time but was not a big part of his illness. He was always a very positive person, treating each day as a new beginning, moving forward to the best of his ability. The few times that he actually complained about his disability were the times when he was clearly depressed. This was heartbreaking. Until the end, he was easily distracted, encouraged, and lifted out of this dark place.

Dementia with Lewy Bodies

Dementia occurs much earlier in Lewy body disease, usually within one year of Parkinson's disease symptoms, and may appear before the movement disorder.

Dementia with Lewy bodies differs from AD in that periods of complete lucidity are common. In addition, patients with DLB typically are aware of what is happening to them.

Without a doubt, Ollie suffered from VaD and DLB. He may also have suffered AD, since his brother had died of the disease several years before Ollie began showing symptoms; and VaD and AD are often found together.

The most aggressive component was DLB, occurring last. It was his awareness of what was happening to him and his periods of near complete lucidity which led me to this conclusion.

The presumptive diagnosis of DLB can be made by testing spinal fluid. There are some unique markers which distinguish it from both AD and PDD.[64] These tests are reserved for research settings because they are expensive and not covered by insurance. Until research finds a treatment and or a cure, knowing the specific diagnosis does not change the outcome.

The genetics of DLB are unique but share some of the genetics of both AD and PDD. On the other hand, AD and PDD do not share common genetic findings.[65] Both Parkinson's disease and DLB are 36 percent heritable. This means, Ollie's descendants have a 36 percent chance of developing one or both of these diseases.

Treatment of PDD and DLB

The treatment of dementia per se remains the same, regardless of the specific diagnosis, typically Aricept® and or Namenda®. See figure 5.

Treatment of the psychotic behaviors such as hallucinations, anxiety, and depression are another matter entirely. Ollie was given a number of drugs to treat these symptoms during his last eighteen months of life. I fought hard to get him off these drugs as soon as possible. It never made sense to me to administer mind-altering drugs to patients whose minds were already compromised. In his case the result of such drug treatment was semiconsciousness and no quality of life. When I was successful in convincing his physicians to remove these drugs, his quality of life improved dramatically, as did his length of life.

Research confirms these drugs are associated with increased death rates in elderly patients with dementia.[66]

The physician's creed is "First, do no harm." On the other hand, it is critical to ease suffering.

In the case of dementia patients, that balance is a real ethical and moral challenge. The American Psychiatric Association (APA) gives us some guidelines.[67] They recognize that dementia patients can be a danger to themselves and others, in which case these mind-altering drugs can be used in an emergency.

Throughout the last eighteen months of his life, Ollie suffered several of these episodes, during which he was a danger to himself and to others. One of these episodes was treated with drugs; the others were resolved without drugs.

The APA recommends trying therapies other than drugs before resorting to their use. Other therapies include psychotherapy and distraction. The APA also recommends that before the drugs are administered, the risks and benefits of these drugs should be discussed with the patient, if feasible, as well as with the patient's family or responsible guardian. If the decision is made to use these drugs, the lowest possible dose should be used, and an attempt to decrease the dose and withdraw the drug or drugs should be made within four months.

CHAPTER 16

Alzheimer's Disease

Alzheimer's disease (AD) is the most common cause of dementia, representing 50 to 70 percent of all cases. It is differentiated from the other dementias by the presence of plaques (comprised of beta-amyloid protein) and tangles (comprised of tau protein). The plaques are found in the brain outside of the nerve cell. These plaques are toxic to the nerve cells. There are normal processes within the brain to remove these harmful substances, but these processes can be overwhelmed, hence the buildup of plaque within the brain. Tangles are found within the nerve cell itself and prevent the cell from functioning normally. Under these circumstances, the cell literally commits suicide. The death of these nerve cells explains the features of AD.

Brain shrinkage is universally found, and the actual weight of the brain at autopsy is markedly less than that seen in normal brains.[68] Our brain cells communicate with each other, much like computer networks. These networks are who we are as individuals. As nerve cells die, these networks are no longer functional. In a very real sense, *we cease to exist.*

It is still unknown whether plaques and tangles are the cause or the result of the disease. A great deal of time, energy, and money have gone into identifying and testing drugs that can remove plaque from the brains of AD patients. Such drugs have been found, and they are both safe and effective in removing plaque from the brain but have little effect on the symptoms or course of the disease. This suggest that plaque is not the cause. Just to make things even more confusing, huge amounts of plaques and tangles can be found in the brains of people with no symptoms of AD and conversely minimal amounts of plaques and tangles can be found in the brains of people with severe symptoms of AD.[69,70]

Researchers are now turning their attention to the tangles and targeting the tau protein at the core of the tangles. The tau protein has many functions within the normal brain.[71] Perhaps the most intriguing function is the role it plays in neurogenesis in the adult brain. It is only recently that scientists have discovered that neurogenesis (regeneration of nerve cells) can and does occur in the normal brain.

Is loss of the brains ability to regenerate itself the cause of AD?

Hopefully, as researchers look more closely at tangles and tau proteins, this question and many others will be answered.

It is now known that AD begins with the deposition of plaques within the brain more than twenty years prior to the occurrence of any symptoms of dementia. This change is followed by a decline in glucose metabolism. This decline in glucose metabolism is an extremely important feature of the disease, so much so that it has led to AD being referred to as type 3 diabetes. Much research is being devoted to the role of glucose metabolism and the role of insulin in the treatment of AD. We will discuss this in more detail in the coming pages.

The final feature of the disease is brain shrinkage.[72]

After the age of sixty-five, a person's risk of AD doubles every five years.

Once the diagnosis of AD has been made, only 3 percent of patients survive fourteen years. Common infections such as urinary tract infections and pneumonia greatly accelerate the process.[73]

Ollie had recurrent urinary tract infections, and while they were treated early and aggressively, I lost a little more of him with each episode. The course of AD can be described as one of *a long goodbye.* Our loved ones are taken from us, one brain cell at a time.

You will frequently hear the term mild cognitive impairment (MCI). While it is often treated like a separate disease state, it is in fact simply the early stage of AD.

Figure 16

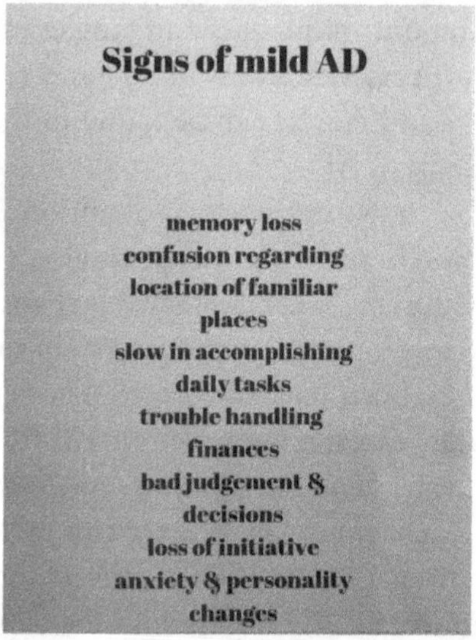

Signs of mild AD

memory loss
confusion regarding
location of familiar
places
slow in accomplishing
daily tasks
trouble handling
finances
bad judgement &
decisions
loss of initiative
anxiety & personality
changes

Figure 17

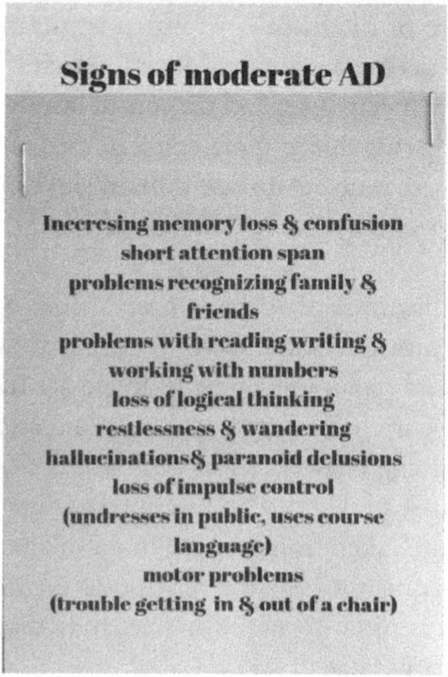

Signs of moderate AD

Increesing memory loss & confusion
short attention span
problems recognizing family &
friends
problems with reading writing &
working with numbers
loss of logical thinking
restlessness & wandering
hallucinations & paranoid delusions
loss of impulse control
(undresses in public, uses course
language)
motor problems
(trouble getting in & out of a chair)

Figure 18

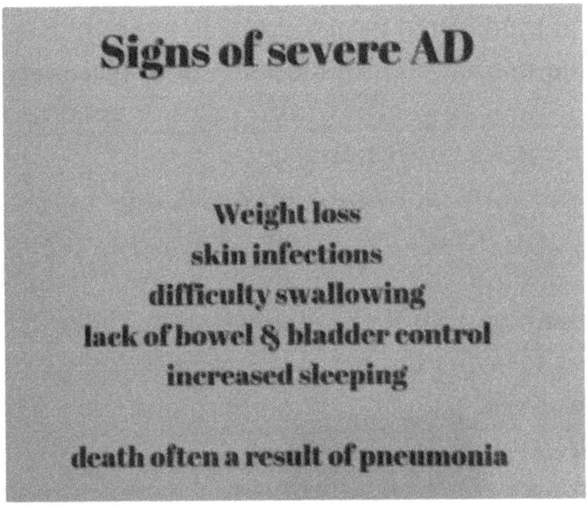

Signs of severe AD

Weight loss
skin infections
difficulty swallowing
lack of bowel & bladder control
increased sleeping

death often a result of pneumonia

Diagnosis

At this time, the diagnosis of AD is made only after symptoms are so obvious that the patient, family, and physician all know there is cause for concern. Then the physician usually administers one of several mental status examinations. The most common of these are the Mini-Mental Status Examination, the Montreal Cognitive Assessment, and the Addenbrooke's Cognitive Examination. These can be administered in the doctor's office, take no more than fifteen minutes, and will show any decline in the patient's ability to perform simple mental functions.[74]

In my view, one of these exams should be administered to all patients over the age of sixty-five on an annual basis. While no one wants to hear, or deliver this diagnosis, it benefits both the patient and the family. The earlier it is diagnosed, the sooner the patient and family can begin to get their affairs in order.

If not already in place, the patient needs to give power of attorney for both health and financial matters to someone whom he or she can trust. In addition, advanced directives can be drafted so that the patient's wishes can be known before he or she becomes incompetent to make these decisions. An elder care attorney can help with this as well as in advanced planning that can help preserve family wealth in the face of staggering long-term health care costs. We will discuss this in more detail in part 3.

For Ollie and me, we had most of this in place very early in our marriage, but we used general attorneys as opposed to an elder care specialist. This was a costly mistake.

On a happier note, an early diagnosis allows patients and families to get to that bucket list. Before the disease becomes too severe, they can do all those things they always wanted to do. These memories will sustain you through the tough times ahead. This was certainly the case for Ollie and me. At the very end, these memories are, of course, lost to the patient, but in Ollie's case, they were sustaining for a very long time.

As shown in figure 10, a definitive diagnosis can only be made at autopsy. Invasive radiology techniques and examination of spinal fluid can often narrow down the diagnosis and distinguish AD from PDD and DLB. Again, these diagnostic methods are reserved for research projects since they are expensive and do not offer a pathway to a treatment or cure at this time. In spite of this, the Alzheimer's Association has published clinical practice guidelines calling for these state-of-the-art tests to be performed.[75]

A new way to confirm the diagnosis of AD is on the horizon. Researchers at Duke University using advanced retinal scanning techniques are able to document changes in the eyes of AD patients. These changes are not present in normal individuals. They can even stage the AD. Patients with more advanced disease show greater retinal changes.[76]

The year prior to this publication, this group of researchers had documented the same findings in a rare pair of ninety-six-year-old identical twins, one with AD and one (normal) without AD.[77] Something other than genetics is at play here. Either the AD twin was exposed to something that caused the AD or the normal twin was exposed to something which prevented the disease. Scientists are coming to the conclusion that we must be able to diagnose AD well before symptoms occur and even before the known biomarkers of plaques and tangles are present. We need to be able to treat the disease early in its course rather than twenty years after it has begun.

There are several promising avenues of research designed to detect the disease early. Three different blood tests are currently being tested. Each tests a different substance found in blood but associated with the brain degeneration seen in AD.[78,79,80,81]

The test developed by researchers at Washington University in St. Louis when combined with genetic testing is 94 percent accurate in predicting the disease and may be able to do so two decades before symptoms begin.[82]

Another blood test being investigated by collaborating German and American researchers shows promise in both inherited AD and sporadically occurring AD. This study shows great promise in early detection (roughly ten years before symptoms begin) and in determining if a treatment regimen is actually working to decrease the damage being done to the brain in AD.[83,84] One or more of these tests, alone or in combination, are likely to help identify a treatment or cure for AD in the future. These blood tests remain research tools for now but hopefully will be available in your doctor's office sooner rather than later.

I am sure you are wondering about the role of genetic testing in the diagnosis of AD. Some cases of AD definitely have a genetic component, and many members of the family will develop AD and usually at a relatively young age. Some specific genes in your DNA give you an increased chance of developing AD, but you do not always develop AD if you have this gene. For that reason, except in the research setting, DNA testing is not advised. Knowing you have an increased chance of developing AD serves little purpose except to increase your anxiety.

Risk Factors/Causes

Genetics

DNA is the blueprint of who we are as individuals and is unique to each person except in the case of identical twins who share identical DNA. We all know this by watching TV and reading crime novels. We use DNA to identify the bad guys. DNA contains thousands of individual genes, each of which is responsible for a specific task. Genes direct the life of every individual cell in our body, its physical makeup, its function and repair.

Genes can be damaged or chemically altered, causing dramatic changes in cell function. The science of epigenetics looks at the effect of environment on genes. It appears that various factors in the environment may turn on or turn off specific genes. These factors may include such things as diet, chemical exposure, or pollution.[85]

Whether a gene is switched on or off may be protective or harmful, helping explain why some individuals develop a disease such as AD, and others do not even when they share specific genes. This also explains the identical twins we discussed earlier, one suffering AD and one normal.

When AD is found to run in families, the disease tends to strike early (between ages thirty and fifty). There are several different single-gene abnormalities, which have been identified in these families, which appear to be the cause of the disease.

Patients with Down syndrome have three copies of one these genes, as opposed to the usual number of two. They usually develop symptoms of AD by age fifty.

Only 5 to 10 percent of AD cases are familial. The rest tend to be late in onset (after age sixty). Here, too, there is some evidence of a genetic risk factor.

The gene Apolipoprotein E (APOE) comes in several forms. APOE 2 is rare but may offer some protection against AD, delaying its occurrence even more. APOE 3 seems to be neutral, neither increasing or decreasing risk, whereas APOE 4 increases the risk of AD. One copy of the APOE 4 gene raises your risk of AD between 8 and 24 percent. Two copies raise the risk to 75 percent.[86]

There is still much we do not know about the genetics of AD, and many studies are underway but suffer from lack of volunteers. Volunteers needed to include both those who are healthy and those who may be showing symptoms or at risk. More information is available at NCRAD (National Centralized Repository for Alzheimer's

Disease and Related Dementias). You may call 1-800-526-2839 or visit this website: http://ncrad.iu.edu.[87] Volunteer!

Plaques (Amyloid) vs. Tangles (Tau)

As we have noted before, beta-amyloid and tau proteins are the diagnostic features of AD. Scientists have been split as to which is the causal protein. Much time and treasure have been invested in finding a way to eliminate beta-amyloid from the brain. Drugs have been found to do just that but have not been shown to affect the course of AD. Some say we must treat earlier, before symptoms appear, and this may be true or maybe we need to move on to other areas of research. We are seeing more studies gearing up to look at tau proteins, but we are also seeing some activity looking outside the box.

Infection

The germ theory as a cause of AD has been considered since 1907 when AD was first described. Researchers are beginning to look at this once again. While prions are not exactly germs in the classic sense, like bacteria, viruses, and fungi, they are infectious. The most widely known prion disease is mad cow disease. Recent work suggests prions may be involved in AD.[88]

Viruses are much better studied and better understood. The herpes simplex virus (cold sore virus) and herpes zoster (chicken pox/shingles virus) are the best studied. Both of these viruses remain in the brain and nervous system of patients after the first infection. Both may be reactivated later, causing a variety of symptoms, and then go dormant again until the next reactivation. According to one of the leading researchers in this field Dr. Ruth Itzhaki, when both the herpes simplex virus and the APOE 4 gene are present in the same individual, the risk of AD is twelve times greater than the risk to the general population.[89]

With respect to the herpes zoster virus, investigators have looked at individuals who had a form of shingles affecting the eye and found that they were roughly three times more likely to develop

AD than the general population. If the shingles patients were treated with an antiviral drug, the incidence of AD was 50 percent less than those who did not receive the antiviral drug.[90] While this is far from conclusive, there is some corroborating evidence. Amyloid is lethal to both viruses and bacteria in the test tube and the mouse experimental model.

According to Harvard neuroscientist Rudolph Tanzi, amyloid is part of the immune mechanism that ramps up when unwanted viruses or bacteria enter the brain. He suggests that this is part of a negative cascade of events leading to the destructive brain disease AD.[91] A contagious mechanism of AD is also suggested by the fact that neurosurgeons are 2.5 times more likely to die of AD than others in the general population.[92] In addition, spouses of AD patients are at a 1.6 times greater risk of developing AD. This risk is even higher if the amount of time the spouse is exposed to the AD patient is taken into consideration.[93] There are many other factors that could explain this spousal risk. These include stress, social isolation, less exercise, and poor diet. We will discuss these factors in more detail later.

To date, in my view, the most exciting evidence that AD may be caused by germs comes from a 2019 study of the bacteria that causes gum disease.[94] It not only suggests a cause but also gives hope for prevention and treatment (not cure). The authors tested the brains of individuals with AD and those without AD. They found evidence of toxic bacterial by products in 96 percent of the AD brains and only 40 to 50 percent of non-AD brains. They also found evidence that these toxins were accumulating in both the plaques and tangles associated with AD. They then conducted mouse experiments, infecting the mice with oral gum disease bacteria. In all cases, the mice were found to have the bacteria in their brain and plaques associated with AD were markedly increased. Mice treated with a drug which inhibits the toxins produced by the bacteria showed significantly less brain plaque and less brain damage. The message here is that oral health may be the key to preventing AD. It also suggests a new way to treat AD may be on the horizon.

Ollie was not inclined to brush his teeth on a regular basis but did visit the dentist at least twice a year for checkups and cleaning while we were married. He had few dental issues until after his dementia diagnosis.

Recently there has been much hype and some research into the composition of gut bacteria and health. Probiotics and prebiotics are everywhere you shop. Evidence does not support this trend.

There is no gold standard for a healthy intestinal bacterial composition. Genetics and environment lead to significant variability from one person to the next. The key seems to be a diverse and stable bacterial composition. Lack of diversity and instability lead to dysfunction. This may progress to leaky gut syndrome, whereby harmful substances associated with gut bacteria begin to cross into the bloodstream.

These substances cause inflammation. Inflammation is consistently associated with many disease processes including dementia and other neurologic disorders.[95]

As research catches up to the hype, we can only say that it is important to keep your gut healthy. The only way we know to do so is to eat a healthy diet.

Stress

Another risk factor for the development of AD is stress. Stress is everywhere, and we all experience it frequently in our lives. Stress at work, meeting deadlines, unpleasant coworkers or bosses affect many of us during our working lives. Economic stress has always been a big one for me, as it is for many. The stress of watching your kids make mistakes in their lives and being powerless to change the outcomes can stress us. Death of a loved one is certainly a stressor. Caring for a loved one with dementia is stressful; for me it was almost overwhelming.

Stress causes the release of a hormone called cortisol. An interesting study of middle-aged individuals who showed no signs of AD showed that those with high cortisol levels were found to have impaired memory and brain shrinkage. This was especially true in women.[96]

Another study published in 2019 showed chronic stress but not single traumatic stress in midlife leads to mental decline within the twenty-year follow-up in women but not in men.[97]

The Alzheimer's Association estimates that one in six women over the age of sixty will develop AD in their lifetime, whereas only one in eleven men will do so. These studies suggest that stress is associated with AD and that women are more affected by this association.

How can we reduce stress in our lives? Getting plenty of sleep, exercise, and relaxation techniques, like meditation, can all be helpful.

Environmental Factors

We have previously suggested that our environment can be a risk factor for dementia, possibly alone or more likely in conjunction with our DNA. So exactly what are those environmental risk factors? To answer this question, a group of investigators from the UK analyzed 4,784 studies of environmental factors deemed possible contributors to dementia.[98]

They concluded metals, trace elements, occupational exposure to lead, inks/dyes, paints/stains/varnishes, gasoline/fuels/oils, liquid plastics/rubbers, vibratory tools, or climate have little to do with the occurrence of dementia. There is, however, moderate evidence that environmental exposure to air pollution, aluminum, silicon, selenium, pesticides, vitamin D, and electromagnetic fields are associated with later development of dementia.

It is interesting to note that Ollie had exposure to three of these risk factors. His company manufactured aluminum windows and building exteriors. He used pesticides in the orchard (using protective gear), and finally Black Horse Orchard was located roughly five hundred yards from the high-tension wires (electromagnetic field) that supplied much of Montgomery and Warren Counties in Missouri.

Air pollution is a major problem in many places around the world. Mexico City is one of these places.

Researchers looked for the diagnostic biomarkers amyloid and tau proteins in the spinal fluid of children, teens, and young adults in both Mexico City and control cities in Mexico with low levels of air pollution. The results were disturbing. The levels of the proteins associated with AD increased significantly faster with age in Mexico City children compared to children living in areas with low levels of air pollution. The children of Mexico City are showing signs of AD in the first two decades of life.[99]

Sleep

Loss of restful sleep is yet another risk factor associated with AD. Researchers have recently found that even losing one night's sleep can increase the levels of tau proteins (biomarker of AD) in cerebrospinal fluid by 50 percent.[100] Similarly, Swedish researchers found increased levels of abnormal tau protein in the blood of subjects with only one night of sleep deprivation.[101] Sleep is the mechanism by which the brain cleans itself of harmful debris such as abnormal amyloid and tau proteins.

Researchers at Washington University in St. Louis have suggested that the relationship of sleep and AD is a two-way street. First, sleep disturbances increase the risk of AD, and secondly, sleep-wake disturbances may be part of the pathology of AD. They have documented the latter.

Their study subjects with increased levels of abnormal tau proteins were getting more sleep, but the sleep was of poor quality as measured by EEG (electroencephalogram) and other sensors. They were not just getting more sleep at night but also were napping more.

Daytime napping was significantly associated with high levels of abnormal tau protein.

In the future, sleep studies and questions about daytime napping may be low-cost screening tools to identify patients with AD.[102]

Anticholinergic Drugs

There is growing evidence that some widely prescribed anticholinergic drugs have a strong association with, if not causation of, dementia when given for a prolonged time, as many as twenty years prior to the diagnosis of AD.

A wide variety of drugs have anticholinergic effects including antihistamines like Benadryl® or Zyrtec®, gastrointestinal antispasmodics such as Donnatal®, and some bronchodilators like Atrovent® and Spiriva®. None of these has been associated with AD.

Drugs with stronger anticholinergic effects such as some antidepressants, drugs used for overactive bladder, and some drugs used for Parkinson's disease (usually for OFF symptoms) are associated with AD.[103,104]

Sinemet® remains the treatment of choice for Parkinson's disease and is not associated with AD.

While the data is compelling and shows a 50 percent increased risk of AD, as long as twenty years after taking these drugs for at least three years, the fact is that both depression and bladder issues have long been linked to AD and may well be early symptoms of the disease. The authors actually make a case for a causal effect of these drugs on AD and estimate that as many as 10 percent of the cases of AD are in fact caused by these drugs.

Alcohol

Is the use of alcohol a risk factor for AD? Evidence suggests that it may increase the risk in some cases and decrease the risk of AD in other cases. Heavy drinking (greater than three to four drinks per day) causes brain shrinkage and mental decline. These changes can be distinguished from AD in the pattern of shrinkage and the fact that the changes due to alcohol can be reversed overtime with cessation of drinking.[105]

Most studies show no real association between AD and alcohol intake. However, a few studies show that moderate drinking (one drink/day for women and two drinks/day for men) may decrease the risk of AD.[106] The benefit may accrue from the anti-inflammatory properties of alcohol. Genetic factors may change this generalization. The presence of the APOE 4 gene may negate the positive effects of moderate alcohol intake.[107]

Obesity

We have long known that being obese is not a healthy life choice. It increases the risk of heart disease, stroke, and diabetes. This is especially true if most of the excess weight is carried around the midsection. We now know that middle-aged people who are obese with a large amount of belly fat are 3.6 times more likely to develop dementia.[108] Even before dementia symptoms are evident, brain shrinkage is seen on MRIs in obese individuals.[109,110]

Obesity is also a risk factor for type 2 diabetes and insulin resistance. Insulin plays an important role in the normal brain. It is important in the regulation of memory, emotion, and other brain functions. Insulin resistance in the brain means that the brain cells do not respond normally to insulin, resulting in malfunction of brain cell communication and normal immune responses, for example, the clearance response to the abnormal amyloid and tau proteins seen in AD.[111] Ongoing research is looking at ways to use insulin to improve the symptoms of AD.

Fat

Fat itself may be key to understanding AD and possibly finding a cure. Normal fat found beneath the skin on all of us produces a hormone which decreases inflammation. In the brain, this helps brain cells function properly As we age, more and more of our normal fat shifts to abnormal fat, located around our bellies. More, instead of less, inflammation occurs. This leads to loss of brain cells.

Researchers at the Medical College of Georgia at Augusta are looking at this fat hormone in mouse models and attempting to find a way to protect the brain from AD using this hormone.[112]

Hospitalization

As I mentioned previously, every time that Ollie was hospitalized, I lost a little more of him.

In a study published in late 2018, my observation was scientifically validated. Researchers found brain shrinkage in a large group of patients hospitalized for routine illness such as severe infections.[113]

Race and Gender

Both race and gender are independent risk factors for AD. The Alzheimer's Association noted that women are disproportionately affected by AD. Nearly two-thirds of the patients living with AD in 2016 were women. It is unclear whether or not women actually have a greater risk of AD; they may just live longer.

The differences between men and women as it relates to AD have been studied. Men and women have an equal chance of carrying the APOE-4 gene. However, the negative effect of AD association is stronger in women than it is in men.[114]

Animal studies suggest that estrogen the female sex hormone may be protective to the brain.[115] Human studies have found that removing the ovaries and precipitating early menopause, with lowered estrogen levels, is associated with an increased risk of AD. This suggest that estrogen is protecting against AD in these women.[116] As an aside, the loss of the male sex hormone testosterone is also associated with an increased risk of AD.[117]

For many years it was suggested that postmenopausal women should receive estrogen replacement as a means to prevent AD. I was happy to take estrogen for this reason alone, until the diagnosis of breast cancer, meant that the risk far outweighed the benefit.

In 2019, new research suggests that estrogen therapy in postmenopausal women is not only not protective but is associated with a 9 to 17 percent increase in the incidence of AD in women who took estrogen, especially for more than ten years.[118] African Americans are between 64 percent and 100 percent more likely to develop AD than Caucasians. The reason for the increased incidence of AD in this population is unknown. but it is thought to reflect both biologic and socioeconomic factors.[119]

Most of the information we have on AD comes from studies conducted on Caucasians. African Americans are reluctant to volunteer. The infamous Tuskegee syphilis experiment remains fresh in their minds. In this highly unethical experiment, the US Public Health service studied untreated syphilis in African Americans for forty years without informing them they had the disease and were not being treated. They were told they were being given free health care and free burial.

An outreach by Washington University in St. Louis is helping us to learn more about AD in African Americans. While the APOE-4 gene in Caucasians triples the risk of AD, it has a lesser effect in African Americans. In addition, if the African American AD patient carried the APOE-4 gene, there was less tau protein in the CSF than normally found in Caucasian AD patients.[120] This suggests that the way the APOE-4 gene is expressed is different in the two races. Also, when CSF is used to make the diagnosis of AD, the threshold for tau should be lower in African Americans.

Much more information on racial differences in AD is needed. We know very little about the disease in Hispanics and Asians.

Intelligence and Education

It has long been assumed that the more intelligent and highly educated you are, the less likely you are to develop AD. In other words, the less educated you are, the greater your risk of developing AD. This is not necessarily so. I have seen professors of medicine sharing the same facility as my husband, Ollie. Nobel laureates and US presidents are also not immune. The most recent information on this subject comes from researchers at Stony Brook University. They suggest that AD is delayed by an average of 2.3 years in those who have four more years of education beyond high school.[121]

Those who speak two languages also enjoy a delay in the onset of AD of five years.[122]

The Nun Study, which looked at most of the Sisters of Notre Dame over many years, had the luxury of extensive archives of auto-biographical data on each sister from the time she entered the convent. Many of these nuns were highly educated and lifelong learners. This did not protect them. Analysis of their writing in their twenties did show that the richness of their vocabulary and idea density (low density is defined as short choppy sentences, whereas high density is defined as dense packing of information in a sentence with complex relationships expressed) was predictive of their risk of developing AD. The nuns with rich vocabularies and high idea density in their twenties did not succumb to AD as they aged.[123] It can be speculated that AD was already affecting the brains of the sisters with low idea density in their twenties. Richness of vocabulary can be taught. *Read to your children.*

Treatment

FDA-approved treatment for AD is the same as for other forms of dementia. Refer to figure 5. These drugs do not stop or reverse AD, and they may have no effect at all after a few months. Would these drugs be more effective if they were given earlier? Possibly, because the disease is present decades before symptoms appear.

World Health Organization Guidelines

Before we discuss current research being conducted to find new treatments, we should discuss some of the simpler methods which may be useful to ease the symptoms. We will start with the 2019 World Health Organization (WHO) guidelines for risk reduction of cognitive decline and dementia.[124]

Physical activity is strongly recommended to reduce the risk of cognitive decline in normal individuals. This recommendation is less strong for the treatment of individuals already showing signs of dementia but still recommended.

Tobacco cessation is strongly recommended.

A healthy diet is recommended, especially the Mediterranean diet. Specific recommendations are fruits; vegetables; legumes such as lentils and beans; nuts; and whole grains such as oats, wheat, or brown rice.

At least five servings of fruits and vegetables should be consumed daily. Starchy roots such as potatoes or sweet potatoes are not considered vegetables.

Sugar should be limited. Sugars are added to many foods and drinks and found naturally in honey, syrup, and fruit juices.

Fats should be limited to 30 percent of intake; and unsaturated fats found in fish, avocado, nuts, canola, and olive oil are preferred to other fats.

Salt should be limited to approximately one teaspoon per day and should be iodized, not sea salt.

WHO strongly recommends against the use of vitamins B, E, fatty acids, and multicomplex supplements.

If alcohol consumption is heavy, interventions should be implemented to return to sobriety.

Cognitive training may be used, but more studies showing improvement in participants is warranted before a strong recommendation can be issued. Cognitive training includes such activities as computer-based exercises, creative writing assignments. and theatre and performing arts workshops.

While social activity is important to overall good health and well-being, there is insufficient evidence that it has any impact on dementia.

The treatment of midlife overweight and obesity is recommended.

The management of high blood pressure in patients without dementia is strongly recommended as a means of preventing dementia. Although it is also recommended in patients with dementia, the evidence that it changes outcome is weak.

The evidence that the management of diabetes changes the incidence or progression of dementia is weak. Management is recommended for reasons other than effect on dementia.

The management of high cholesterol and other lipid abnormalities is recommended to reduce dementia progression, although the evidence is not strong.

The evidence for treating depression in order to alter the occurrence and progression of dementia is insufficient to support a recommendation.

Likewise, there is insufficient evidence to suggest that hearing aids in the hearing impaired will change the course of dementia.

Diet

Researchers have found that they can *reverse* AD symptoms in mice using substances found in a plant-based diet—specifically, substances found in green tea, carrots, tomatoes, rice, wheat, and oats. While mice do not always represent humans, it is certainly worth recommending a Mediterranean-type diet in AD patients.[125]

The keto diet has long been known as the best weight loss diet when supervised by a physician. Recently, it has become so popular that many are using it without physician supervision, not just for weight loss but as a way of life. The long-term risks and benefits of this diet remain to be seen.

In AD, the brain loses its ability to use sugar as an energy source. Researchers are now looking at ketones, produced by the keto diet, to see if the brain is able to replace sugar with ketones for energy production. Preliminary results suggest that this dietary change might be helpful in early stage AD.[126,127]

We have heard for years that excessive salt intake is unhealthy, especially as it relates to high blood pressure and heart failure. A 2018 study gives us evidence that it is also plays a significant role in AD.[128] This study shows a causal link between dietary salt intake and the accumulation of tau proteins in the brain (one of the harbingers of AD), along with signs and symptoms of dementia in a mouse model. It is important to keep in mind that the hazard of added salt intake is not just from the salt shaker but also from preprepared and restaurant foods.

Blood Pressure Control

Consistent with the findings that tight blood pressure control (targeting a blood pressure of 120/80 as opposed to 140/90) reduces the risk of heart disease, it also reduces the incidence of AD by 19 percent.[129]

Another study suggests that the specific blood pressure medication being used may be important.

The drug Valsartan® and others like it, that can reach the brain after oral administration, are associated with greater memory preservation and less brain shrinkage than other commonly used blood pressure medications.[130] Many orally administered medications do not reach the brain. Recent evidence suggests that the time of day you take your blood pressure pills may be important. The Hygia Chronotherapy Trial has shown a nearly 50 percent reduction in heart attacks, strokes, and heart failure in patients who took their blood pressure medicine at bedtime instead of in the morning.[131] This study did not specifically address AD. However, the close association of AD with stroke and vascular disease make it worth noting.

Supplement Hype

The FDA has begun cracking down on companies selling supplements and unproven cures for AD on websites, on social media, and in stores. Warning letters have been sent to both US and foreign companies engaging in misleading and or fraudulent marketing.[132] At this time, there is no cure for AD, nor is there a completely reliable, preventative measure. Always consult your physician before taking nonprescription drugs.

Antidepressants

The jury is still out when it comes to the use of antidepressants in AD. A class of antidepressant drugs known as tricyclic antidepressants are not recommended in older adults due to their anticholinergic effects. As we noted earlier, anticholinergic drugs are a known risk factor for AD. A 2018 study suggests that antidepressants are not effective for the treatment of depression in AD patients.[133] In fact, this study suggested that antidepressants might actually be harmful to AD patients. A more recent but smaller study suggests that the combination of Namenda®, usually given for moderate to severe AD, and the antidepressant Lexapro® achieved not only improvement of

SUSAN WILSON KRECHEL MD

depression but also improvement in AD symptoms in patients with early AD.[134]

The antidepressants that Ollie was taking made him excessively sleepy, thereby robbing him of any quality of life. The rare symptoms of depression he showed were easily managed with positive suggestion and distraction.

Marijuana and Other Plants

Marijuana has been cultivated and used by humankind for centuries. Europeans used it as a textile of sorts, while ancient Egyptians were well acquainted with its narcotic, antispasmodic effects as well as its mind-altering properties.

The widespread interest in the legalization of both medical and recreational marijuana has led to numerous studies. Not only is the human brain hardwired to use some of the substances found in the plant, but it is also known that these substances can function in such a way as to cause cells within the brain to regenerate.[135] This early finding may be extremely important in the search for a cure of not only AD but also stroke and multiple sclerosis.

Early evidence suggests that the active components of marijuana decrease the amount of beta-amyloid associated with the plaques found in AD.[136] By itself, this finding means nothing. Other rigorously tested drugs that also reduce plaques do not change the course of AD. However, medical marijuana has been found to be safe and effective for symptom relief in elderly patients with nerve damage due to many diseases such as Parkinson's disease and AD. Modest symptom relief of pain, sleeplessness, and anxiety were achieved. However, usefulness may be further limited by side effects such as sleepiness and balance problems.[137]

Like marijuana, California's "holy herb" shows promise in decreasing inflammation and protecting brain cells in diseases such as AD.[138] This work is in the preliminary stages. Many more studies are needed.

Anti-inflammatory Drugs

Inflammation of the brain is known to be an accompanying feature of AD. Intuitively, one would think that the use of anti-inflammatory drugs would be helpful in relieving symptoms, preventing or delaying onset of the disease. This does not appear to be the case. Rheumatoid arthritis is a well understood inflammatory disease. Studies of these patients both with and without AD and with and without the use of anti-inflammatory treatments are conflicting. One 2017 study suggests that the use of anti-inflammatory drugs for rheumatoid arthritis actually increases the risk of AD.[139] Another 2017 study shows the exact opposite. This study found a significantly decreased risk of AD in rheumatoid arthritis patients who were taking anti-inflammatory drugs.[140]

Since the brain is affected by AD long before symptoms occur, studies performed on normal individuals can be very valuable in predicting efficacy of various drugs.

A well-done study of individuals showing no signs of AD were randomly assigned to receive the anti-inflammatory drug Aleve® or a placebo (identical-looking pill with no active ingredients). The incidence of symptomatic AD nor the diagnostic tests suggesting AD were different between the two groups.[141] This 2019 study suggests that the use of anti-inflammatory agents have little or no effect on the progression of AD.

Therapy for Plaques (Beta-Amyloid) vs. Tangles (Tau)

Far more research has gone into the idea that removing plaque from the brain could reverse the symptoms of AD and if given early enough to asymptomatic patients might prevent the disease. There are two classes of drugs being tested for plaque removal at this time. One class is BACE inhibitors; several have been tested. Some of the drugs tested have failed because they proved damaging to both the liver and the eye. Others have been shown to be well tolerated and very effective in preventing plaque formation but minimally effective in showing improvement in symptoms or slowing progression of AD. The second class of drug for plaque removal are plaque anti-bodies. Some early studies were halted due to problems with brain swelling. Changes made to dosing schedules have since eliminated this problem.

In the last three years, at least two research trials using drugs in this class have been halted because while they were safe and seemed to work well on plaque removal, they showed disappointing results for AD reversal and or progression.[142] (That, after all, is the point).

One of these drugs aducanumab, manufactured by Biogen, was pulled from clinical trials in March 2019 after the company had reportedly spent over 18 billion in development costs. However, after further review, Biogen deemed the drug worthy and as of October 2019 were awaiting FDA approval sometime in 2020. This is a highly unusual course of events for both manufacturers and the FDA. If approved, the drug will likely be very expensive and probably not widely available. Its use will probably be restricted to a small subset of AD patients who meet specific criteria. It will also be the first AD drug approved in a very long time.

Tau tangles correlate better with the degree of dementia than do amyloid plaque. Work on finding a way to remove tau tangles is in its infancy relative to work on amyloid plaque which is a decade or so in existence.[143] Beginning the search for the cure with amyloid plaque makes sense because tau tangles seem to occur after amyloid. The way in which the two interact to cause memory loss is unknown. Targeting tau tangles with antibodies in mice has shown intriguing information. Removing tau tangles not only improved dementia symptoms but also decreased amyloid levels. This suggests a complex relationship between plaques and tangles and suggests that targeting the tangles may be the best way to begin treatment.[144] Another way to target tau tangles is to prevent tau from forming tangles in the first place. It is the tangles which appear to cause harm, not the tau protein itself.

LMTX is a drug developed to prevent tangles from forming. Trials in AD patients failed to show improvement in symptoms, daily functioning, or brain shrinkage.[145] However, when the investigators looked at patients who had never been treated with the currently available drugs Aricept® and Namenda®, they found an improvement in symptoms, functioning, and brain shrinkage.

Yet another way to attack tau tangles is to use an enzyme to untangle tau. CyP40 has been shown to do this both in the test tube and in a mouse model.[146] It is unknown if the enzyme treatment has any effect on AD symptoms.

Although still very early in the developmental stage, the most exciting news to come out of AD research is a look at the role of brain immune cells called microglia and their interaction with tau tangles in symptomatic AD. In October 2019, a study was published online in the *Journal of Experimental Medicine*. This study comes from Washington University in St. Louis. Researchers showed that mice given a compound to reduce these brain immune cells showed almost no brain shrinkage, whereas comparable mice which did not receive the compound showed severe brain shrinkage. This suggests, to me, that AD is at least in part an autoimmune disease, like rheumatoid arthritis and inflammatory bowel disease among others, in which the body's immune system attacks itself. While the compound used in the mice is not suitable for humans, it offers a starting point to find at least an effective treatment for patients already diagnosed with AD. It is also important to note that potentially traumatic brain injury could also be treated in a similar fashion, as it, too, involves tau tangles.

Repurposing an Old Drug

As drugs become more and more expensive to develop, they become more and more costly to patients. Consequently, researchers on occasion look to repurposing old drugs for new indications. It is not uncommon for such research to lead to off-label use of the drug studied. Off-label use refers to a use which has not been approved by the FDA. An example of this with regards to AD is the use of lithium, a drug commonly used for the treatment of bipolar disorder and major depression. Patients with bipolar disorder treated with long-term lithium therapy have been shown to have a decreased incidence of AD. In a very small study published in 2011, researchers found a decrease in the number of patients who progressed from mild AD to more advanced AD when treated with lithium. They also demonstrated lower levels of tau protein in cerebrospinal fluid in patients treated with lithium, concluding that lithium treatment may have a protective effect, thus slowing progression of AD.[147] Research looking at this drug continues.

Another example of an old drug which could be repurposed to slow the progression of AD is the oral anticoagulant Pradaxa®. A recent study in the AD mouse model suggests that Pradaxa® does delay the progression of AD.[148] Certainly, this addresses the common association of vascular dementia with AD.

Insulin and Related drugs

Type 2 diabetes and AD share a common factor, that is insulin resistance. Insulin plays a role in signal transmission in the brain. Because signs of insulin resistance have been found in the brains of AD patients, scientists have been studying the effects of insulin and insulin sensitizers like Avandia® and Actos® in AD patients.[149]

A July 2019 report of the use of intranasal insulin is very encouraging. This study found that treatment with intranasal insulin for twelve months slowed the progression of AD by one to two years. In addition, the abnormal proteins found in the cerebrospinal fluid of AD patients were reduced in the treatment group. This suggests a positive effect on brain health.[150] Studies continue in the hopes that longer treatment may show even more beneficial effects. This study also suggests that the earlier in the course of AD that treatment with intranasal insulin is begun, the more beneficial it is likely to be.

The advantage of using intranasal, as opposed to intravenous or skin injections, is the fact that the intranasal route puts the drug directly into the brain, avoiding the complication of low blood sugar.

In the long-term the administration of Avandia® has not proven useful in slowing AD.

Early studies of the effect of Actos® in patients with both type 2 diabetes and AD have been encouraging. However, the drug may be associated with bladder cancer.

Stem Cells

Researchers at the Pennsylvania State University have been doing amazing work transforming human stem cells into functioning nerve cells.[151]

The same investigators have shown in a mouse model their "drug cocktail" can induce nerve cell growth in the areas of the brain most affected by AD. This is exciting work that holds promise not only in AD patients but also in stroke victims and those with traumatic brain injury. This is very early work and is certainly not yet ready to be offered to the public as a cure. I say this as a word of caution because there are stem cell clinics across the country offering unproven cures for many different ailments that are often staffed by unqualified practioners.[152]

Young Blood

Another study from Washington University in St. Louis, although not specifically related to AD at this time, is intriguing. A blood component eNAMPT declines in the blood of both mice and humans as they age. When this protein substance is taken from young mice and given to old mice, it has been shown to slow the decline in health and extend the life span of these older mice by 16 percent.[153] These findings need to be replicated in humans.

In addition, there are many other proteins in blood that decline with age; these, too, are being studied.

In the summer of 2019, a study was being contemplated by the Institutional Review Board at St. Louis University, which would administer blood from young healthy individuals to those with advanced AD. If approved and implemented, it would be the only study being done on persons with advanced AD.

I had offered to enroll Ollie in this study, but sadly, it did not become a reality before his death.

As with stem cell clinics, there are also "young blood" clinics. At least some of these have been shut down by the FDA (Food and Drug Administration) on the basis that the science was unproven.[154]

Modalities

Noninvasive techniques such as transcranial electrical stimulation, light therapy, transcranial magnetic stimulation, low-level laser treatment, and ultrasound therapy are all being investigated. While these treatments in many cases seem to have a positive effect following treatment, long-lasting results seem elusive.

Conclusion

While there is a lot going on in AD research, some of it exciting, we need to keep in mind that the diversity of this disease makes it unlikely that a single magic bullet will emerge to treat or cure this devastating condition.

Prevention

AD is associated with both age and genetic risk factors. We cannot roll back time and at this point cannot change our DNA. There are, however, some lifestyle changes we can make to decrease our risk of AD or to delay its onset, even in the presence of high genetic risk.[155]

One study finds that older individuals with healthy memory were more likely to be female, more highly educated, engaging in many social activities, displaying a lower heart rate, a faster walking gait, and tending to be slightly overweight, and more engaged in activities to make themselves look and feel better. The reverse was true of individuals who displayed signs of AD.[156]

The University of California Irvine's ninety-plus study shows us that people who drink moderate amounts of alcohol and coffee live longer than those who abstain. Those who are slightly overweight in their seventies live longer than those who are normal weight or underweight. Finally, those who show a poor performance on physical activities such as walking are at an increased risk of dementia.

The US Department of Health and Human Services attempts to help prevent diseases like AD in the elderly by offering the Welcome to Medicare visit at age sixty-five and the Annual Wellness visits. The Welcome to Medicare visit is a comprehensive screening assessment and aims to uncover previously undiagnosed conditions such as diabetes and high blood pressure among others. The Annual Wellness visit is designed to keep you up to date on immunizations and other health maintenance exams and in most cases should include tests to look for early signs of AD.

Too few seniors avail themselves of these services. In 2013, only 6.8 percent of new Medicare enrollees took advantage of the Welcome to Medicare visit. In 2014, while 16 percent of Medicare recipients had an Annual Wellness exam, only 7 percent received all the recommended preventative services.[157] Avail yourselves of all that Medicare offers in the way of preventative services, and ask your doctor to follow the Medicare guidelines.

Anti-inflammatory Agents

An article in the business section of *The Washington Post* on June 4, 2019, states that the drug company Pfizer had information as early as 2015 that their rheumatoid arthritis drug Enbrel® could reduce the risk of AD by 64 percent. Enbrel® is an anti-inflammatory agent with a different mode of action from Aleve®, which we discussed previously. Studies on Aleve® did not show any promise in decreasing the incidence of AD. Pfizer has chosen not to pursue the testing required to prove that Enbrel® has any effect on the occurrence of AD. The drug is not able to enter the brain after administration, suggesting that it should not have any direct effect on processes occurring within the brain. It will be interesting to see if anyone else is willing to pursue repurposing Enbrel® for use in AD. At this time, off-label use is not warranted.

Tight Control of Blood Pressure and Stroke Prevention

Perhaps the most important thing you can do to help prevent AD and other dementias is to maintain your blood pressure at 120/80. Maintaining blood pressure just twenty points lower than the previous standard of 140/90 was able to reduce the incidence of dementia by 17 to 19 percent in just three years of treatment. [158] Tight control of blood pressure goes a long way toward stroke prevention.

A multinational panel convened at the 2019 World Congress of Neurology concluded that in order to reduce the incidence of dementia, societies around the world must reduce the incidence of stroke. Half of all patients who suffer a stroke go on to develop dementia within three years. [159]

Social Engagement and Other Brain-Stimulating Activities

The Whitehall II study from the United Kingdom has been studying a large group of people over the last thirty to forty years. A treasure trove of information can be obtained by the long-term follow-up of a single group of individuals. The latest published results from this study suggest that frequent social contact in mid to late life reduces dementia risk. The results suggest it is contact with friends or acquaintances, not relatives, which was the critical factor. While speculative, it is suggested that those who are socially engaged are exercising their minds, using memory, language, and other important mind skills, thus building brain reserve capacity. [160] It is also known that the more mental activities in which an individual engages in late life, the less likely he or she is to develop dementia.

Mentally stimulating activities which were studied included reading, socializing, playing games, using a computer, and crafting. [161]

Physical Exercise

Just like exercising your mind, exercising your body has been shown to decrease the risk of AD. A 2006 study showed a 38 percent decrease in AD in individuals who exercised regularly compared to those who did not. Regularly was defined as fifteen minutes or more at least three times per week. Qualifying exercise included walking, hiking, aerobics, calisthenics, swimming, water aerobics, weight training, and stretching. [162]

Those who exercise have known for a long time it makes us feel good. This is due to the hormone-like substances endorphins, which are released during exercise. Endorphins are the body's own natural narcotic. More recently, another hormone has been found to be released during exercise. This hormone is known as irisin and is thought to promote the growth of nerve cells in the part of the brain which controls memory. Irisin is reduced in the brains of AD patients. Studies in mice suggest that this hormone is responsible for the positive effects of exercise in improving memory and decreasing the incidence of AD.[163] A 2018 study suggests that it is never too late to start exercising. In this study, six months of aerobic exercise was able to improve function in patients with very early AD.[164]

Diet

We are constantly advised to eat a healthy diet. This we are told will ward off each of the chronic illnesses we face as we age. There is ample but sometimes conflicting evidence that eating a healthy diet will help prevent AD. Just exactly, what is a healthy diet? Evidence suggests that it is a diet consisting of whole grains; fruits and vegetables; and low sugar, fats, salt, and red meats. What makes food taste good? Sugar, fat, and salt. If it tastes good, spit it out. This is exactly why a healthy diet is so hard to follow.

The most highly recommended diet is the MIND diet, which is a combination of the Mediterranean diet and the low-salt DASH diet. Research from Harvard University suggests that high adherence to the MIND diet is associated with a 53 percent decrease in AD and moderate adherence can lower the risk of AD by 35 percent. The diet emphasizes green leafy vegetables, other vegetables, nuts, berries, beans, whole grains, fish, poultry, olive oil, and red wine (one glass per day). It restricts red meat, cheese, fast foods, sweets, and butter or margarine.

Other studies do not replicate these findings. The latest report from the Whitehall II study mentioned above failed to show that a healthy diet reduced the incidence of AD. This 2019 report contradicts earlier work by the same study group which did suggest a benefit.[165]

Specific components of a healthy diet recently studied include pomegranate juice and mushrooms; both have been shown to independently reduce or slow the onset of AD.[166,167]

Recent studies also show that caffeine may be a useful component of an AD prevention strategy. A key brain cell maintenance factor NMNAT2 is positively impacted by caffeine. This factor is known to be reduced in AD and Parkinson's disease. Work in mice suggests that caffeine may boost memory by boosting production of this important factor.[168]

Diet does matter.

Smoking Cessation

If you smoke, *quit*. Smoking is associated with dementia, both AD and vascular dementia. Those who never smoked were 18 percent less likely to develop dementia.[169] This study suggests quitting lowers your risk of dementia substantially. Long-term quitters' risk of dementia was 15 percent, nearly the same as those who had never smoked. Even those who had quit only recently lowered their risk of dementia by 8 percent.

Get Married and Stay Married

Marriage is associated with a lower risk of dementia as compared to those who are divorced, separated, widowed, or never married.[170] Divorced men are nearly three times more likely to develop dementia than married men, whereas divorced women are only 30 percent more likely to develop the disease than married women. One can only speculate on why this may be the case. Couples are able to support each other emotionally and financially. They have combined social networks, thereby increasing their social interaction.

Divorce is an extremely stressful event, and men tend to take the biggest hit. They lose the emotional support and health reminders—time for your checkup, don't smoke, don't drink so much, etc. They also take a big hit financially.

Get Plenty of Quality Sleep

We covered the fact that both lack of sleep and poor-quality sleep is associated with AD. While we sleep, the brain's immune system rewires, repairs, and cleans our sick and injured brain cells.[171]

Since this trash removal repair mechanism is active *only* while we sleep, it is easy to see how the system can be overwhelmed and overburdened when we do not get enough sleep.

Hearing and Vision

To engage in the world around us, we need to hear and see. As we age, both hearing and vision become less acute. Hearing aids and glasses can be expensive, but they are critical to keeping us engaged in the world around us. A recent study showed that hearing aids reduced dementia risk over a three-year period by 18 percent.[172] A significant decrease in the rate of memory decline has been found after individuals begin using hearing aids.[173] Work with a reputable audiologist before you purchase hearing aids. You want aids which amplify only the auditory frequencies you need. Aids which amplify all sound will make background noise so loud that you will still not hear the speech sounds you need to hear.

Cataract surgery has been shown to significantly improve memory scores in some cases and to slow the decline in memory.[174]

It is critical to pay attention to sensory health. Improving our ability to see and hear the world around us helps prevent AD or at least slow it down.

Vaccines

Many would say that the ultimate goal in prevention of a disease is a vaccine. Vaccines work well for many diseases, measles, chicken pox, diphtheria, whooping cough, tetanus, hepatitis, polio, and more. The search for a vaccine for AD and related dementias is ongoing. Much of the work has focused on a vaccine against amyloid plaques. More recently work has expanded into vaccines that target both amyloid plaques and tau tangles.

A vaccine targeting amyloid plaques is already in the human-testing phase. Results as of January 2019 show that it is both safe and effective in generating an immune response. The researchers noted a positive trend in memory and function in the AD patients tested. Further testing is underway with results expected in 2021.[175] There are at least two other vaccines being tested in animals, one targets both amyloid plaque and tau tangles.[176] The other targets tau tangles only.[177] While these trials are encouraging, we must realize we are many years and perhaps billions of dollars away from eradicating AD with a vaccine. Until then, all we can do is begin a lifelong regimen to protect our brains. This should include diet, exercise, sleep, socializing, blood pressure control, and paying attention to our total health including sensory. Together, we can help prevent AD. *We can do this.*

Addendum

As I draw close to finishing this book, a new study has been published which could have important ramifications on the treatment of not only early AD but also early PD, as well as many other neurological disorders such as amyotrophic lateral sclerosis and multiple sclerosis. The work is conducted on animal models but represents a new way of looking at causation of these devastating diseases. It also suggests a new way to treat these diseases, if treatment can begin early, before major nerve damage has occurred. While still very preliminary, I believe this work deserves mention.[178]

PART 3

Navigating the Minefield of Dementia Care

As you can discern from the memoir, Ollie and I had a wonderful fun-filled life together. We were able to do things together that neither of us would have done alone. We were a team. After we were both retired, I took care of the cooking and day-to-day running of the household and the finances. He did everything else, growing a lot of the food, managing the farm chores, and advanced planning for the farming businesses as well as maintenance decisions for the home.

Life was good.

After his stroke, the decline was slow. Gradually more and more of the tasks he normally took care of found their way to my to-do list. Sadly, his favorite form of relaxation, hitting golf balls, was no longer of interest to him. I believe he was losing the fine mind-and-body control he needed to make those long drives and short putts.

We found ourselves spending a lot of holiday weekends in the hospital with Ollie suffering fever and delirium. The usual cause proved to be a urinary tract infection. A full workup of fever and delirium always includes a head CT or MRI. His doctors kept me informed to a point, so thank God for the patient portal and my medical education. Although I had made multiple attempts to teach him computer skills, Ollie was not computer literate. Consequently, I set up his patient portal and managed it for him. This gave me access to all his test results. I watched his brain shrink in real time. This was horrifying.

I knew what the future had in store for us and it would be hard. Little did I know just how hard it would be and what a toll it would take on me and our finances. We thought we had plans in place. We had established a revocable living trust. We had powers of attorney established for each other, living wills and other legal documents. They had been revised periodically over the years, and all our assets were actually in the trust. We had money set aside for nursing home care if needed. Since I was seventeen years younger, I was confident that I would be able to provide most of the care he needed. I was able to do so but at a cost to my health. When things were the most difficult, I explored options for care and soon found that costs of $10,000 per month far exceed our expectations and planning.

Although Ollie was a veteran, he did not qualify for assistance because we had too much in savings. We would need to spend down all of it before he would be eligible. That in effect would eliminate my own safety net entirely.

I continued to care for him until I simply could not do it anymore. Then we were at the mercy of the system, as I like to call it, and it is a very complicated, confusing minefield of a system.

It is my hope that you will be able to benefit from the wisdom, which I try to convey in this section of the book. It is wisdom I acquired often the hard way.

Caregiving

Being the caregiver for a dementia patient is a lot like child rearing. They become more and more childlike as the disease progresses. Instead of starting in the diaper phase, you end in the diaper phase. A baby in this phase is cute and portable; a dementia patient in this phase is sad and difficult. On the other hand, giving care to someone you love is rewarding. It is my own belief that caring for another being is a basic human need. That need can be met by caring for a loved one or caring for a pet.

Until the very end, Ollie thought of himself as my caregiver. He refused to travel late in his illness, because he knew he could not help me if I got into trouble while we were traveling. He still felt confident he could protect me in the St. Louis area. In reality, I knew this was not true, but it gave him comfort to believe that this was the case.

While your loved one is still the same person, even though they now suffer from dementia, the way you interact with them needs to be different. Now you need to think about *what* you say and *how* you say it, *what* you do and *how* you do it.

Be patient. Your loved one has lost his or her ability to process information quickly.

Limit the amount of information you ask them to process. Give them two, no more than three, choices to make; but *do* give them choices. This allows them to feel connected and in control.

Try not to raise your voice especially when it is tainted with anger or frustration. *This is hard to do.* Your loved one is likely to react as if wounded if they sense your anger and frustration. Then both of you feel bad about yourselves.

Stimulate your loved one mentally when you can. If your loved one enjoyed putting together puzzles, you will need to choose age-appropriate puzzles. A puzzle designed for a six-year-old may well be appropriate for someone with early moderate-stage dementia. No one likes to *fail*. Try not to set them up to *fail*.

Give your loved one a job of some kind. Ollie used to say, "I want to achieve something"

Ask them to carry the laundry for you or help you bring in the groceries; the simplest task will give them a sense of achievement. If they do it wrong, just redo it when they are not looking. Do not let them know that they failed. It was my experience, in contrast to a child, it is not possible to teach them the right way to do things. Understanding this will help both of you deal with the situation and reduce stress and frustration. *Focus on your loved ones ability, not their disability.*

Quality of life, in my opinion, requires some degree of self-reliance. There is a very fine line between protecting your loved one and standing in their way while they try to maintain their own self-reliance.

Falls are inevitable; most result in no injury or only minor injury. Some falls may be serious, or even life-threatening. It is important to remember *quality of life is far more important than quantity of life.* Hospitals and nursing homes fear lawsuits and consequently limit quality of life in dementia patients as they go to extremes to prevent falls. An example of this in Ollie's case was the memory care facility that used chair alarms. Each time he attempted to get up and walk, he was cajoled into sitting back down. My complaints led to the next step-up, a Merry-chair. A Merry-chair is basically a cube made of PVC piping with a seat in the middle and four wheels on the bottom. Ollie called it a cage. Using it did increase his mobility; however, it removed social contact. Since he was no longer a fall risk, he was largely ignored by the staff. Since he was the highest-functioning person on the unit, he became socially isolated, leading me to move him once again.

There is no point in arguing with a dementia patient. He or she may be convinced of something that is not real, for example, that there is a basement or elevator in a building that does not have one. Often there is a fantasy surrounding something going on in that basement or travel on the elevator. Just listen to the story; the fantasy is not harmful and may be comforting on some level to the patient.

Avoid the use of force in any form. Placing yourself between your loved one and something they desire, even if it is bad for them, may well be interpreted as force, and a dementia patient *will* fight back. Their base instinct is to protect themselves, and only after they have hurt you will they realize they hurt someone they love. They are *devastated.*

Assisting them with taking medications by trying to place the pill in their mouth can result in the caregiver being bit. Human bites are serious and need immediate medical attention. Behaviors such as those I just described are common in the later stages of dementia. *Any wounded animal, including humans, will try to protect themselves from further harm.* Dementia patients are wounded, and they may hurt their caregiver and themselves as a result.

Encourage your loved one's efforts, and praise their success. Do this in a genuinely thankful way. This will make both of you feel good about yourselves.

Dementia patients often understand that they are losing mental function and experience joy in being able to be successful, even in the smallest task. *Encourage and praise success, no matter how small.*

Modifications

There are some necessary modifications to your loved one's lifestyle and environment that need to be made.

Taking away the car keys is the most significant. The ability to get in the car and just go is one of the most liberating aspects of life. At some point in the disease process, the dementia patient becomes an impaired driver. They are not just a danger to themselves but also a danger to others. This cannot be allowed.

Sometimes, a physician in concert with other health care professionals will make the determination that the patient is a danger to others if allowed to drive. While this information is passed on to law enforcement and the driver's license may be revoked until the keys and or the car are removed, there is no certainty that the dementia patient will not simply drive without a license. I was fortunate that Ollie voluntarily gave up driving. To remove any temptation, I gave up my beloved hardtop convertible, leaving only one practical car in the garage and the keys in my pocket.

Cooking can be another difficult issue; life-threatening fire hazards can result from forgotten foods left cooking or ovens and stovetop burners left unattended. Disconnecting the stove and encouraging the use of devices with automatic shutoff features, such as a microwave, can mitigate this problem.

Silver alerts are issued for endangered seniors with dementia who have wandered away from home. This is an all too common occurrence. They will often wander in severe weather without proper clothing. Hospitals and nursing homes provide patients with a bracelet, which will set off an alarm if the dementia patient crosses the threshold. A medical alert device may be helpful if someone finds the wanderer and tries to help. Unfortunately, the dementia patient is usually not able to use these devices and frequently will simply discard them. This was certainly the case with Ollie. A security door chain placed high (well above eye level) on the outside doors along with a wood or metal bar placed in the slide track of any sliding glass doors opening to patios or decks will usually prevent dementia patients from gaining access to the outside.

It is important to modify the residence of the dementia patient in order to enhance safety. Be sure that electrical cords including extension cords are secure and do not encroach on walkways. Unsecured, they can be a trip hazard. Handrails in tubs and showers as well as near the toilet are extremely important. Many dementia patients have balance and lower-body strength issues, the rails offer security and assistance. Tubs and showers should be fitted with a nonskid bath mat to avoid slipping. All throw rugs should be removed; they are an extreme fall hazard. Make sure all walking paths within the home are free of clutter.

Encourage the use of a walker or wheelchair. Older homes may need extensive remodeling to accommodate wheelchairs.

Many older adults, including dementia patients, do not see well in low light. Be sure the home has adequate lighting, including night-lights. Ollie was unable to use a flashlight. Consequently for us, the only way to prevent nighttime falls was to let him sleep with the lights on all night. Sadly, I had to leave the marital bed since I was unable to sleep with the lights on. He had no problem sleeping this way, and the nighttime falls stopped.

In early and moderate stages of dementia, the patient may be able to manage his or her medications as long as the dosing schedule is simple, such as all drugs given once a day in the morning. Ultimately, the caregiver will need to take over the job of medication administration.

This can become problematic if the dementia patient is living alone and using the assistance of caregiver organizations such as Visiting Angeles® or Home Instead Senior Care®. These agencies usually do not allow workers to give medications. What they can do is hand an envelope containing the medication to the dementia patient so they can take the medication themselves. This system worked for us when I had surgery and was temporarily unable to be the caregiver. I sorted all of Ollie's medication into envelopes labeled with date and time they were to be given. The agency worker just handed him the envelope and a glass of water so he could take the medication.

At some point, it will be necessary to have your loved one declared incompetent so that the person who has the power of attorney for health care and financial decisions is able to take over those duties. Depending on the state laws and or personal desires, either one or two physicians must certify that the patient is incompetent. The patient's primary care physician and neurologist or nursing home physician will be happy to provide you with letters certifying incompetence. File these with the patient's legal documents. If proof of incompetency is requested, these documents will provide the proof.

As a caregiver, there are modifications you will need to make to your own lifestyle. This is where it gets really hard. While you may be giving care out of love, you are still giving up a part of your own life in order to add quality of life for your loved one.

In late early stage and early moderate-stage dementia, I found myself driving myself to exhaustion, trying to keep Ollie busy and engaged. We both enjoyed live theatre and symphony music, so I planned many days around these activities. We also spent many hours at the art museum and other museums in the St. Louis area. I truly enjoyed these activities and the time we spent together; but the constant planning, executing the plan, and making sure Ollie was safe and secure was exhausting. I was paddling two canoes, mine and his. At this stage, you must expect that even simple things will be hard. This is also the stage at which toileting is an issue from time to time. Putting your loved one in Depends® is easy, but they are always at liberty to remove them. Consequently, the bed may be wet. Toilet seats can become mysterious to your loved one. On occasion, Ollie would forget to raise the toilet seat and have a large bowel movement on top of the seat and environs. The cleanup was always difficult and stressful. A toddler can be toilet-trained; the dementia patient cannot be trained. This knowledge weighs heavily on you. Things will not get better; you simply need to get through it one day at a time. The love and appreciation that I received from Ollie helped me carry this burden, but it was heavy.

The most important modification to your life as a caregiver is to carve out time for yourself. I failed to do this. Ollie and I both paid the price for my failure to do this. It led to severe health problems for me and ended with Ollie entering a memory care unit. It was all downhill from there, as you will recall from the memoir.

For both your sake and that of your loved one, find the time to take care of yourself. Exercise, eat right, and enjoy some peace and quiet. Find someone who will give you the break you need.

Dealing with Behaviors

It is important to remember dementia is not just about memory. The patient's personality may change completely at times, while at other times, they may seem to be their familiar selves. The dementia patient is often not able to express to you a problem they may be having such as a need to go to the bathroom, hunger, thirst, or boredom. This often leads to very uncharacteristic behaviors. These behaviors can be very disturbing to both the patient and the caregiver, as well as others who may witness these behaviors.

Anxiety

Anxiety is least troubling to caregivers but most troubling to the dementia patient. Anxiety and fear are two sides of the same coin. Ollie suffered anxiety for the last six years of his illness. It was manifest most often by clinginess. He felt secure if I was within his sight. This meant that unless I held his hand as we walked, he would follow me rather than walk beside me. My head was often on a swivel, checking behind me to see if he was all right. After he was in the nursing home system, he would cling to his favorite caregiver. It was sometimes a problem, as they tried to care for others, but most often, they found it endearing. He was well loved wherever he went.

Occasionally, anxiety will manifest itself by cries for help. Unable to understand and cope with a situation, they may ask for help from visiting relatives, or even strangers. Ollie did this several times. He was never able to verbalize the problem; it was up to me to try to understand what was wrong.

In one case, he asked his brother to help him after Ollie's daughters were urging me to put him in assisted living while I had surgery. Although Ollie was willing to go along with the plan, he did not really want to leave home even for a short time unless we were together. I figured this out quickly, and as soon as I made arrangements for an in-home caregiver, while I recovered from surgery, the behaviors disappeared.

There are drugs to treat anxiety; and in younger people, who are in otherwise good health, they are useful to help them cope. In the elderly dementia patient, they are more likely to cause distressing side effects than they are to be helpful. Excessive sleepiness and more frequent falls are among the side effects observed.

Showing love, support, and understanding will do more to safely calm anxiety than any pill can ever do.

Aggression

In some, anxiety leads to aggression. This is a behavior distressing to everyone. The aggression can be either verbal or physical. Yelling, swearing, hitting, and biting are all observed.

Yes, my dear sweet, loving Ollie displayed all of these. On the occasion of one of our excursions away from the memory care unit in which he was residing, he refused to go back and called me the B word. The staff came out, and they were able to persuade him to go back inside quietly. I was devastated; he had never treated me like this previously. It made me wonder if I was being foolish trying so hard to improve his quality of life. The next time I visited to take him out to lunch, I asked him if he remembered what he had said to me the last time we were together. Very sheepishly, he said, "Of course, I do, and I am ashamed of myself." The incident was heart wrenching for both of us. Not all dementia patients will be able to recall incidents of bad behavior, but those with Lewy body dementia often do.

In the fall of 2018, shortly after Thanksgiving, I moved Ollie back home. Seeing him in the nursing home was almost as hard on me as caring for him at home. I also wanted him to be home for his birthday and Christmas. My strategy was to hire someone to bathe and dress him in the morning and then take him to adult day care and pick him up each evening. This person would also take him on excursions each Saturday. It was the aggressive behaviors which caused my plan to fail. He had public outbursts of kicking and hitting the caregiver I had hired. On one occasion, I needed to go get him because he would not get out of her car after getting her in a stranglehold with the seat belt.

On New Year's Day 2019, he bit me because I tried to put his medicine in his mouth. In his damaged brain, this was viewed as an act of aggression, so he defended himself. I went to the emergency room. Each morning after a restful night, he was his charming, polite, loving self. As the day wore on, anxiety and aggression resurfaced.

In early February of 2019, the Missouri Veteran's Home called to tell me they had a room available for him. It was with a heavy heart; I took them up on the offer.

As I mentioned earlier, all behaviors result from some unexpressed issue. In retrospect, I think that in this late stage of dementia, I was giving Ollie too much stimulation with the day care program and Saturday excursions. I just could no longer do the 24/7 care.

There are a number of medications that are used to help quiet the agitated, aggressive dementia patient. These include antidepressants, antipsychotics, marijuana, and combinations of these. Ollie was given both antidepressants and antipsychotics. They did quiet him but left him in a stupor. Quetiapine®, an antipsychotic, was best tolerated in a very low dose but made him more prone to falls. It is also associated with stroke and death in elderly dementia patients.

Nondrug therapy is currently favored.[179] Researchers found that outdoor activities were the most effective for reducing agitation and aggression. Outdoor activities, massage, and touch therapy were best for treating verbal aggression. Exercise and the modification of daily activities were best for physical aggression.

If your loved one is displaying aggressive behavior, *stay calm, stay clear, and do not put yourself in harm's way.*

Try to think of a reason for the behavior—is the TV too loud? Would soothing music be more calming? Is the room too hot or too cold? Offering food or water may help. Make these simple modifications.

Plan ahead. Make sure your loved one does not have access to guns, knives, or other objects with which they could harm themselves or others. During an outburst is not the time to make these modifications.

Distraction is very effective, redirect the mind and thinking. Go for a walk outside, or lead your loved one to another room. Add another person to the room—anything to change the dynamic of the situation.

Depression

Depression is very common in dementia patients. How could it not be? In the early stages, patients may even be suicidal. In later stages, they often can-not function at a high enough level to achieve suicide.

Institutionalized patients are often given antidepressants. On the surface, this seems kind, however, in most cases it leaves them with more confusion and a propensity for falls. It really is hard know, what is best for these patients. When Ollie was not taking these medications, his quality of life was much better and he and I were able to have some good times together.

There were only two instances in which I heard Ollie express that he was tired of living, because he was so dysfunctional. In these cases, I was able to lift him up and convince him, that he was loved and valued.

My God-daughter, Anna, explained to me once, that there are four ways that people are able to give and receive love. First there are those who need affirmation, they need reassurance that they have value. Second are those who need gifts, given or received. Third are those who wish to serve or be served. Finally, there are those who give and receive time.

Ollie had a need to show his love by service and his loss of ability to do so, was very hard for him. One day as we sat together for lunch, in the Veteran's Home, I asked him what he had done that morning, he told me had gotten these guys fed as he gestured to the other dementia patients in the room. In his mind, he was still being of service.

Affirmation and time are something we can and should, give our loved ones with dementia.

Delusions and Hallucinations

Both delusions and hallucinations are very common among those with dementia. Your loved one is delusional if they firmly believe in something that either does not exist or never happened. For example, they may believe that there is an elevator next to their room when the building does not have an elevator or that some activity occurred in the basement of a building that has no basement. *Do not try to convince them that these beliefs are false.* They will not be able to grasp the fact that something they believe so firmly is untrue. Reassure them, if the belief is distressing. Simply acknowledge the belief if it is not distressing to your loved one. Attempting to impose your reality on them will only cause them anxiety and possibly agitation and aggression.

Hallucinations are occurring when your loved one sees, hears, or feels something that is not real. Poor vision or hearing can certainly exacerbate hallucinations. It is easy to say be sure they are wearing their glasses and or hearing aids but very difficult to achieve.

The eye exam itself in later stages of dementia can be problematic. The dementia patient is being asked to respond to questions like, "Do you see better with this lens or that lens?" This can be a very confusing question to the dementia patient, and if the exam is hurried, the glasses prescribed may only make their vision worse, not better.

The same is true of being fitted with hearing aids. The exam requires accurate responses to questions about hearing. In addition, dementia patients often have difficulty with speech understanding, and hearing aids may not help them at all.

Dementia patients ultimately lose their ability to keep track of things, even important things like glasses and hearing aids. Hearing aids are expensive and very vulnerable.

In Ollie's case, he took one out of his ear and ate it like candy. Fortunately, this behavior was observed and the battery (which can be harmful if swallowed) was retrieved. His remaining aid was destroyed when he removed it from his ear, dropped it on the floor, and his roommate ran over it with his wheelchair.

Fortunately, Ollie's hallucinations were entertaining to him. He would point out something he saw with great wonder. "Look at that," he would say. In other cases, hallucinations can be frightening to the dementia patient.

As with delusions, do not dispute what your loved one is experiencing. If the hallucination is distressing, reassure or pretend to remove the offending object—for example, step on the bug or open the door to let the snake crawl outside.

Hiding and Hoarding

Hiding and or hoarding are also commonly seen in dementia patients. This is often seen in nursing care situations. Patients will take things belonging to someone else. They do so because they remember a similar object and believe it belongs to them. This can be a source of conflict between residents of a nursing facility.

In my experience, it is best to ignore this transfer of stuff. Diffuse a conflict with acquiescence if you can. *Do not put yourself in harm's way*; blows may be exchanged.

For Father's Day one year, Ollie's daughter brought him an engraved paperweight that read "World's Best Dad." Someone placed it front of Ollie's army photo. For weeks, Ollie would carry this picture around with him and then put it in odd locations. "This is a picture of my father," he would declare as he hugged it close to his chest.

It was not unusual to find items in the trash or moved to some bizarre location. Be proactive. *Remove any object you do not want to lose* from your loved one's environment.

Do not attempt to interfere with a dementia patient's desire to move an object. They may well interpret this as a threat and become physically aggressive.

Sexual Behaviors

While the dementia patient in the later stages of the disease may still have a normal sex drive, often sexual behavior is the result of other sensations being confused as sexual urgings. For example, a need to go to the bathroom or the discomfort of a urinary tract infection. The result is that the dementia patient may remove his or her clothing in public or begin to masturbate in public. They may also make sexual demands of a spouse or others.

This can be very embarrassing and disconcerting to a caregiver. Keep in mind, dementia is a very common disease, and this behavior is very common in dementia patients.

Do not become embarrassed, do remove your loved one from public view, do distract them, and do not chastise or shame your loved one. Give them some space. If you need to refuse advances, do so very gently. A hard, forceful refusal may provoke anger and aggression. *Do not let your loved one hurt you.*

Sundowning

Often behavioral problems become worse in the evening, hence the term sundowning. This for me was very hard to deal with. I was tired in the evening and wanted to decompress. The behavioral issues prevented me from relaxing and decompressing, thereby adding to my stress and compromising my ability to cope. There were nights when he would awaken me in the wee hours of the morning, thus interfering with my ability to rest at night.

When the nighttime wandering was frequent, I hired people to sit with him at night while he slept. These people can be found through home health care agencies. They are not easy to find and are expensive. They would bathe and dress him in the morning. This allowed me to get much-needed rest.

You cannot deal with this alone. Get help.

While friends and family seem a logical choice. This is not always the case. The hours you need them can often be irregular and unpredictable. To many, the disease is frightening, and they will go to great lengths to avoid contact with dementia patients. This further isolates the caregiver.

Other Caregiving Issues

Falls

Dementia patients fall frequently. Usually, the falls result in minor injuries only. Occasionally, the fall is serious enough to cause a severe injury such as a broken bone or head injury. Common sense precautions can be instituted around the home to decrease the likelihood of falls. These were discussed previously under "Modifications."

Beyond this, my own feeling is further intervention to prevent falls is counterproductive. Freedom of movement is an important part of quality of life. *Dementia is a progressive, incurable, and ultimately fatal disease.* Preventing falls with chair alarms or Merry-chairs are effective in preserving *quantity of life* but do just the opposite for preserving *quality of life.*

Determining if the injury is serious or not will be very difficult for nonmedical family members. You *cannot* rely upon the dementia patient to tell you if they are seriously injured. At the end of his life, Ollie fell out of bed twice. In one of these falls, he sustained a shoulder injury. He never complained, but it was obvious that he had pain when the Veteran's Home staff would try to assist him into a standing position by pulling on his arms. "Oh, don't do that to me," he would cry. Look for subtle signs like this one after a fall.

Trouble breathing after a fall may indicate a severe chest injury and or a broken rib. Injuries like this can lead to pneumonia and death.

In the case of a fall involving the head, excessive sleepiness; a seizure; episodes of vomiting; or a new weakness often in a leg, arm, or both are among the signs that a severe head injury has occurred. *Never blame yourself* if you miss a serious injury and do not call for help early. Dementia patients are dying an unpleasant death if the disease is advanced. *Nothing you do or don't do* is going to change this.

Helping your loved one get up may be hazardous to you, the caregiver. Often you can get them up by putting a chair in front of them so they can pull themselves up. Bystanders are often willing to help or calling a family member or friend may be necessary. Dialing 911 is also an option. If 911 responders are called, they often want to transport your loved one to an emergency room. You risk hospital-ization in this case, and dementia patients seldom leave the hospital with as much functional ability as they have when they enter. If you do try to get your loved one up after a fall, remember to lift with your knees, not your back, and assist rather than do all the lifting. If you allow yourself to be injured, you will no longer be able to give care.

Dealing with End-Stage Dementia

In order to understand what is happening to your loved one in the last few weeks of life, you need to realize that the brain controls *all body functions.* You and your loved one have already been through so much, and now it gets even harder. Infections become more com-mon including skin infections. Crusty lesions may develop on the face and head. The immune system is shutting down and can no longer fight these infections. Difficulty swallowing occurs, so your loved one does not want to eat or drink. Weight loss is profound and dehydration occurs. They get weaker and can no longer walk or talk much. If they do eat or drink at this stage, they often have food and drink going into the lungs, resulting in pneumonia.

The brain also controls body temperature. At the end of life, you will see both chills and fever as this vital center shuts down. The inability to swallow allows saliva to build up in the throat, causing a rattling sound. Breathing becomes very irregular, with many shal-low breaths, followed by one big deep breath, and then only shallow breaths. The lips turn blue as insufficient oxygen is delivered to the body. The heart is the last vital organ to shut down. Hearing is retained until the end and your loved one may respond to something you say, even in a small way, and it may comfort both of you. I personally feel that releasing them is helpful to both of you. I told Ollie to go when he was ready. He died soon after.

You and your loved one do not need to go through this alone. *Seek help* through *hospice care*. There are a number of different hospice providers. They may differ in services and most of all in attitude. Nearly one year before his death, Ollie's doctor recommended hospice care but did not recommend a specific provider. After talking with friends, I had a number to call for an agency that had provided care for a friend's sister at the end of her sister's life. I called and spoke to someone who told me Ollie was not eligible for hospice because he could still walk and did not have bed sores. In addition, they were too busy to provide care.

This conversation proved to be a great disservice to both Ollie and me. Had I pursued the idea of hospice with other providers, the end of life might have been much easier for both of us.

Much later, I met a hospice care nurse at a medical meeting we were both attending. She spoke to me in detail about the benefits of hospice for both the person approaching the end of life and those they will leave behind. Within a month, Ollie was enrolled in Heartland® Hospice Care. They helped him transition from life to death in a pain-free, comfortable manner. They were also there to help me deal with my grief.

I will discuss hospice in more detail in the section of this book, which deals with available resources.

Dealing with the Stress of Caregiving

Being a caregiver for a loved one who has dementia extracts a toll on you, both emotionally and physically. Certainly, you will feel sadness. This may well become chronic depression. You are losing your loved one, one brain cell at a time. Watching this happen is devastating. Ask your doctor to prescribe an antidepressant. I did, and it helped.

You will experience frustration which will likely lead to verbally lashing out at your loved one. You must remember you are only human and your loved one has no control over his or her abilities. No one is at fault, but both of you will be hurt.

Researchers at Baylor University in Texas recently reported that dementia caregivers lose 2.5 to 3.5 hours of sleep per week due to difficulty going to sleep and staying asleep. This can be due to chronic stress or due to nocturnal caregiver awakenings by dementia patients.[180]

When you add sleep loss to the stress, grief, and sadness, caregivers are at high risk for physical as well as emotional problems. Physical problems will vary with the individual but often include headaches, back pain, and stomach pain. Some people deal with stress by overeating, and thereby gain weight. Others will be unable to eat and lose weight. Neither of these responses are healthy but are likely to occur unless you can manage the stress.

Broken Heart Syndrome

Stress can literally break your heart. Chest pain, shoulder pain, shortness of breath, and other symptoms of a heart attack may develop in persons under extreme stress. Most often, testing shows that the blood vessels supplying the heart are not responsible for the symptoms, as they usually are in heart attacks. Instead, the heart muscle itself is damaged and does not effectively pump blood into the circulation. Fortunately, the condition is usually short-lived. It is likely to resolve within a month or two, but complications can occur, resulting in death. The condition is very much like congestive heart failure and is treated the same way.[181,182]

Stress Mitigation

So how do we prevent this extreme manifestation of stress and control the others?

Take time for yourself.

Exercise regularly.

Avoid unhealthy coping habits (drinking, smoking, overeating).

Develop healthy coping skills (listening to music, chatting with friends, shopping, jogging).

Surround yourself with friends and family.

Search for support groups or professional services.

While this is good, solid advice, it may not be so easy to achieve these goals. It was not easy for me. While I did not have unhealthy coping habits, I did not have any healthy ones either. Taking care of Ollie was my sole purpose in life. Anything I did, I did with him. So I was always paddling two canoes. It was exhausting.

Friends and family all advised me to institutionalize him for my own sake. I simply could not do this until I was physically unable to go on. Even then I was always fighting for him, to gain a little more quality of life.

Support groups do exist. I found that nearly all long-term care facilities had them. I just never availed myself of the help they offered. I am not entirely sure why I did not seek help. Denial was perhaps a big part of it. This was not happening to us. I could deal with it no matter what it took. The fact is, it was happening to us and I was no more able to deal with it than anyone else. I knew too late to help me that palliative care and hospice is also there for the living family as well as the dying patient. Establish a relationship with palliative care and hospice, sooner rather than later.

Facebook has a number of dementia support groups. Just use the Facebook search menu to connect with one or more of them. One of my step daughters did use this support and found chatting with others dealing with dementia patients helped her to cope a little better.

The Alzheimer's Association has a 24/7 help line; (800) 272-3900. You can also reach them online at www.alz.org. The National Institute on Aging (NIA) oversees an Alzheimer's Disease Education and Referral (ADEAR) Center: (800) 438-4380.

Clergy may be very helpful. Many in their flock have gone through this process, and they can often offer some insight.

Frequently, clergy will help with a crisis situation, even if you are not a member of the church.

Hopefully, this book answers many of your questions, and you may use not only the book but me, the author, as a resource. I wrote this book to help others, so do not hesitate to contact me with questions or for conversation. My e-mail is susan_krechel@icloud.com.

Legal Matters

They don't just matter; they are critical.

I am not a lawyer, but the information I put forth here is widely available from many different sources.

Everyone over the age of eighteen needs an estate plan of some kind. Simple forms can be downloaded online, and then either two witnesses can sign, or the document can be notarized.

With a *power of attorney*, you give another person (spouse, relative, or trusted friend) the power to make decisions on your behalf when you are incapacitated and unable to make decisions on your own. Appointing a power of attorney allows you to choose the person who will make these difficult decisions. Not doing so means the court may step in and assign a guardian who will then make these very personal decisions.

You generally need a power of attorney (POA) for health care and a POA for financial affairs. To assist your doctors and your POA for health care, you should execute a living will. The living will is only in effect if you are permanently unconscious or unable to make any informed decisions. It needs to stipulate what life-saving measures you want in this event. Do you wish to be on life support? Do you want to have a feeding tube? In some states, one doctor or in other states two doctors must stipulate that you are in an irreversible coma or terminally ill before the living will takes effect. In some states, a living will may be known as an advanced directive, a medical directive, a health care declaration, or physician instructions.

Keep in mind a POA ends with your death. Whomever you chose to manage your affairs will be unable to pay your final bills and distribute your estate. The court can then take possession of all your assets and assign someone to pay your bills and distribute the remainder to any known heirs. This takes time, and nearly all estates are lost in legal fees.

If you leave a last will and testament, you make your wishes known to the court, and they may honor those wishes, or they may not.

To keep your affairs private and out of the court system, you need a trust.

A revocable living trust is the most flexible and the most common type of trust employed. In a revocable trust, you as a grantor or you and your spouse as grantors execute a legal entity which will hold *all* of your assets—your house, your car, your bank accounts and brokerage accounts, etc. You appoint yourself as the trustee of the trust, thereby allowing you to do anything you want with the assets in the trust as though they were not in the trust. You name successor trustees—for example, a child or dear friend—to manage all your assets if you become incapacitated. While you are incapacitated, your trustee will be able to manage your assets, pay your bills, and in the end pay final expenses and distribute your assets according to your specified wishes.

The most common mistake people make is to set up a trust and fail to transfer *all* their assets to the trust. The title to your home must be in the name of the trust. It takes time and effort to do this; legal documents must be produced for every asset you retitle to the trust.

Smaller items, such as your car, you may want to leave in your name with a transfer on death (TOD) clause so that the asset goes to your trust when you die. Any asset *not* titled to your trust will be lost to *probate* when you die.

It is *critical* that you execute these documents before you become mentally incapacitated. If you do not, the court may step in and appoint a guardian/conservator. The guardian will be given the legal authority to determine where and how you will live. The conservator will have the legal authority to manage all your financial affairs.

An irrevocable trust is similar in most respects to a revocable trust but is much more restrictive. Once assets are in the trust, you do not normally have authority over them. The assets in an irrevocable trust are, to a large extent, protected against financial judgments against you. They are also not considered your assets when it comes to Medicaid applications. Using a trust like this will allow you to get nursing home care without bankrupting yourself and most importantly your family. We will discuss this in more detail when we consider options for care.

Early in life, it is important to set up these legal documents, but they need to be reviewed at least every five years because things change. One of your successor trustees may have died, and you may no longer want to have your estate divided in the same way you did five years earlier.

Simple changes are not costly but may be essential to the success of your plan.

As you age, it is important to consider the services of an elder care attorney. They can be essential to protecting your family and any legacy you may want to leave, even if you fall victim to dementia. Ollie and I were diligent about setting up and reviewing a revocable trust, but we did not have the knowledge and foresight to consult an elder care attorney until many possible options were no longer available.

Ollie was already legally incompetent when I consulted an elder care attorney for the first time. I was desperate to find a way to give Ollie the best possible care without bankrupting myself. At this time, my options were limited, but I did have options. What I learned was valuable, and much of what I learned I will pass on to you in subsequent pages.

A word of caution, be sure to read all the documents that are drafted on your behalf very carefully. I ran into a problem with Ollie's financial power of attorney after he had been declared incompetent. The document date and the date stipulated by the notary did not match. The lawyer acted as his own notary, and this likely would not have happened if a second person had been involved. In any event, the bank refused to recognize the document. This only involved our safe deposit box, so it was not a huge problem. I still had the authority to close the box and transfer the contents to another box in my own name.

I was able to do this because the elder care attorney had suggested that I transfer all assets out of our joint trust into a new trust in my name only.

Establishing the new trust and transferring assets from the joint trust before Ollie's death made things a lot easier for me at the time of his death. There was little paperwork to be done when he died.

In spite of the fact that I knew very well what was coming, I was not prepared and not very functional for at least six weeks after he died. Having already done most of the paperwork was indeed a blessing.

Covering the Cost of Care

Dementia is a long-term illness; care may well be required for a decade or more. The cost of care is staggering and continues to increase as the need for care becomes greater. The cost of memory care in a private facility that does not take Medicaid patients will cost $10,000 per month or more for a semiprivate room. The cost of a private room in such a facility will cost $14,000 per month. A facility that does accept Medicaid patients will cost $8,000 per month for a semiprivate room. These fees are not all inclusive. You will still pay for medications and Depends®, as well as other extras.

Medicare will not pay for long-term care. They will pay for a skilled nursing facility if you have been hospitalized and need rehabilitation care as a result of that hospitalization. Once you reach a minimal level of functioning, they will no longer pay for your care. Medicare may pay for home care in some instances. You must be homebound. A doctor must certify a plan of care, and that care cannot be provided for more than thirty-five hours per week or eight hours per day. They may also provide a home health aide for some personal care such as bathing.

The majority of dementia patients will need additional financial assistance or pay these high costs. The Veterans Administration may offer aid and assistance to help with the costs, and state-sponsored Medicaid programs can also help cover some of the costs. However, in both cases you and your spouse must be impoverished before these programs will pay the cost of care. This basically means that you will need to pay for your care until you and your spouse have little to nothing left in financial resources.

Long-term care insurance is an option you might want to consider. The younger you are when you purchase the insurance, the lower the premium, but like most insurance, it will increase as you age. Policies are often restrictive as to what they will pay and for how long they will pay. You may find that once you have exhausted the benefits of your long-term care insurance, you will again be paying the bills yourself and again facing bankruptcy.

Long-term care insurance may make sense for families wanting to care for aging parents while preserving a legacy when they die. Sharing the cost with siblings can make sense.

You will, of course, need to make the decision to purchase long-term care insurance before you need it.

The financial strength and reliability of the insurance company is also important. Insurance companies can come and go, leaving you with an expensive policy that is worthless at the time you need it. State regulators can lessen this eventuality, but risk is still involved.

Ollie and I made the conscious decision to self-insure. Since I was seventeen years younger than he and a physician, we planned on my being able to care for him for most of any long-term illness. We set aside what seemed an adequate amount of money to cover long-term care if needed. This strategy, for the most part, worked. However, I would have been bankrupt had he lived another three years in a memory care facility. It was this realization that prompted me to seek the services of an elder care attorney. In addition to his advice on how I could protect myself from bankruptcy, he also told me about the Missouri Veterans Home. This proved to be our very best option. We did have to apply and wait for availability (six months on average). Our cost for *full care*, medicine, Depends®, and barber care all included was $2,000 per month. The care that he received there was better than what he had received at the more costly facilities.

Medicaid is a joint federal and state health insurance program administered by the individual states. It is primarily for low-income persons, both over the age of sixty-five and younger persons who are disabled. It is, of course, taxpayer funded.

Medicaid does cover skilled nursing facilities when deemed medically necessary by a physician. Indeed, most of the costs of long-term care in the USA are paid for through the Medicaid program.

While each state has different rules, in general, you must have low income and few assets. They do not consider your home or your car in determining your assets. They do look back at your finances five years before you make application. In that time if you have given away or transferred assets out of your name, they will be counted as though you still owned them, and you will not qualify for Medicaid.

There are ways for persons to qualify for Medicaid without bankrupting themselves and being unable to leave a legacy to their children or other heirs. It requires planning, timing, and an elder care attorney. In my case, in the state of Missouri, I could have applied for Medicaid for Ollie by using our remaining assets to improve the house or buy a new car (home and car are exempt assets). I would also have been allowed to keep the money in my IRA because it was a small amount, but anything else would have needed to go into a Medicaid annuity. I would have been entitled to receive the income from the annuity, but upon my death, the principal would go to the state. The state will, in nearly all cases, try to recoup anything they spend on the Medicaid recipient. This may include a lien against a home.

The rules governing Medicaid eligibility are complex and fluid. For example, if the Medicaid recipient receives an inheritance from a spouse or other person, they will lose their Medicaid eligibility. Eligibility may also be lost due to certain financial actions of a community dwelling spouse. The services of an elder care attorney may be an ongoing need.

Planning ahead can save your family from the devasting costs of long-term health care.[183] In the case of a couple, if family history or current events suggest that one of you may need long-term care, you have at least three possible options. One is to establish an irrevocable trust and put all of your assets in this trust. You can live off the assets in the trust but have little or no control of them. This would need to done a least five years before making a Medicaid application. Since predicting when and even if a dementia patient may need long-term care is difficult to impossible, a useful strategy may be to buy a five-

SUSAN WILSON KRECHEL MD

year term long-term care insurance policy. If care is needed in the five-year period before Medicaid eligibility, the insurance company would pay some, if not all of, the costs. A second option is to divorce, with all of the assets, except for a minimum amount, going to the healthy spouse. The third option is to just say *no*. Simply refuse to pay for the care of your spouse. The authority to just say *no* was actually granted in 1988 with the passage of the Medicare Catastrophic Act. Technically, this is the law of the land and pertains to all fifty states.

To date, only New York and Florida have voluntarily changed their statues to provide for this provision. Connecticut was forced to comply after losing a suit to force implementation.

The law should apply in all states but may require litigation, according to the laws of the individual state.[184]

Be aware, some states have laws which can force children to pay their parents' bills. If your parents are aging, you would be wise to consult an elder care attorney for your own sake, as well as the sake of your parents.

Care Options

Your options are many and, even with a guide, will at times seem overwhelming. All are expensive in one way or another and some can be prohibitively expensive. Here are your options:

- You as the caregiver
- Home caregivers.
- Aid and assistance
- Health care aid (medication delivery, physical therapy, etc.)
- Adult day care
- Group homes (often associated with adult day care)
- Assisted living
- Skilled nursing facility (traditional nursing home)
- Memory care facility
- Veterans' homes
- Continuing care retirement communities (CCRC)
- Hospice and palliative care

In most cases, we begin with option 1. It is our pleasure to care for our loved one. As a spouse, it is simply a loving duty. As a child caring for a parent, it is simply life's full circle. The parent cares for the child, and the child cares for the parent. The cost of this care does not come out of the checkbook. It is much more subtle. If you have a job, it may mean missing work or taking time at work to answer the phone or make calls to solve problems. Even if you are not working, the cost is a negative impact on your own well-being. You are taking time you might spend on your own physical and mental health and devote it to your loved one's physical and mental health. The result, as it was in my case, may be extreme stress both physical and mental, including depression. This option may also be a burden to the dementia patient. Most older people express the desire to live and die in their own homes. As a single person living alone, this may be more of a prison sentence than a comfort. Loneliness is not a comfort. Getting out is often not an option; the dementia patient should not be driving, and it is often difficult to find someone to take the dementia patient out for social activity.

Actually, caring for the home is difficult to impossible for the dementia patient. Living in the home includes utility bills, telephone, Internet, TV cable service, house cleaning, and many more expenses. All these costs must be considered if a move to another level of care is being contemplated.

If your loved one has a long-term care insurance policy, check to see if it will pay for home care provided by a family member or by another home service provider. If so, it may ease the burden to some extent.

You as the caregiver may work well in early stage dementia. As dementia progresses, the task becomes more and more difficult.

Adult Day Care

The next step for Ollie and me was adult day care. He loved it. It gave him a real social outlet. He made friends, and he proudly introduced me to his new friends when I picked him up in the evening. Day care centers open early and stay open until late evening to accommodate working spouses or caregiving sons and daughters. Many offer a full range of services which include an onsite nurse to administer medications and monitor health issues. Many services such as transportation, bathing, toileting, and feeding are also available at an extra charge over the base charge.

Keep in mind, as you traverse this particular minefield of care options, *extra charges* for services rendered beyond a basic level of care are almost always *added to your bill*, and the cost can be substantial.

Genworth Financial has provided a 2019 cost of care survey available at genworth.com.[185] This survey lists the cost of adult day care as $19,500 per year. In our case, the annual cost including the extra care was closer to $30,000 annually.

Shopping for the best care for the lowest cost is always wise, but it is time-consuming. The choices are many and varied. Often communities and religious organizations will offer adult day care services which are less costly than privately owned centers.

Group Homes

Some adult day care centers also operate group homes. This is a niche market in senior care and is generally self-pay (Medicaid is not accepted).

Group homes are large private residences with all the amenities of home. Eight to ten bedrooms with one or more shared baths are available. Cost includes five days a week at the day care facility, all meals and transportation. Twenty-four-hour supervision is provided, and residents are kept busy with activities. Here again, extra costs quickly add up, making this a lovely but expensive option.

Group homes are also available without the day care option.

The Dementia Village

A similar concept to the group home is the dementia village. This is an idea developed ten years ago in the Netherlands by Elroy Jespersen. His idea coincides with my own belief, and that is to remove "the surplus of safety" and embrace the "dignity of risk."[186]

In a sense, this is a private reality for dementia residents only. They live in group homes and can wander the village at will. The village contains vegetable plots, petting zoos, coffee shops, bistros, salons, and community centers. They can wander at will and *find* their *purpose*. They wear tracking bracelets and are well monitored, as well as gently supervised. They cannot leave the confines of the village (about five acres).

British Columbia, Canada, now has a dementia village, but none are available in the United States.

In-Home Assistance

As dementia progresses, they will need more and more assistance. Bathing, dressing, toileting, and fixing simple meals become impossible.

Again, your choices for in-home assistance are many and varied. Begin by asking friends and acquaintances if they know someone who does home care. Beauticians and church secretaries are great sources for information of this sort. You may be able to find someone reliable but less costly than what you will find using an agency. The downside of this approach is that an independent contractor like this does not have backup. If they are sick or experience a family emergency, you will need to find a replacement on short notice.

There are a number of home health care agencies; some operate nationwide as franchises. Visiting Angels® and Bright Star® are two which come to mind. They can usually accommodate any schedule you may need.

My first experience was with Visiting Angels® came about because Ollie was waking me in the middle of the night on a regular and continuing basis. I called for help on Thanksgiving Day, and the owner came to our house to do the initial assessment of needs and paperwork that very evening. The next day, I had someone come to stay with him all night while I got uninterrupted sleep. It was often a different person every night, but someone always showed up. When I had surgery, I used them on a 24-7 basis. Three people would rotate in a week. They are not allowed to give medication but will hand a labeled envelope to the dementia patient containing the pills. This worked for us.

The annual cost for home health care of this type according to the Genworth 2019 survey is $51,480.[187]

Workers in this industry are not highly paid; as a result, we will likely see increasing costs as demand for higher wages increases.

Community and religious groups also provide services in home care. Depending on your zip code, you may be able to find extraordinary services for much less money.

In-home nursing care is also available locally. Services vary but may include wound care, catheter care, ostomy care, diabetic care, delivery of medication, and many other nursing services.

Telemedicine is also available in many instances. Nurses can monitor a patient from a remote location and actually interact with the patient verbally.

Medicare and Medicaid may pay for some of these services.

I do not have an average cost of care for these services but expect to pay more than the cost of home care alone. Compensation for nursing care is considerably higher than compensation for basic home care.

Assisted Living

Assisted living is the step between independent living and a skilled nursing facility. Assisted-living facilities vary greatly one from the other, both in what they do or do not offer and what is expected of the dementia patient.

Dementia patients do not deal with change very well. Change tends to bring about deterioration in their condition. *Goal number one, keep them in the same facility as long as possible.* This is where I made the first mistake in choosing Ollie's care. I did not fully understand how assisted-living facilities were licensed and what that meant in how long he would be able to stay in the facility we chose. The facility was level 2. It had a locked memory care unit to which he was accepted. He was required to be able to make his way out of the building unassisted if the fire alarm was sounded. The staff thought he could do this, I was not so sure, but his room was adjacent to the exit, and they had frequent fire drills. His care was excellent, and there were no additional charges beyond the base memory care fee with room and board.

The unforeseen problem arose when he was hospitalized. He could no longer make his way out of the building unassisted. The hospitalization had caused him to be too weak to walk unassisted. He would never be able to return to this facility. He had been there only six weeks.

Had this been a level 3 facility, he could have been assisted from the building in case of fire. *Be sure to run a worst-case scenario.* Ask questions about what if this happens, what if that happens when you choose a facility so you know what to expect when things go from bad to worse.

Many assisted-living facilities will automatically transfer a dementia patient to a psychiatric hospital if the all-too-common bad behaviors begin to occur. They may or may not allow the patient to return following discharge from the psychiatric hospital.

Be sure to include this in your *worst-case scenarios.*

All too often, assisted-living facilities charge a base room and board fee, and everything else is extra. This can lead to unanticipated very large bills. Be sure you know exactly what is included in the rate you are quoted.

You will find that many skilled nursing facilities offer an assisted-living wing and a memory care lockdown wing. Transition in this case may be a little easier for the dementia patient as they continue to decline. In my experience, this was a more expensive option.

Another important question to ask is if they are Medicare and Medicaid certified. Many times, they will be Medicare certified but will not take Medicaid patients. These facilities are usually privately owned and can pick and choose the patients they will or will not care for. Ollie was rejected by at least two private assisted-living memory care facilities because he would have required more care than other residents of the facility. They can expel a patient if they become a problem. Some facilities will take Medicaid but only after the patient has paid full charges for eighteen months.

The Genworth survey[188] found the average annual cost of care for a private one-bedroom apartment in an assisted-living facility to be $48,612. Memory care is substantially more expensive but was not specifically addressed in the Genworth survey. In my experience, the cost was between $96,000 and $120,000 per year.

Memory care is care specifically geared to dementia patients. Nonetheless, you find dementia patients in all levels of long-term care.

Skilled Nursing Facility (Nursing Home)

When the dementia patient needs care 24/7, the next step is a nursing home or a memory care facility which provides care 24/7 (most do).

Many of these facilities have a waiting list, so it is important to plan ahead. Trying to place a dementia patient urgently is extremely stressful. Among the urgent situations you may encounter are death or illness of the primary caregiver, eviction from an assisted-living facility, or a psychiatric hospital admission with a discharge recommendation of advanced care.

Facilities vary greatly. In some cases, your primary care physician may be able to assume responsibility for the dementia patient's care. In other cases, the facility will have a house physician who will assume this responsibility.

In my experience, the philosophy of the responsible physician makes all the difference in the dementia patient's quality of life. If the attending physician treats depression and agitation with pharmaceuticals, nearly all the patients residing in the facility will be quiet, docile, and missing out on life. If the physician's philosophy is to avoid mind-altering drugs in the dementia patient, the residents will have the occasional dust up with other residents and staff but will appear much happier and more social. I prefer the latter; however, it can be argued that the quiet, docile dementia patient is at peace.

Tour these facilities ahead of time, and find several which are suitable and add your loved one's name to the waiting list. The paperwork you will need to do is substantial. You will need to provide documents for both health care and financial powers of attorney, as well as other documents. A deposit may also be necessary. If you have already done the paperwork and accepted a spot on the waiting list, the need for emergent placement may put you at the top of the list.

The Genworth survey[189] found the national average cost of nursing home care was $90,155 for a semiprivate room or $102,200 for a private room.

Continuing Care Retirement Communities (CCRC)

Another option which may be especially appealing to a couple is a CCRC. These are communities which offer independent living, assisted living, and nursing home care all on one campus.

Independent living offers nice apartments with kitchen and laundry facilities but also offer meals, activities, and all the amenities of a resort.

These communities are of three types: A, B, and C. The A community is really a long-term care contract community. You buy into the community with a fee based on the size of the unit you chose. In my case, selling my house would have qualified me for a one-bedroom apartment with 890 square feet of space. I would have paid an additional monthly fee, which in my case was equivalent to my monthly costs of staying in my home. This fee would have gone up annually based on inflation but would never go above this base fee even if I required skilled nursing care. If I ran out of money through no fault of my own, the facility would find the resources to continue my care. This is basically a life contract and is referred to as such.

For Ollie and me, my thought was that I could live in the independent-living wing while he was in the nursing home wing, putting us close together, allowing me to visit daily. Since Ollie was already in the late stage of dementia, he was not eligible for a life contract; and I would have needed to pay full cost of care, $9000 per month, to keep him in the skilled nursing center.

Had we known about CCRCs early in his illness, we could have both had a good quality of life together in independent living, with less stress on both of us and a smoother transition into higher levels of care for him.

I would urge any couple with one partner facing dementia to investigate a type A CCRC to see if it will improve your quality of life together.

A type B facility generally offers all the same amenities at a lower cost (both buy in and monthly charges) but does not offer life care. It is often structured to help you with costs of care beyond independent living but is more a shared cost situation with no long-standing obligation on the part of the CCRC.

I also visited several type C CCRCs. Three of these were built in the time I was looking for a place where Ollie and I could be together. Typically, there is no buy in fee, but monthly fees tend to be higher for independent living. Meals are extraordinary and abundant. The atmosphere is very resort like. In-home services are available but not included in the monthly charges. Fees for assisted living and skilled nursing are market rate. If you run out of money, you are out on the street. They do not accept Medicaid.

I found this vision disconcerting.

Be aware of the differences in the three types of CCRCs when shopping CCRCs.

You will likely need a medical evaluation before entering a type A or B CCRC. These facilities are underwriting your care, all or in part, and therefore want to know if you have any chronic or costly diseases. Early Parkinson's disease or Alzheimer's patients can still be accepted but with a delay in onset of the life contract. They also will look at all your financial documents so they can be assured that you can actually pay your fees over your projected lifetime.

All three types of CCRCs typically have a waiting list of six months or more. If you are interested in a CCRC, put your name on the waiting list. If you are still not ready to make the move when your name comes up, ask them to put you back on the list. They will then offer the apartment to the next person on the list.

As baby boomers are rapidly becoming seniors and in the market for all of the types of care we have discussed, the marketplace is expanding. More and more businesses are starting up to service this growing market. There are also mergers and acquisitions of existing properties. This may pose a problem with respect to all of the choices we have spoken of above. When properties change hands, rules and eligibility may change. Care may also change as employee turnover (already high in most places) removes familiar faces. Be sure to pay close attention to these types of changes as they occur and explore your options in advance.

Another important thing to look for is financial viability. This is especially important in the case of a type A CCRC. Be sure to take into account how long the CCRC has been in business and any recent or pending mergers and acquisition.

Options for Veterans

In some cases, veterans benefits may pay all or part of senior care. In order of priority, the Veterans Administration (VA) considers service-related disability, disability, and income. These aid and assistance and homebound benefits may also be available to a veteran's spouse. To qualify, both income and assets owned must be meager. For those in need, these benefits are substantial and well deserved.

In addition, a veteran may qualify for long-term care in a VA long-term care facility or in a community facility which contracts with the VA to provide care. In some cases, the veteran may be required to pay a copay up to $3,000 per month.

In addition to VA long-term care facilities, each state has one or more state veterans homes. State veterans homes date back to the Civil War. They were established to provide care to homeless and disabled veterans. They are owned, operated, and managed by state governments. They may be accredited by and operate under the rules of the Federal Department of Veterans Affairs.

It was in one of these veterans homes that Ollie spent his final days.

If your state has more than one veterans home, it is likely that they are located across the state in a way that maximizes accessibility. As was the case with skilled nursing facilities, the veterans homes may look very different depending on the attending physician's philoso-

SUSAN WILSON KRECHEL MD

phy with respect to pharmaceuticals. Even though you may need to drive farther to visit your loved one, look at all your available options.

The admission process is similar to the admission process for a skilled nursing facility but includes the need to produce military discharge papers and proof of any service-related disability, if any. All this needs to be done in advance in order to have your loved one placed on the waiting list. The wait time is often six months to a year.

I chose a veterans home that was about a ninety-minute drive from my home. This made a visit a day trip. This limited my visits to once or twice a week; but with daughters Claudia and Gloria also visiting, Ollie had a visitor three or four times a week. On one occasion, a large group of us drove up to take him out to lunch. He clearly enjoyed this reunion which included four generations. Two months later, he was gone.

The staff at this facility all had the same attitude, and that was it was their pleasure to care for these veterans who had honored our country with their willingness to serve it and if necessary to die for it.

Here, for the first time in our experience, the care was all inclusive. We paid a $2,000 monthly, copay and nothing else. Medicine, Depends®, and even the barber were included.

When his time came, I stayed at his side in a vigil. I was given a room with a pullout bed where I could rest and the kitchen brought food and drink for me and other family members.

A ceremony including the playing of taps was held, as his flag draped body was carried from the veterans home.

If your loved one is a veteran, I strongly recommend that you investigate the veterans homes in your state.

Resources

You do not need to navigate the minefield on your own. There are resources to help you find caregivers or facilities near you. Among these are A Place for Mom® and Caring.com. I used both these resources from time to time. Because Ollie was a veteran, they gave me information on veterans aid, and even connected me with a VA representative.

The service is free. They keep large databases of caregiving organizations and facilities all over the country. They have no firsthand information about these organizations or facilities. They do offer you a place to start your search. If you choose one of their recommendations, they will receive a finder's fee from the agency or facility you have chosen.

If you live in a city like St. Louis, Missouri, which borders another state, in this case, Illinois, the advisors will give you listings in both states. You may find that the facilities in the adjacent state, of which you are not a resident, are closer, nicer, and cheaper than those in the state of your residence. *Beware*—there are issues to be considered such as state taxes, residency requirements if Medicaid is needed at some future time, and possibly other issues.

The local Alzheimer's Association will also provide a list of facilities and services in your area.

Fortunately for me, I found Rob Howe of Assisted Living Locators of St. Louis. As a certified senior advisor (CSA), he had firsthand knowledge of all care facilities in the St. Louis area, adult day care, group homes, assisted living, and skilled nursing care.

After determining our needs and budget, he scheduled appointments at facilities that fit our situation. I made the tours with him and later we took Ollie to visit the facilities on our short list. Rob was gracious and helpful. His services were free to us as clients. He collected a finder's fee from the facility we selected. Rob kept track of us as our journey through dementia continued. I was both grateful and amazed to see him at the funeral home visitation.

Rob is not unique; he is part of a growing industry of people dedicated to helping families find the best services for their loved ones.

The one-on-one navigation services offered are comforting and help reduce the stress associated with senior living placement.

Wherever you live, there is likely to be a professional who can help you. I suggest an Internet search looking for care placement services or senior placement services in your area.

Every community has a local area agency on aging. It is a government-mandated resource acting as a clearing house for information.

They can provide you with valuable information about transport services, meals, day care, legal assistance, caregiver training programs, and much more. In many cases, these community-based services are free or very low cost to seniors. *Make your local area agency on aging one of your first calls for assistance.*

Support groups are everywhere—churches, nursing homes, hospitals, community centers, and other locations. They may address specific groups such as the newly diagnosed or caregivers only. They are all different, finding one that addresses your needs may be difficult. These groups can reaffirm that you are not alone. That, in itself, makes them valuable. The journey through dementia with a loved one can be a very lonely journey.

Another valuable resource is the Alzheimer's Disease Education and Referral Center (ADEAR). They manage a list of government-funded research centers and may be able to help you get referrals for diagnosis and medical treatment, including access to clinical trials.

I cannot overemphasize the value of clinical trials, especially to society as a whole. You never know, one of these days someone's loved one will be the first to be cured.

I have volunteered both myself and Ollie for various clinical trials. Sometimes you will meet the criteria for the study, and sometimes you will not, and as be the case with Ollie, sometimes you die of the disease before the trial is approved and funded.

Blogs, chat rooms, and Facebook® groups are another source of support. An Internet search can help with blogs and chat rooms, and Facebook® groups can be located on Facebook®. Some of these sites are monitored by a sponsor, and some are not. I have no direct experience with any of these, but my stepdaughter found a Facebook® group that was a comfort to her. Unlike groups that meet face-to-face in public places, you can seek solace right at home. *However, I urge caution in revealing things to the unknown and unseen.*

Predators lurk; and as a caregiver, you and your loved one are vulnerable.

Hospice and Palliative Care

Medicare will pay for hospice care for dementia patients, but in order to eligible for hospice, the *dementia* patient must meet very rigorous criteria:

- inability to speak more than six intelligible words in the course of a day or an intensive interview,
- inability to walk without assistance,
- inability to bathe or dress without assistance, and
- incontinent with respect to bladder and bowel.

In addition, one or more of the following medical complications related to dementia must have occurred in the past year:

- pneumonia,
- severe urinary tract infection,
- blood infection,
- skin breakdown as a consequence of being bedridden,
- recurrent fever after antibiotic treatment,
- inability or unwillingness to take food or water, and
- unintentional weight loss in the last six months.

Finally, a physician must suggest hospice care and project the opinion that death will occur within six months.[190] It should also be noted that if the patient is not covered by Medicare, Medicaid, or private insurance may also pay for hospice services.

Hospice care is mind, body, and spirit care for both the dementia patient and the family

Hospice care can be delivered in the home, a skilled nursing facility, or in some cases, a special hospice facility. They provide all medications and all equipment needed for comfort.

Hospice can also provide respite care by arranging temporary nursing home care if the patient is still residing at home and the primary caregiver is sick or dealing with another crisis.

If a medical crisis occurs, hospice nurses can provide eight to twelve hours of in-home care to deal with a symptom crisis. The goal being to prevent another hospitalization. If a hospitalization does occur, hospice will continue supporting both patient and family in a loving caring way.

My own personal experience with hospice began almost a year before Ollie's death. Our physician suggested that I should consider hospice. My first call was to a local hospice care group recommended by a friend. The person I spoke with was not very comforting, in fact rude and abrupt. She began by outlining the criteria we just covered and ended by telling me they were too busy anyway.

At this time, Ollie did not meet the criteria for hospice care, so I thought nothing more of it until the next spring when I met Margaret Terranova, RN, at a medical meeting on the topic of dementia. I was there gathering new material for this book, and she was there staying up to date. We chatted, and I learned that she was affiliated with Heartland® Hospice Care. When I told her of my struggles in caring for Ollie, she encouraged me to look at hospice again. She explained what the hospice experience means to both patient and family. I arranged to meet with Margaret to interview her for this book. Much of what I say about hospice has come out of that interview. A week before the interview, Ollie began a very steep decline in awareness and mobility. He fell and for the first time expressed pain. When anyone tried to help him, he would say, "Don't do that to me." His shoulder was injured, although a bedside X-ray showed no obvious abnormality. Both the social worker at the veterans home and Ollie's daughter recommended Heartland® Hospice Care. Having met Margaret previously, it was an easy choice. My journey with hospice care began with Heartland®. They quickly came to assess Ollie and communicated with me after every visit. They kept him comfortable and pain-free.

As Margaret would tell me later, the body is as efficient at dying as it is at living. Death is a normal process and follows a sequence which may vary from person to person but often has a common thread. It was comforting for me to learn this process. No, it was not taught in medical school, nor did I learn it in medical practice. My job was to prevent death, and I did so efficiently many times.

Ollie had already begun the dying process by the time I called hospice. He had begun to *withdraw*. He showed little interest in food or anything around him, including me. Had I understood this at the time, I would not have been hurt. Please understand when your loved one begins to withdraw, it is part of the normal process. Some will be *disoriented* with one foot in this world and one in the next. They may well speak to others who have already died. In a way, this is both comforting and reaffirming.

Physical changes occur. Blood pressure is lower, and heart rate may be very slow or very fast. Temperature fluctuates; body temperature may be high enough to constitute a fever or much lower than normal. The skin may be clammy and is often bluish in color. Breathing changes from regular to irregular. Rapid shallow breaths may be followed by periods of no breaths at all, followed again by rapid shallow breathing.

Death is a normal process and will come in its own way in its own time.

The hospice nurse is there to not only keep the dying patient comfortable but to also comfort the living. *Ask questions* about the process and anything else you do not understand.

The dying, like the living, can be comforted. The dementia patient has regressed to infancy. Just like cuddling a baby comforts, so does cuddling. Comfort the dying dementia patient. Hearing remains until late in the dying process, and words of comfort and soothing sounds will help.

No one wants to die in pain. Giving pain relief is not given to help them die; it is given to make them comfortable as they die a natural death. *This is comfort.*

Death does not need to be awful; it should be comfortable, and it is normal.

Until the moment of death, *the mind, body, and spirit are there to be comforted.* Hospice will help the family learn how to make this connection with their loved one.

This is death with dignity.

SUSAN WILSON KRECHEL MD

There are several other points about hospice care that I would like to share with you even though they are not necessarily applicable to the dementia patient.

Most people wish they had started hospice sooner. Getting information about hospice is not a commitment; it simply allows you to understand your options. Hospice is not depressing; it is rich, fulfilling, and a blessing. In some cases, hospice can help you finish your bucket list. (Some hospice companies like Heartland® operate a 501(C)(3) nonprofit fund which is used to assist patients and families.) Hospice can help the patient become reassured that the family they are leaving behind will be okay. (Concern for those they are leaving behind weighs heavily on the dying). Hospice determines your own personal vision of dying in peace and tries to make that happen for you. Finally, hospice is there for those left behind. They will check in with you regularly for thirteen months. Grief counselling is offered; *they are there for you.*

While the dementia patient must be close to death before they actually qualify for hospice care, they can qualify at any time for palliative care. Palliative care is another layer of care provided by a team of physicians, nurses, social workers, counselors, and spiritual advisors. Like hospice care, it addresses psychological, social, and spiritual distress that accompanies many illnesses. It addresses the issue of *quality of life* while relieving suffering.

Palliative care offers patients with terminal or incurable illnesses support in making the hard choices about how they wish to deal with their disease. In the case of dementia patients, the sooner they are enrolled in palliative care, the better. This is also true of most serious neurological diseases such as Parkinson's disease and multiple sclerosis. Unlike hospice care, palliative care allows for aggressive treatment to continue and enrollment in research studies is also permitted. Palliative care does not have a separate funding stream through Medicare like hospice care enjoys. It is, however, usually covered on a fee for service basis through Medicare, Medicaid, and private insurance.

238

Ollie and I did not avail ourselves of palliative care, but we should have done so. I believe that it would have relieved a great deal of the stress we both experienced.

Do investigate palliative care for your loved one.

Grief

As I write this section, Ollie has been gone for nearly seven months. I am still grieving.

Everyone grieves in their own way.

Losing a loved one to dementia is to lose them one brain cell at a time. To some extent, this prolongs your grief. It also puts you in a better position to cope with life after they are gone. As Ollie's ability to contribute to our life together disappeared, I slowly assumed all those tasks, he typically performed. I was now head of household and responsible for home maintenance decisions, repairs, landscaping, and many more tasks that he had assumed responsibility for during our marriage partnership. I was spared the shock of needing to figure all this out when he died. I had already learned to stand alone. I was a stronger person.

My grieving began when Ollie had the small stroke, and I was told it was not the first, just the first to display symptoms. As a physician, I knew the prognosis and how the disease would be likely to progress. My role was now supportive, and in spite of grieving my loss, I also treasured every happy, loving moment we still had.

Grief is not something you should go through alone; we need other people to help us recover and those other people cannot be those who are dealing with their own grief. While my step children tried to be supportive, they were dealing with the loss of their father, both before and at the time of his death. There are many sources of support, grief counselors, community grief support groups, church grief support groups, and of course, hospice. There are also many books written on the subject and as many theories regarding stages of grief and advice on how to get through the process.

I read the *Grief Survival Guide* by Jeff Brazier,[191] and much of what follows concerning grief, I learned from this book.

Some very powerful emotions occur with grief. These include the following:

- denial
- guilt
- loneliness
- resentment and or anger
- shock and or numbness

In spite of the fact that I knew very well how our journey through dementia would end, I still felt shock and numbness. I attribute my trip to the emergency room with a 103-degree temperature and diagnosis of pneumonia the day after Ollie's death as a form of shock. The next two months were pretty much a blur. I was existing and not much more. Work on this book was halted.

Grief has been described as an upward spiral. I believe this is a good description. You hit bottom and then begin to rise. At the top of the spiral is acceptance and moving on.

Guilt is a very common emotion associated with grief. If only I had done this and not that.

Guilt serves no effective purpose. Especially in the case of dementia, nothing is going to change the course of the disease.

Grief, in a way, allows us to rise from the ashes. It can be a great motivator for change.

You need never forget your loved one. They would want only the best for you.

What better way to honor a loved one than to *move on and be happy?*

ENDNOTES

1   Cole, Laurence A., and Peter R. Kramer. *Human Physiology, Biochemistry and Basic Medicine.* Amsterdam: Elsevier, 2016.

2   https://en.wikipedia.org/wiki/Army_Specialized_Training_Program

3   NYWF64.COM

4   Peterson, Jordan B., Ethan Van Sciver, and Norman Doidge. *12 Rules for Life: an Antidote to Chaos.* Toronto: Random House Canada, 2018.

5   Lavey, K. "What's the Future for Great Lakes Salmon." *Lansing State Journal,* May 26, 2016.

6   Krechel, Susan W., and Judy Bildner. "CRIES: a New Neonatal Postoperative Pain Measurement Score. Initial Testing of Validity and Reliability." *Pediatric Anesthesia* 5, no. 1 (1995): 53–61. https://doi.org/10.1111/j.1460-9592.1995.tb00242.x.

7   Sparano, Joseph A., Robert J. Gray, Della F. Makower, Kathleen I. Pritchard, Kathy S. Albain, Daniel F. Hayes, Charles E. Geyer, et al. "Adjuvant Chemotherapy Guided by a 21-Gene Expression Assay in Breast Cancer." *New England Journal of Medicine* 379, no. 2 (December 2018): 111–21. https://doi.org/10.1056/nejmoa1804710.

8   Editors of Encyclopaedia Britannica, (2011) Yangtze River Floods, Encyclopaedia Britannica URL https://www.Britannica.com/Science/Yangtze River Floods

9   https://en.wikipedia.org/wiki/Petra

10   The Editors of Encyclopaedia Britannica. "Masada." Encyclopædia Britannica. Encyclopædia Britannica, inc., October 23, 2019. https://www.Britannica.com/place/Masada.

11   Peterson, Jordan B., Ethan Van Sciver, and Norman Doidge. *12 Rules for Life: an Antidote to Chaos.* Toronto: Random House Canada, 2018.

12   Peterson, Jordan B., Ethan Van Sciver, and Norman Doidge. *12 Rules for Life: an Antidote to Chaos.* Toronto: Random House Canada, 2018.

13   "2010 Alzheimers Disease Facts and Figures." *Alzheimers & Dementia* 6, no. 2 (2010): 158–94. https://doi.org/10.1016/j.jalz.2010.01.009.

14   "2010 Alzheimers Disease Facts and Figures." *Alzheimers & Dementia* 6, no. 2 (2010): 158–94. https://doi.org/10.1016/j.jalz.2010.01.009.

15   Hurd, MD, Martorell, P et al NEJM (2013) 368:1326-1334

16 "National Alzheimers Project Act." ASPE, April 10, 2020. http://napa.alz.org/national-alzheimers-project-act-background.

17 "2010 Alzheimers Disease Facts and Figures." *Alzheimers & Dementia* 6, no. 2 (2010): 158–94. https://doi.org/10.1016/j.jalz.2010.01.009.

18 Alzheimer's Disease International. (n.d.) World Alzheimer's Report (2015): The global impact of dementia. (http://www.co.uk/research/world-report-2015)

19 Taylor, Jill Bolte. *My Stroke of Insight a Brain Scientists Personal Journey*. London: Hodder & Stoughton Ltd, 2008.

20 Gorelick, Philip B., Angelo Scuteri, Sandra E. Black, Charles Decarli, Steven M. Greenberg, Costantino Iadecola, Lenore J. Launer, et al. "Vascular Contributions to Cognitive Impairment and Dementia." *Stroke* 42, no. 9 (2011): 2672–2713. https://doi.org/10.1161/str.0b013e3182299496.

21 Kang, Ju-Hee, Magdalena Korecka, Jon B Toledo, John Q Trojanowski, and Leslie M Shaw. "Clinical Utility and Analytical Challenges in Measurement of Cerebrospinal Fluid Amyloid-β1–42 and τ Proteins as Alzheimer Disease Biomarkers." *Clinical Chemistry* 59, no. 6 (January 2013): 903–16. https://doi.org/10.1373/clinchem.2013.202937.

22 "Stroke Prevention Best Path to Dementia Reduction, Experts Say." Medscape, July 23, 2019. https://www.medscape.com/viewarticle/915916.

23 Taylor, Jill Bolte. *My Stroke of Insight a Brain Scientists Personal Journey*. London: Hodder & Stoughton Ltd, 2008.

24 "Stroke Prevention Best Path to Dementia Reduction, Experts Say." Medscape, July 23, 2019. https://www.medscape.com/viewarticle/915916.

25 "Statins Overlooked for Secondary Stroke Prevention." Accessed April 20, 2020. https://www.medscape.com/viewarticle/883933.

26 "Heart Meds May Prevent Vascular Dementia After Stroke." Accessed April 20, 2020. https://www.medscape.com/viewarticle/912635.

27 "Home." Onward Healthcare. Accessed April 20, 2020. https://medicalexpress.com/news2019-01-drug-alzheimer-disease.html.

28 "Stroke Prevention Best Path to Dementia Reduction, Experts Say." Medscape, July 23, 2019. https://www.medscape.com/viewarticle/915916.

29 "MIND Diet May Slow Cognitive Decline in Stroke Survivors." Accessed April 20, 2020. https://www.medscape.com/viewarticle/891957.

30 Morris, Martha Clare, Christy C. Tangney, Yamin Wang, Frank M. Sacks, Lisa L. Barnes, David A. Bennett, and Neelum T. Aggarwal. "MIND Diet Slows Cognitive Decline with Aging." *Alzheimers & Dementia* 11, no. 9 (2015): 1015–22. https://doi.org/10.1016/j.jalz.2015.04.011.

31 Coronado, Victor G., Lisa C. Mcguire, Kelly Sarmiento, Jeneita Bell, Michael R. Lionbarger, Christopher D. Jones, Andrew I. Geller, Nayla Khoury, and Likang Xu. "Corrigendum to 'Trends in Traumatic Brain Injury in the U.S. and the Public Health Response: 1995–2009 ☆' [J. Saf. Res. 43 (2012) 299-307]." *Journal of Safety Research* 48 (2014): 117. https://doi.org/10.1016/j.jsr.2013.12.006.

[32] "Mild TBI Doubles Dementia Risk, Even Without LOC." Medscape, September 27, 2018. https://www.medscape.com/viewarticle/902589.

[33] Department of Defense Coding Guidance for Traumatic Brain Injury Fact Sheet http://www.dcoe.health.mil/ForHealthPros/Resources.aspx

[34] Johnson, Victoria E., Janice E. Stewart, Finn D. Begbie, John Q. Trojanowski, Douglas H. Smith, and William Stewart. "Inflammation and White Matter Degeneration Persist for Years after a Single Traumatic Brain Injury." *Brain* 136, no. 1 (2013): 28–42. https://doi.org/10.1093/brain/aws322.

[35] https://link.springer.com/article/10.1007%2Fs11916-015-0522-z

[36] Baugh, Christine M., Clifford A. Robbins, Robert A. Stern, and Ann C. Mckee. "Current Understanding of Chronic Traumatic Encephalopathy." *Current Treatment Options in Neurology* 16, no. 9 (2014). https://doi.org/10.1007/s11940-014-0306-5.

[37] "Statins May Cut Postconcussion Dementia Risk." Accessed April 20, 2020. https://www.medscape.com/viewarticle/913830.

[38] Kordower, Jeffrey H, Yaping Chu, Robert A Hauser, Thomas B Freeman, and C Warren Olanow. "Lewy Body-like Pathology in Long-Term Embryonic Nigral Transplants in Parkinsons Disease." *Nature Medicine* 14, no. 5 (June 2008): 504–6. https://doi.org/10.1038/nm1747.

[39] Reyes, Juan F., Christopher Sackmann, Alana Hoffmann, Per Svenningsson, Jürgen Winkler, Martin Ingelsson, and Martin Hallbeck. "Binding of α-Synuclein Oligomers to Cx32 Facilitates Protein Uptake and Transfer in Neurons and Oligodendrocytes." *Acta Neuropathologica* 138, no. 1 (November 2019): 23–47. https://doi.org/10.1007/s00401-019-02007-x.

[40] Katz, M Parkinson's Disease Audio Digest 66, (13) 2019.

[41] Grosset, D, L Taurah, D J Burn, D Macmahon, A Forbes, K Turner, A Bowron, et al. "A Multicentre Longitudinal Observational Study of Changes in Self Reported Health Status in People with Parkinsons Disease Left Untreated at Diagnosis." *Journal of Neurology, Neurosurgery & Psychiatry* 78, no. 5 (2006): 465–69. https://doi.org/10.1136/jnnp.2006.098327.

[42] Pfeiffer, Ronald F. "Gastrointestinal Dysfunction in Parkinson's Disease." *Current Treatment Options in Neurology* 20, no. 12 (2018). https://doi.org/10.1007/s11940-018-0539-9.

[43] Pfeiffer, Ronald F. "Gastrointestinal Dysfunction in Parkinson's Disease." *Current Treatment Options in Neurology* 20, no. 12 (2018). https://doi.org/10.1007/s11940-018-0539-9.

[44] Katz, M Parkinson's Disease Audio Digest 66, (13) 2019.

[45] Katz, M Parkinson's Disease Audio Digest 66, (13) 2019.

[46] Hauser, Robert A., Stuart H. Isaacson, Aaron Ellenbogen, Beth E. Safirstein, Daniel D. Truong, Steven F. Komjathy, Deena M. Kegler-Ebo, Ping Zhao, and Charles Oh. "Orally Inhaled Levodopa (CVT-301) for Early Morning OFF Periods in Parkinsons Disease." *Parkinsonism & Related Disorders* 64 (2019): 175–80. https://doi.org/10.1016/j.parkreldis.2019.03.026.

[47] Katz, M Parkinson's Disease Audio Digest 66, (13) 2019.

[48] https://medicalxpress.com/news/2017-12-laser=parkinson-patients.html

[49] Abeyesekera, Anita, Scott Adams, Cynthia Mancinelli, Thea Knowles, Greydon Gilmore, Mehdi Delrobaei, and Mandar Jog. "Effects of Deep Brain Stimulation of the Subthalamic Nucleus Settings on Voice Quality, Intensity, and Prosody in Parkinson's Disease: Preliminary Evidence for Speech Optimization." *Canadian Journal of Neurological Sciences / Journal Canadien Des Sciences Neurologiques* 46, no. 3 (2019): 287–94. https://doi.org/10.1017/cjn.2019.16.

[50] Pagan F, et al Nilotinib Effects in Parkinson's Disease and Dementia with Lewy bodies J Parkinsons Dis (2016) Jul 11; 6(3):503-17

[51] https://www.news-medical.net/news/20190313/Study-unravels-how-cancer-medication-works-in-brains-of-Parkinsonsons-patients.aspx

[52] https://www.medicalnewstoday.com/articles/318257.php

[53] Monti DA N-acetyl Cysteine is Associated With Dopaminergic Improvement in Parkinson's Disease Clin Pharmacol Ther (2019) Jun 17. Doi: 10.1002/cpt. 1548

[54] Whone AL et al Extended Treatment with Glial Cell Line-Derived Neurotrophic Factor in Parkinson's Disease Journal of Parkinson's Disease 9 (2019) 301-313.

[55] Bekris LM et al The Genetics of Parkinson's Disease J Geriatr Psychiatry Neurol. (2010) December;23(4):228-242

[56] Wirdefeldt K et al Epidemiology and etiology of Parkinson's disease: review of the evidence European Journal of Epidemiology (2011(, 26:1

[57] Parkinson's May Spread From Gut to Brain via Vagus Nerve-Medscape-Aug 06, 2015

[58] Peter, I et al Anti-Tumor Necrosis Factor Therapy and Incidence of Parkinson Disease Among Patients With Inflammatory Bowel Disease JAMA Neurol. (2018);75(8):939-946

[59] Tetz, G et al Parkinson's disease and bacteriophages as its overlooked contributors Scientific Reports (2018) 8:10812g

[60] De Pablo-Fernandez E et at Association between diabetes and subsequent Parkinson disease A record-linkage cohort study Neurology July 10, 2018;91 (2)

[61] Gregory M, et al. An Association between bipolar disorder and Parkinson disease. Neurology May 2019; DOI:10.1212/WNL.

[62] Kovacs G.G. et al Mixed Brain Pathologies in Dementia: The BrainNet Europe Consortium Experience Dement Geriatr Cogn Disord (2008);26:343-350

[63] http://www/alz.org/dementia/parkinsons-disease-symptoms.asp

[64] Mukaetova-Ladinska E.B. et al Cerebrospinal Fluid Biomarkers for Dementia with Lewy Bodies International Journal of Alzheimer's Disease (2010) Article ID 536538. 17 pages

[65] Guerreiro R et al Investigating the genetic architecture of dementia with Lewy bodies: a two-stage genome-wide association study Lancet Neurol (2018) 17(1):64-74

66 Maust DT et al Antipsychotics, Other Psychotropics, and the Risk of Death in Patients with Dementia Number needed to Harm JAMA Psychiatry (2015):72(5):438-445

67 Reus VI et al The American Psychiatric Association Practice Guideline on the Use of Antipsychotics to Treat Agitation or Psychosis in Patients with Dementia https://doi.org/10.1176/appi.ajp.2015.173501

68 Lakhan SE et al Alzheimer Disease. http://emedicine.medscape.com/article/113 4817-print

69 Sahyouni R et al Alzheimer's Disease Decoded (2017) World Scientific Publishing Co. Pte. Ltd.

70 Snowdon D Aging with Grace, what the Nun Study teaches us about leading longer, healthier and more meaningful lives (2001) Bantam Books.

71 Morris M et al The Many Faces of Tau (2011) Neuron. 70(3):410-426.

72 Triple Threat: Alzheimer's Biomarkers Occur in Sequence-Medscape-Feb 06, 2018

73 Sahyouni R et al Alzheimer's Disease Decoded (2017) World Scientific Publishing Co. Pte. Ltd.

74 Albin RL, Highlights from Dementia: What Now? AudioDigest Internal Medicine (2019) vol. 66 issue 15.

75 Alzheimer's Disease Clinical Practice Guidelines (2018)-Medscape-Aug 09, 2018.

76 Yoon SP et al, Retinal Microvascular and Neurodegenerative Changes in Alzheimer's Disease and Mild Cognitive Impairment Compared with Control Participants, Ophthalmology Retina (2019): 3 (6) 489-499.

77 Dilraj S et al. Assessment of Differences in Retinal Microvasculature Using OCT Angiography in Alzheimer's Disease: A twin Discordance Report Ophthalmic Surg Lasers Imaging Retina. (2018); 49:440-444.

78 Schindler SE et al. High Precision Plasma amyloid—beta 42/40 predicts current and future brain amyloidosis. Neurology. August 1, 2019.DOI:10.121/WNL.0000000000008081

79 https://www.news-medical.net/news/20190508/Fatty-molecules-which-induce-sleep-may-help-with-diagnosing-alzheimers.aspx

80 Preische O et al. Serum neurofilament dynamics predicts neurodegeneration and clinical progression in presymptomatic Alzheimer's disease Nature Medicine 25,277-283 (2019)

81 https:www.news-medical.net/news/20190423/Study-provides-evidence-that-blood-tests-can-detect-Alzheimers28099s-risk.aspx

82 Schindler SE et al. High Precision Plasma amyloid—beta 42/40 predicts current and future brain amyloidosis. Neurology. August 1, 2019.DOI:10.121/WNL.0000000000008081

83 Preische O et al. Serum neurofilament dynamics predicts neurodegeneration and clinical progression in presymptomatic Alzheimer's disease Nature Medicine 25,277-283 (2019)

84 https:www.news-medical.net/news/20190423/Study-provides-evidence-that-blood-tests-can-detect-Alzheimers28099s-risk.aspx

85 http://www.nia.nih.gov/health/alzheimers-disease-genetics-fact-sheet

86 Sahyouni R et al Alzheimer's Disease Decoded (2017) World Scientific Publishing Co. Pte. Ltd.

87 http://www.nia.nih.gov/health/alzheimers-disease-genetics-fact-sheet

88 Atsushi A et al ABeta and tau prion-like activities decline with longevity in the Alzheimer's disease human brain Science Translational Medicine (2019) 11 (490).

89 More Evidence Herpes Virus Strongly tied to Alzheimer's-Medscape-Oct 19, 2018.

90 More Evidence Herpes Virus Strongly tied to Alzheimer's-Medscape-Oct 19, 2018.

91 Infectious Theory of Alzheimer Disease Draws Fresh Interest-Medscape-Nov 14, 2018.

92 Lollis SS, et al Cause-specific mortality among neurosurgeons. J Neurosurg (2010);113:474-478.

93 Vitaliano PP An Ironic Tragedy: Are Spouses of Persons with Dementia at Higher Risk for Dementia than Spouses of Persons without Dementia? J Am Geriatri Soc. (2010) 58(5);976-978

94 Dominy SS, et al Porphyromonas gingivalis in Alzheimer's disease brains: Evidence for disease causation and treatment with small-molecule inhibitors Sci. Adv. (2019);5:eaau3333

95 https://www.medscape.com/viewarticle/841748

96 Echouffo-Tcheugui JB et al Circulating cortisol and cognitive and structural brain measures in the Framingham Heart Study Neurology (2018);91 (21)

97 Munro C et al Stressful life events and cognitive decline: Sex differences in the Baltimore Epidemiologic Catchment Area Follow-Up Study International Journal of Geriatric Psychiatry (2019). DOI: 10.1002/gps.5102

98 Killin LOJ et al Environmental risk factor for dementia: a systematic review BMC Geriatrics (2016) 16: 175

99 Calderon-Garciduenas et al Air pollution linked with development of Alzheimer's in Mexico City children J Alzheimers Dis (2018) 66; 1437-1451

100 https://www.news-medical net/news/20190322/Exploring-pathophysiologic-factors-link-sleep-problems-and-Alzheimers-disease aspx

101 Acute Sleep Loss Increases Blood Levels of Alzheimer's Biomarker-Medscape-July 11, 2019

102 Poor Quality Sleep Tied to Early Signs of Alzheimer's-Medscape-Jan 14, 2019

103 Richardson K et al Anticholinergic drugs and risk of dementia: case-control study BMJ (2018)361:k1315/doi:10.1136/bmj.l1315

104 Coupland C et al Anticholinergic Drug Exposure and the Risk of Dementia A Nested Case-Control Study JAMA Internal Medicine (2019);179 (8):1084-1093.

[105] Tyas, SL Alcohol Use and the Risk of Developing Alzheimer's Disease Alcohol Research & Health (2002);25(4) 299-306.

[106] Tyas, SL Alcohol Use and the Risk of Developing Alzheimer's Disease Alcohol Research & Health (2002);25(4) 299-306.

[107] Neafsey EJ et al Moderate alcohol consumption and cognitive risk Neuropsychiatric Disease and Treatment (2011):7 465-484.

[108] Caroline Cassels. Central Obesity in Midlife an Independent Risk Factor for Dementia-Medscape-Mar 27, 2008

[109] Obesity Tied to Brain Volume Loss-Medscape-Nov 21,2014

[110] Overweight, Obesity in "Early Old Age" Tied to Cortical Thinning-Medscape-Jul 24, 2019

[111] Arnold SE et al Brain insulin resistance in type 2 diabetes and Alzheimer disease: concepts and conundrums Nature Reviews Neurology (2018) 14, 169-181.

[112] https://www.news-medical.net/news/20190521/Researcher-explore-link-between-aging-fat-cells-and-Alzheimers.aspx

[113] Hospitalizations, Critical Illness Linked to Dementia-Related Brain Changes-Medscape-Oct 24, 2018.

[114] Rocca WA et al Sex and gender differences in the causes of dementia: a narrative review (2014) 79(2):196-201

[115] Yue X et al Brain estrogen deficiency accelerated A-beta plaque formation in an Alzheimer's disease animal model (2005)PNAS 102(52) 19198-19203

[116] Rocca WA et al Oophorectomy, estrogen and dementia: A 2014 update (2014) Mol Cell Endocrinol,;389(0):7-12

[117] Pike CJ et al Protective actions of sex steroid hormones in Alzheimer's disease (2009) Front Neuroendocrinol; 30(2):239-258

[118] Savolainen-Peitonen H et al Use of postmenopausal hormone therapy and risk of Alzheimer's disease in Finland: nationwide case-control study (2019) BMJ;364:1665

[119] Steenland K A Meta-Analysis of Alzheimer's Disease Incidence and Prevalence Comparing African Americans and Caucasians (2016) Journal of Alzheimer's Disease 50(1):71-76

[120] Morris JC et al Assessment of Racial Disparities in Biomarkers for Alzheimer Disease JAMA Neurology (2019);76(3):264-273

[121] Clouston S et al Education and Cognitive Decline: An Integrative Analysis of Global Longitudinal Studies of Cognitive Aging The Journals of Gerontology Series B, gbz053, (2019) https://doi.org/10.1093/geronb/gbz053

[122] Craik F et al Delaying the onset of Alzheimer disease: bilingualism as a form of cognitive reserve Neurology, (2010);75(19)1726-9

[123] Snowdon D Aging with Grace, what the Nun Study teaches us about leading longer, healthier and more meaningful lives (2001) Bantam Books.

[124] Risk reduction of cognitive decline and dementia: WHO guidelines, Geneva; World Health Organization 2019

[125] Takashi M et al Combined treatment with the phenolics (_-)-epigallocate-chin-3 gallate and ferulic acid improves cognition and reduces Alzheimer-like pathology in mice Journal of Biological Chemistry (2019) 294:2714-2731

[126] Boosting Brain Ketone Metabolism: A New Approach to Alzheimer's-Medscape-Aug 03, 2017

[127] Keto-Like Diet May Improve Cognition in MCI, Early Alzheimer's-Medscape-Jul 03, 2019

[128] Faraco G et al Dietary salt promotes neurovascular and cognitive dysfunction through a gut-initiated TH17 response (2018) Nature Neuroscience 21, 240-249

[129] The Sprint Mind Investigators for the Sprint Research Group Effect of Intensive vs Standard Blood Pressure Control on Probable Dementia A Randomized Clinical Trial JAMA (2019) 321(6):553-561

[130] Does an ARB a day Keep Dementia at Bay?-Medscape-Jul 26, 2019

[131] Hermida RC et al Bedtime hypertension treatment improves cardiovascular risk reduction:the Hygia Chronotherapy Trial (2019) European Heart Journal. doi:10.1093/euroheart/ehz754

[132] FDA Cracks Down on Illegal Sale of Alzheimer's "Cures"-Medscape-Feb 11, 2019

[133] Antidepressants Lack Effectiveness for Depression in Dementia-Medscape-Sep 07,2018.

[134] Alzheimer's drug Plus SSRI May Cut Depression, Improve Cognition.-Medscape-Mar 06, 2019

[135] Galve-Roperh I et al The Endocannabinoid System and Neurogenesis in Health and Disease Neuroscientist (2007) 13(2):109-114

[136] Eubanks LM et al A Molecular Link Between the Active Component of Marijuana and Alzheimer's Disease Pathology Mol Pharm, (2006);3(6): 773-777.

[137] Medical Cannabis Safe, Effective for Neurologic Symptoms in the Elderly-Medscape-May 06, 2019

[138] California "Holy Herb" a Potential Treatment for Alzheimer's?—Medscape-Feb 25, 2019.

[139] Chou MH et al DMARD use is associate with a higher risk of dementia in patients with rheumatoid arthritis: A propensity score-matched case-control study Toxicology and Applied Pharmacology (2017) 334; 217-222.

[140] Judge A et al Protective effect of antirheumatic drugs on dementia in rheumatoid arthritis patients Alzheimer's &Dementia: Translational Research & Clinical Interventions (2017) 3: 612-621.

[141] Meyer PF et al INTRAPAD A randomized trial of naproxen to slow progress of presymptomatic Alzheimer disease Neurology (2019); 92:e2070-e2080

[142] Alzheimer's Disease and Amyloid: Time to move on?-Medscape-Jan 19, 2017

[143] Sigurdsson EM Tau Immunotherapy Neurodegener Dis. (2016): 16(0): 34-38

ENDNOTES

[144] Castillo-Carranza DL et al Tau Immunotherapy Modulates Both Pathological Tau and Upstream Amyloid Pathology in Alzheimer's Disease Mouse Model The Journal of Neuroscience, (2015); 35(12): 4857-4868.

[145] Alzheimer's Disease and Amyloid: Time to move on?-Medscape-Jan 19, 2017

[146] https://www.medicalnewstoday.com/articles/318138.php

[147] Forlenza OV et al Disease modifying properties of long-term lithium treatment for amnestic mild cognitive impairment:randomized control trial (2011) Br J Psychiatry 198(5):351-6

[148] Cortes-Cantreli M et al Long-Term Dabigatran Treatment Delays Alzheimer's Disease Pathogenesis in the TgCRND8 Mouse Model Journal of the American College of Cardiology (2019) 74(15): 1910-1923

[149] Morris JK et al Insulin: an Emerging Treatment for Alzheimer's Disease Dementia? Curr Neurol Neurosci Rep (2012);12(5):520-527

[150] Striking Benefit of Intranasal Insulin in Slowing Dementia—Medscape-July 19, 2019.

[151] Jin JC et al Chemical Conversion of Human Fetal Astrocytes into Neurons through Modulation of Multiple Signaling Pathways Stem Cell Reports (2019) 12: 488-501.

[152] Fu W et al Characteristics and Scope of training of Clinicians Participating in the US Direct-to-Consumer Marketplace for Unproven Stem Cell Interventions JAMA (2019);321(24):2463-2464

[153] Yoshida M et al Extracellular Vesicle-Contained eNAMPT Delays Aging and Extends lifespan in Mice; Cell Metabolism (2019)

[154] "Young Blood" Clinics Shut Down after FDA Action-Medscape-Feb,20 2019.

[155] Lorida I et al Association of Lifestyle and Genetic Risk With Incidence of Dementia JAMA (2019):322(5):430-437

[156] https://www.ualberta.ca/science/science-news/2019/april/healthy-memory-preventing-alzheimers.

[157] Morbidity and Mortality Weekly Report.2018;67(37):1036-1039 © 2018 Centers for Disease Control and Prevention (CDC)

[158] Richard S Isaacson. Can Tight Blood Pressure Control Prevent Dementia?—Medscape-Oct 29,2018

[159] Prevent Stroke to Prevent Dementia?-Medscape-Oct 31,2019

[160] Sommerlad A et al Association of social contact with dementia and cognition: 28-year follow-up of the Whitehall II cohort study (2019) https://dol.org/10.1371/journal.pmed.1002862

[161] Krell-Roesch J et al Quantity and quality of mental activities and the risk of incident mild cognitive impairment Neurology®(2019);93:e548-e558.doi:10,1212

[162] Mayer S Regular exercise reduces risk of dementia and Alzheimer's disease BMJ, (2006);332(7534);137.

[163] Lourenco MV et al Exercise-linked FNDC5/Irisin rescues synaptic plasticity and memory defects in Alzheimer's models, Nature Medicine (2018).doi:10.1038/s41591-018-0275-4

164 Damian McNamara, Six Months of Aerobic Exercise Cuts MCI Risk-Medscape-Dec 20, 2018.

165 Sommerlad A et al Association of social contact with dementia and cognition: 28-year follow-up of the Whitehall II cohort study (2019) https://dol.org/10.1371/journal.pmed.1002862

166 Pomegranate Juice May Slow Age-Related Decline-Medscape-Mar 05, 2019

167 Mushrooms May Cut Cognitive Impairment Risk-Medscape-Mar 20, 2019

168 Ali YO et al Screening with an NMNAT2-MSD platform identifies small molecules that modulate NMNAT2 levels in cortical neurons Scientific Reports (2017); 7:43846

169 Choi D et al Effect of smoking cessation on the risk of dementia: a longitudinal study Annals of Clinical and Translational Neurology (2018) 5(10) 1-22

170 Hui Liu et al Marital Status and Dementia: Evidence from the Health and Retirement Study, The Journals of Gerontology. Series B gbz087, https://doi.org/10.1093/geronb/gbz087

171 Stowell RD et al Noradrenergic signaling in te wakeful state inhibits microglial surveillance and synaptic plasticity in the mouse visual cortex Nature Neuroscience (2019):doi:10.1038/s41593-019-0514-0

172 https://labblog.uofmhealth.org/rounds/hearing-aids-linked-to-lower-risk-of-dementia-depression-and-falls-study-finds (2019)

173 Cataract Surgery, Hearing Aids may Curb Cognitive Decline-Medscape-Oct 30, 2018.

174 Cataract Surgery, Hearing Aids may Curb Cognitive Decline-Medscape-Oct 30, 2018.

175 UB-311 Alzheimer's News Today https://alzheimersnewstoday.com/ub-311-vaccine-alzheimers-beta-amyloid-protein/

176 Davtyan H et al Alzheimer's disease Advax CpG—adjuvanted MultiTEP-based dual and single vaccine induce high-titer antibodies against various forms of tau and A beta pathological molecules Scientific Reports (2016) 6:28912 doi:10.1038/srep28912

177 https://www.farrlawfirm.com/alzheimers-3/reality-of-a-vaccine-to-protect-against-alzheimers/

178 Heo JY et al Aberrant Tonic Inhibition of Dopaminergic Neuronal Activity Causes Motor Symptoms in Animal Models of Parkinson's Disease (2020) Current Biology DOI;https://doi.org/10.1016/j.cub.2019.11.079

179 Watt J et al Comparative Efficacy of Interventions for Aggressive and Agitated Behaviors in Dementia: A Systematic Review and Network Meta-analysis. Ann Intern Med. 2019;171(9):633-642

180 Gao, MA etal Sleep Duration and Sleep Quality in Caregivers of Patients With Dementia A Systematic Review and Meta Analysis JAMA NetworkOpen.2019;2(8) e199891.doi:10.1001/jamanetworkopen.2019.9891

[181] Bybee KA et al Systematic Review: transient left ventricular ballooning: a syndrome that mimics ST-segment elevation myocardial infarction Ann Intern Med. (2004);141(11)858.

[182] Desmet WJ et al Apical ballooning of left ventricle: first series in white patients Heart (2003);89(9):1027

[183] Heiser, KG Attorney, How to Protect Your Family's Assets from Devastating Nursing Home Costs—Medicaid Secrets. Eleventh Edition (2017) Phylius Press, Laredo TX.

[184] Heiser, KG Attorney, How to Protect Your Family's Assets from Devastating Nursing Home Costs—Medicaid Secrets. Eleventh Edition (2017) Phylius Press, Laredo TX.

[185] Genworth 2019 Cost of Care Survey, genworth.com

[186] "Dementia Village" Creates Artifical Reality-Medscape-Sep 11, 2019.

[187] Genworth 2019 Cost of Care Survey, genworth.com.

[188] Genworth 2019 Cost of Care Survey, genworth.com

[189] Genworth 2019 Cost of Care Survey, genworth.com.

[190] https://www.cms.gov/medicare-coverage-database/details/lcd-details.aspx

[191] Brazier J. The Grief Survival Guide—how to navigate loss and all that comes with it (2017) Hodder & Stoughton Ltd, London, UK

ABOUT THE AUTHOR

The author was born Susan Lee Wilson, shortly before the end of WWII in Chicago, Illinois. She spent her early childhood through preteen years there, enjoying Lake Michigan beaches and horseback riding in Lincoln Park. When the family moved to St. Louis, she spent her teen years working in her father's medical office practice. Her interest and passion for medicine developed there. She graduated from Washington University in St. Louis and went on to graduate from the University of Louisville with an MD degree in 1972. Following residency in anesthesiology at Washington University's Barnes/Children's Hospital, she began an academic career which included an assistant professorship at UCLA, associate professorships at Washington University in St Louis, and finally as chief of pediatric anesthesiology at the University of Missouri in Columbia, Missouri. She is the author of numerous scientific papers and edited the first textbook of geriatric anesthesia. She currently resides in San Diego, California.

CPSIA information can be obtained
at www.ICGtesting.com
Printed in the USA
FSHW011846220421
80739FS